D1038134

WARRIORS OF THE 106TH

WARRIORS OF THE 106TH

The Last Infantry Division of World War II

MARTIN KING, KEN JOHNSON & MICHAEL COLLINS

CASEMATE | publishers

Philadelphia & Oxford

Published in the United States of America and Great Britain in 2017 by
CASEMATE PUBLISHERS
1950 Lawrence Road, Havertown, PA 19083, USA
and
The Old Music Hall, 106–108 Cowley Road, Oxford OX4 1JE, UK

Hardcover Edition: ISBN 978-1-61200-458-7
Digital Edition: ISBN 978-1-61200-459-4

A CIP record for this book is available from the Library of Congress and the British Library

Printed and bound in the United States of America
Typeset in India by Lapiz Digital Services, Chennai
Cartography by Stig Söderlind

For a complete list of Casemate titles, please contact:

CASEMATE PUBLISHERS (US)
Telephone (610) 853-9131
Fax (610) 853-9146
Email: casemate@casematepublishers.com
www.casematepublishers.com

CASEMATE PUBLISHERS (UK)
Telephone (01865) 241249
Fax (01865) 794449
Email: casemate-uk@casematepublishers.co.uk
www.casematepublishers.co.uk

MIX
Paper from
responsible sources
FSC
www.fsc.org
FSC® C011935

Disclaimer

We the authors gratefully acknowledge the support and encouragement of Leon Goldberg, President of the 106th Infantry Division Association, Jim West of www.indianamilitary.org and all American members of the 106th Infantry Division Association. We received neither assistance nor cooperation from any other organization outside the United States claiming to represent the 106th Infantry Division Association. Fifty percent of all proceeds from this book will be donated to the "Official" 106th Infantry Division Association.

CONTENTS

This volume is dedicated to our dearly respected friend, World War II veteran and official 106th Infantry Division Association Historian, Mr. John Schaffner and his lovely wife Lil.

When the history of the Ardennes fighting has been written, it will be recorded as one of the great strategic Allied successes of the war in Europe. Tactically, for the 106th, and the other American divisions involved, it was a bitter and costly fight. But it becomes increasingly clear that the Germans expended in that last futile effort those last reserves of men and material which they so badly needed a few months later. The losses and sacrifices of the 106th Infantry Division paid great dividends in eventual victory. These pages are dedicated to those gallant men who refused to quit in the darkest hour of the Allied invasion, and whose fortitude and heroism turned the tide toward overwhelming victory.

—Major General Donald A. Stroh
Commanding General 106th Division from February 7, 1945

It's surprising to me that Bastogne has an honorable place in American military history and St. Vith is hardly mentioned! The Battle of the Bulge was not fought solely at Bastogne, or by the admirable arrival of Patton's Third Army; here at St. Vith were all elements of tragedy, heroism, and self-sacrifice, which go to make up human experience at its most acute. The actions of our army around St. Vith exerted a great influence on the result of the German purpose in many ways, briefly: the schedule of the right wing of my army—a whole army corps was delayed by your defense around St. Vith, in spite of the ill-fated elements of the 106th Division. The troops in this area held up the German Corps five days longer than our time-table allowed, forcing us to detour the attacking forces so much that the [Sixth SS Panzer Army] on our right had no success. The 106th Division was outflanked, encircled, and overwhelmed by powerful German forces who were superior in numbers and arms. It is in my opinion very wrong to blame the 106th Infantry Division.

—General der Panzertruppe Hasso von Manteuffel
Commander, German Fifth Panzerarmee
Letter (paraphrased) to Colonel Robert Ringer, 1970

In remembrance: Kenneth Raymond Johnson, A Company, 424th Infantry Regiment, 106th Infantry Division

FOREWORD

Beginning shortly after the end of hostilities in Europe in 1945 certain armchair generals who thought themselves journalists began to write their versions of the history of the Battle of the Bulge. These writers accepted hearsay for fact and published their accounts of what they thought happened to my outfit. A lot of their material came from panic-induced "reports from the front." Some of the veterans of the 106th Division would not admit to being there since these accounts of the battle embarrassed them. They were not true. Nobody in the 106th Infantry Division ran from the attack in panic. They fought a much stronger enemy with what they had on hand and without resupply. Only when all means of resistance were expended did a surrender rather than suicide become an option. This became the fate of many of the soldiers as ordered by their commanders. Nobody was offered a vote. Those units still able to relocate and establish resistance to the German attack did so. They suffered the casualties inflicted by superior forces but held the line.

This book has been compiled from first-hand experiences of the soldiers who were there in harm's way. If you are looking for little mistakes along the way you may not be disappointed. I can tell you about a night in a foxhole with another soldier. He has a different account of what I remember happened that night. This book will take you there for your enlightenment of what it can be like to be in life or death action for the first time. Remember, it really was the first time for the soldiers of the 106th Infantry Division. None of them faced the enemy before December 16, 1945. This accounting is arguably the most comprehensive and inclusive story of a green division that was subjected to the threat of annihilation before a shot was fired.

—John Schaffner
106th Infantry Division veteran and official Division historian

ACKNOWLEDGEMENTS

Thank you first and foremost to my wife Freya for her continued support despite all the adversity, and grateful thanks to John Schaffner, Leon Goldberg and Jim West. Posthumous thanks to my late grandfather, Private 4829 Joseph Henry Pumford, who fought at Passchendaele in World War I and provided invaluable inspiration for my early interest in military history. He was promoted to corporal but then demoted for punching out a sergeant. He was unique in managing to terrify both sides in that particular conflict. Also and not forgetting offspring Allycia and Ashley Rae, brother Graham, sisters Sandra and Debbie, brother-in-law Mark, nephews Ben and Jake and niece Rachel. Treasured long-time friends Andy Kirton, Mike Edwards, Mike Collins, Lt. Col. Jason Nulton (ret'd), Commander Jeffrey Barta (ret'd), General Graham Hollands (ret'd) and Betsy Jackson, for their wonderful support and encouragement. Grateful thanks to my dear friend Mr. Roland Gaul at the National Museum of Military History, Diekirch, Luxembourg, and to Helen Patton.

Thank you also to Dan and Judy Goo in Hawaii, Mrs. Carol Fish and the staff at the United States Military Academy, West Point; Rudy Beckers and Greg Hanlon at Joint Base McGuire, Dix, Lakehurst, for their wonderful ongoing support. Many thanks to Doug McCabe, former curator of the Cornelius Ryan Collection, Ohio University; my friends Brian Dick, John Taylor and the excellent SHAPE kids; World War II veteran John Schaffner and Madam Ambassador Denise Campbell Bauer.

Also grateful thanks to Ruth Sheppard, Michaela Goff, Chris Cocks, Hannah McAdams, Rajni Varsani and the tremendous staff at Casemate, including former editor Steve Smith, who continue to inspire me.

—Martin King

Special thanks go to Martin King, Mike Collins, Carl Fischer, Craig Snow, Michael Hamill, Noel Ellis, and Dr. Ralston Robertson for their tireless and critical review over the two years during which the story took shape. Col. David Hugus (USAR ret'd), Col. Todd Garlick (USAR ret'd), and Lt. Col. Mark Wroth (USAR ret'd), who were instrumental in the continuous process of review and comment from the beginning. All spent countless hours discussing approaches and details as the story evolved and most definitely helped us understand aspects of warfare and military details. Lt. Gen. Brian Arnold (USAF ret'd) was an encouragement from the start and provided many ideas along the way.

—Ken Johnson

Thank you first to my amazing son, Daniel Edward, for continuing to make me realize how important it is to preserve history for when you are old enough to read it and understand it. To my co-authors, Martin King and Ken Johnson, for their support, patience, and friendship throughout the writing of this book. To John Schaffner, 106th veteran and historian of the 106th Division Association, for his humor, advice, and help with writing this book. To my parents, John and Joanne Collins, for their continued support in my writing endeavors. My brothers John and Chris, my sisters-in-law Melissa and Maria, nieces and nephew, Morgan, Katie, Keira, Margo and Henry. To the King and Johnson families, for their support and understanding during the writing of this book. My friends Michael Aliotta, Christopher Begley, Patrick Healy, Howard Liddic, Mike Edwards, John Vallely, Sean Conley, Christian Pettinger, Mark Weber, Dirk De Groof, Rudy Aerts, and all those who support me during my many travels. To Kathleen Reilly and Ann-Marie Harris and the staff in the Local History Department at the Berkshire Athenaeum who continue to support my research endeavors. Thank you to the staff at Casemate and editor Ruth Sheppard for the continued professional work and help throughout the publishing process. Finally to the members of the 106th Infantry Division, may this book help preserve your memory, accomplishments, and history. Long Live the Golden Lion Division!

—Mike Collins

INTRODUCTION

I always knew my parents named me after my father's brother. I also knew that he served in the army during World War II and did not come home when the war ended; but that is all I knew. As a boy, I spent part of the summers with my grandparents in Florida. On their bedroom dresser, just as in a million other homes, was a faded black and white photograph of their son, Kenneth Raymond Johnson, in uniform.

When my grandparents died my father got the pictures, letters, and newspaper clippings they had on Ken. My dad and I have talked quite a bit about what he knew of his brother and the war. In 1955, he went to Germany to see where it happened, but that's all he knew. As I grew a little older and grey, I began to wonder what happened, so I started digging.

It took a while to find a lead to Ken. I had his name. I knew his hometown, and I knew that for 16 years he was MIA—but I had no idea which outfit he served with or what he did. After several hours, I hit pay dirt, or so I thought when I found an official table of MIA and KIA from World War II with the name Kenneth Johnson. I now had three leads—and I took the wrong path.

Kenneth E. Johnson, Army Serial Number 32288744, was from Rockland County just like Kenneth R. Johnson. I spent several days searching for Kenneth E. Johnson of the 102d Infantry Division, learned that he was in the 1276th Engineers, and had it all wrong. To the family of Kenneth E. Johnson, Rockland County, New York, may he rest in peace.

My father corrected my mistake and I went in search of Kenneth R. Johnson, Army Serial Number 12226733. The date of his death was the first thing that caught my interest—December 17, 1944—which was the second day of the Battle of the Bulge. I had no idea that my namesake died in the Battle of the Bulge. After a little more work, I found the 106th Infantry Division Honor Roll, which told me that Ken was in the 424th Infantry Regiment, 106th Infantry Division. With that, I read everything related I could find.

The men and families of the 106th Infantry Division have done an excellent job collecting and chronicling their stories before, during, and after the war. I learned that the 106th Infantry Division was in the Battle of the Bulge, and in fact, they played a pivotal role in the first seven days of the battle. During my research, I discovered the Camp Atterbury album, a photo album of the men taken before they went overseas. I knew Ken was in the 424th Infantry, so I studied the photographs of over 3,400 men in the 424th Infantry and, sure enough, I found him among the men of A Company. He's in the top left of the picture, back row, third from the left, and looks just like the picture on my grandmother's dresser.

When I showed the picture to my mom and dad, they confirmed that it was Ken. Sixty-five years later, I had found a picture nobody in the family had. And with that, my search for the story of my uncle, and the men of the 106th Infantry Division, was on.

—K.J.

PREFACE

In 2014 I stood in the Pentagon at a rostrum opposite a 90-year-old World War II veteran I'd known for some time. I'd asked him to join me when I was presenting my latest book to an audience of Pentagon employees. I knew John Schaffner had been with the 106th Division during the Battle of the Bulge but that wasn't the only reason I'd invited him to join me on that day. I knew from experience that John could captivate an audience with his inimitable talent for putting across a story, and on that day he didn't disappoint. He was as always charming, entertaining and precise in his recollections. When he ended his perfectly timed monologue he added that he had one more ambition to fulfill. I should add that John also had an innate capacity for being wonderfully unpredictable. "I'd like to be shot by a jealous husband," he said straight-faced but with a glint in his eye that illuminated and brought down the whole room. Later that day we shared a drink and I promised John that someday I would attempt to write the story about his division: therefore most of the "eye-witness" accounts in this volume are from him and in many ways this is very much his story.

It's time to right the wrongs and put the 106th Infantry Division right up there with the best of the best where they belong. There's a monument to the 168th Combat Engineers up on the Prümerberg ridge east of St. Vith. Respected author Charles MacDonald erroneously referred to it in his book *Decision at St. Vith* as a monument to Colonel

Riggs. It isn't. It's actually a monument to the 168th Combat Engineers and with all respect to the man, Riggs's name isn't even mentioned on it. I know this whole area very well indeed because at the time of writing I've lived in Belgium for 35 years and, prior to that, visited it many, many times.

I'd got to know about the 106th Infantry Division while assembling my first book *Voices of the Bulge* with Mike Collins. Theirs was an unusual story and Mike and I had noticed that the esprit de corps between veterans was particularly intense. There was no other World War II story in my opinion that had such incredible polarity. For some it was a story of victory and for others it was a resounding defeat but for each and every member of that division it's a story of remarkable courage, heroism and fortitude. It took courage to face a determined enemy but it took equal courage to survive the deprivations and cruelty of the German stalags. I hope that Ken Johnson, Mike Collins and I can do their story justice and finally give them the credit they truly deserve.

—M.K.

The 106th were destined to be a division with a difference. These young men were fresh, raw and eager to serve their country. The division would be one of the first to have a multicultural element to it years before this became the norm. They would hammer the parade ground, participate in numerous preparatory exercises and be drilled to perfection until they crossed the Atlantic and went to war, a war that would emblazon their name in the annals of military history for all time. Some historians would recall their name ignominiously while others would get it right and allocate the credit this division deserves for their tremendous sacrifice and indomitable courage. As with previous volumes we will attempt to be as comprehensive and meticulous as possible, but some details may be omitted for continuity purposes. There will always be those who say, "It didn't happen like that" or "Why have they left that out?" To these dissenters the only feasible suggestion would be: write your own book. Speaking of which, the 106th Infantry Division story has been referred to in a few notable volumes and even appears on a few rogue websites run by amateurs hoping to make a buck off the backs of these indomitable men, but all this team can do is their level best to get to the core of the story. This is their story recounted mostly by those who were there.

—M.K., K.J., M.C.

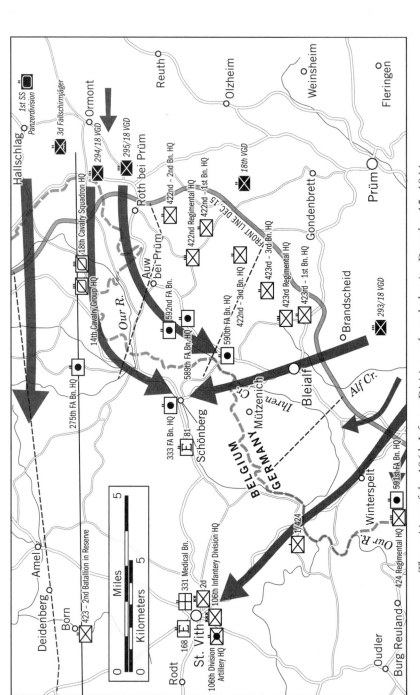

The positions of the 106th Infantry Division and attached units, December 15, 1944.

CHAPTER I

BIRTH OF THE LAST INFANTRY DIVISION

It was noon on Monday, March 15, 1943, when a limousine drew to a measured halt at the entrance to Outdoor Theater 2. A blue flag emblazoned with a white crescent in its upper corner and a white palmetto palm in its center was attached above the vehicle's radiator. As the rear door opened and the Honorable Olin Johnston, Governor of South Carolina, stepped out, he was greeted in accordance with the prestige his office demanded, and duly escorted to the stage. A truly notable and distinguished assemblage awaited him. Among them was Major General William Simpson, Commanding General, XII Corps. On the stage sat Brigadier General Alan Walter Jones with the staff of the division about to be born. In the body of the theater sat the cadres furnished by the 80th Infantry Division and a few recruits who had arrived over the past few days. As the Governor took his place, those assembled were ordered to present arms. When they returned to order, the Division Chaplain, Major John Dunn, stepped to the rostrum and gave the invocation. The Division Adjutant General, Lieutenant Colonel Frank Agule, then read the 106th Infantry Division's official birth certificate, the War Department order for their activation.

Agule returned to his seat and Master Sergeant Jay Bower, representing the parent 80th Infantry Division, summoned Private Francis Younkin from the ranks of the 422d Infantry Regiment. Bower delivered the National Colors to Younkin, thereby entrusting them to the new division. Younkin delivered them to the color guard and took the seat Bower vacated while Bower took the private's place in the ranks.

Jones introduced Governor Johnston and General Simpson. Johnston extended a brief greeting to the men of the division; Simpson welcomed the new division to membership in XII Corps. Jones then delivered a brief message concluding with the words, "In your hands is held the opportunity to fashion an instrument which will demonstrate to the world that our way of life develops men superior to any other."

With those words and the benediction, the ceremony ended. The troops were dismissed and the 106th Infantry Division, the last infantry division created in the war, assumed its place on the rolls of the United States Army. As the units defiled from the theater, the Commanding Officer of Troops turned to his adjutant and recited the words of American poet Richard Hovey:

> I do not know beneath what sky,
> Nor on what seas shall be thy fate:
> I only know it shall be high,
> I only know it shall be great.

The CO didn't quote the words verbatim but the sentiment hit the spot. Those words were to prove quite prophetic.

Three days later Brigadier General Alan Walter Jones was promoted to major general and appointed Commander of the 106th Infantry Division. Their emblem was a golden lion's head on a blue background. Jones had just turned 50, a stocky man with a full round face, jet-black hair, heavy eyebrows, and a pencil moustache. He was regular army, but hadn't attended West Point Military Academy. He had attended the University of Washington, where he'd studied chemical engineering on an ROTC scholarship. In World War I, he was commissioned as a second lieutenant with the 43d Infantry Division. To his regret, like Eisenhower, he never saw combat during the Great War. Following the war, Jones rose through the ranks, served with the 45th Infantry Division, and attended infantry and artillery schools. At the outbreak of World War II, he was Assistant Division Commander, 90th Infantry Division.

Jones's new division was an archetypal United States infantry division based on organizational groupings of threes. Now Jones was given the task of finding 14,000 men to fill the ranks and prepare them for war.

To keep his division running Jones had a standard complement of support companies. The 106th Quartermaster Company obtained and managed all the food, clothing, and material. The 106th Signal Company made sure Jones could communicate to his superior commands and subordinate commanders. The 106th Headquarters Company administered the day-to-day operation of the division. The 331st Medical Battalion handled the division's medical needs. To keep all his machinery working he had the 806th Ordnance Light Maintenance Company. A contingent that became known as the 106th Military Police was created to maintain soldierly conduct and whatever other tasks they might be allocated.

When it came to building the roads, bunkers, bridges, and housing the division needed Jones had the 81st Engineer Combat Battalion who when required could pick up a rifle and jump into a foxhole. When it came to mechanized infantry he could rapidly send the 106th Reconnaissance Troop where needed.

To help manage the affairs of the division, Jones had a general staff reminiscent of Napoleon's Grande Armée, whereupon each position in the headquarters was assigned a letter prefix corresponding with the unit's element, and a number specifying the role. This was standard for most U.S. infantry divisions at the time. The letter G was reserved for division and above, anything below division level was an S. G-1 handled all the administration and personnel in the division. G-2 was responsible for collecting and analyzing intelligence about the enemy to determine what they were doing, or might do, to prevent the accomplishment of the unit's mission. The same function at regimental level and down was S-2. G-3, or operations section, was responsible for everything the unit needed to accomplish the mission such as training and planning. G-4 handled the logistics, and, while there were five more staff positions, they were less involved in the combat operation of the division. Under his command Jones had the last three infantry regiments created during World War II, the 422d, 423d, and 424th.

All regiments were composed of squads, platoons, companies, and battalions. At normal strength, each squad consisted of 12 men: ten were armed with M-1 rifles, one with a BAR (Browning Automatic Rifle), and one with an M-1903 Springfield bolt rifle. Three such rifle squads formed a rifle platoon. Three rifle platoons plus a weapons platoon (armed with one .50-caliber machine gun, two .30-caliber machine guns, three bazookas, and three 60mm mortars) made up a rifle company of six officers and 187 men. Three rifle companies and a heavy weapons company made up an infantry battalion of 871 men. Three battalions plus a headquarters and support unit constituted an infantry regiment of 153 officers and 3,049 men.

These would be his primary fighting units. For firepower he had three battalions of light artillery, the 589th, 590th, and 591st, which were assigned to a regiment, and one battalion of medium artillery, the 592d, that he kept under division control. If there were enemy aircraft bombing or strafing his troops, he could rely on the 119th and 574th Anti-Aircraft Artillery battalions. Each of the three infantry regiments was comprised of three infantry battalions numbered 1st, 2d, and 3d. Every regimental commander held the rank of colonel, with 3,400 men at his disposal along with a headquarters company whose job was to coordinate, plan, and carry out the regiment's activities, keeping the colonel informed of all developments regarding intelligence and reconnaissance (also known as the I&R Platoon). His service company managed logistic matters to provide the trucks needed to carry supplies and troops.

Each regiment had an anti-tank, or AT, company comprised of three anti-tank platoons equipped with three wheeled 57mm cannons, and an anti-tank mine platoon of three squads. A cannon company with three cannon platoons of two self-propelled 105mm howitzers each provided immediate fire as needed.

The regimental medical detachment, consisting of a headquarters section and a battalion section, was deployed with each of the three battalions. The battalion sections established medical aid stations and provided aide men to each rifle and heavy weapons platoon in the battalion. Litter teams were also assigned to the battalion sections to evacuate the wounded from the front lines to the aid station.

When the bugle sounded reveille on Monday, March 29, 1943, training of the new 106th Infantry Division began and it was time for barracks inspections, colors, and breakfast. By 0700 hours, the rumbling stomachs and ravenous appetites of more than 10,000 young men had been satiated. The army breakfast mess was a place of both derision and reverence to these new recruits.

They peered through sleep-heavy eyes at watery coffee and ate from cereal boxes to the background cacophony of multitudinous tin trays slamming against garbage cans and the monotonous drone of interlaced voices chorused by the bronchial protestations of those indulging the first cigarette of the day. Dinner was just as desultory. Men forced smiles and vainly asked attendants to put potatoes here and the meat there. This request would be ultimately ignored as something that went *slop* hit the trays to the accompaniment of remarks such as "Just like Momma's, eh" from men whose hygienic standards were at best dubious and at worst downright unsound. Some men waved their trays about. Most tried to find a friendly face before sitting to eat. Loners sat wherever they could find a place. After the meal, they hurried back to the barracks hoping for a mail call.

More than 10,000 men were in training under regimental and battalion control. Twenty thousand feet hit the pavement in unison. Soon bridges began to creak, so the marching soldiers had to break step when they approached one. They sang old cadences and learned new ones. When units passed each other, their cadences changed:

Hold your head up high and turn your eyes this way,
Company L is passing by.
Swing your arms and cover down,
Keep your eyes off of the ground.
You aren't behind the plow,
You're in the Army now.
There ain't no need of going home,
Jody's done got your gal and gone.

Young Thomas Riggs's first duty with the 106th Infantry Division began when it was activated and his engineers were attached to the new outfit. Most of the enlisted men in the new division were 18-year-old draftees, so the average age of the division was well under twenty-two. With an excellent cadre of officers and noncoms, the division was ready for tough training. What impressed Riggs most was that the Division Chief of Staff,

Colonel William Baker, was an engineer; it was good to have an engineer on the division staff.

Later that summer Riggs was ordered to establish a new Engineer Combat Battalion at Camp Gordon, Georgia. Lieutenant Colonel Himes, then Commander of the 81st, insisted Riggs select the best officers from the 81st to make up his cadre. Sixty days after starting the new battalion, Riggs was ordered back to the 81st to replace Himes who was moving on to command an Engineer Corps. It was now Lieutenant Colonel Thomas Riggs. He began his military career in February 1941 when he graduated from the University of Illinois and received an ROTC commission as a second lieutenant. After a refresher course at the U.S. Army Engineer School, he became platoon leader for a training battalion at the Engineer Replacement Training Center in Fort Belvoir, Virginia. The next two years passed quickly, and by 1943, Riggs had a regular army commission, completed the Engineer Officer Advanced Course, and became a battalion commander with the rank of major. Riggs quickly tired of being a training instructor, and looked into transferring to a combat division.

John Schaffner, Scout, Battery A, 589th Field Artillery Battalion, 106th Infantry Division

I passed my 18th birthday on August 11, 1942. The war in Europe was in full swing with the Nazi armies taking victories everywhere they went. The U.S. had officially declared war on Japan after the Japanese attack on Pearl Harbor on 7 December 1941. Nazi Germany declared war on the U.S. on December 11. The world was having big troubles. All American "boys" between the ages of 18 and 45 were ordered by an Act of Congress to register for the draft. There were few shirkers. It became a matter of pride to be "in" some branch of the service. Some of my classmates quit school in their senior year to enlist.

February, 1943, I graduated from high school (Baltimore City College) and immediately became eligible for the call. On March 7, 1943, at about quarter to seven in the morning, I kissed my Mom goodbye, and with my little suitcase, walked three blocks with my Dad to the street-car line. We had a short conversation about taking care of myself, a quick hug and a brave "so-long." He was going off to work and I walked another three blocks. I reported to my local draft board and was selected to serve. We draftees were then put on a bus, driven to downtown Baltimore and ushered into the 5th Regiment Armory to be subjected to all kinds of physical and psychological examination. As I recall, we were stripped down to our socks and a doctor probed, poked and squeezed all sorts of places. Then we were asked all kinds of questions to find out if our head was on straight. The only one that I remember was, "Do you like girls?" Of course, I said, "Yes." That was it. I was in. Then somebody asked me what branch of the service I preferred. I said, "Navy." (Some of my friends had gone in the Navy and that was the only reason that I requested Navy.) He said, "No, we have too many in the Navy." I said, "How about the Air Corps?" He said, "No, you need to wear glasses. I have to put you in the Army." Then he took my papers and stamped them with "LIMITED SERVICE" (whatever that meant). When all of that business was finally over we were "sworn in." We were then read "The Articles of War" (by a PFC) and made to realize that any disobedience from then on would incur punishment that nobody could possibly recover from. As I recall, the penalty for any and every infraction was "DEATH or WORSE." We boarded a bus, and were driven to Fort G.G. Meade, Maryland.

At Fort Meade, the army placed us in groups, assigned us to a bunk in a barracks building and proceeded to try to make us look like soldiers. We were issued uniforms and dog tags, given shots for every disease known to man, and told how to stand, walk, sit, and never refuse an order from somebody with one more rank than what you had. They even tried to teach us Close Order Drill. We had a lot to learn just to survive, and that guy back in the Armory did stamp my papers with "LIMITED SERVICE." I wondered just what <u>that</u> was going to mean. A few days later I would find out. Nothing! My civilian clothes were packed in the little suitcase and sent home, courtesy of the Army.

I, along with a whole train load of 18-year-old draftees, joined the 106th Infantry Division at Ft. Jackson, S.C. in March 1943. My first morning at Fort Jackson was anything but satisfactory. The sergeant came into the barracks making a lot of noise and told us to "Get up, get dressed, and get going." It was still dark and cold. The wind was blowing sheets of rain against the barracks. I thought the inclement weather would keep us inside for the day. I was wrong. A powerful voice shouted, "Everybody out for roll call!" With steel helmets and raincoats, we lined up on the battery street and sounded off when the sergeant called our names. I stood there with the rain beating on my helmet and running *down the back of my neck. The pelting rain on my helmet sounded like I was sitting in an attic with a tin roof. It immediately became clear to me that the weather, regardless of conditions, would have no impact on what we had do.*

I was assigned to A Battery, 589th Field Artillery Battalion and placed in the Instrument Section under S/Sgt. Clyde Kirkman. My particular job was Scout, MOS 761. This was probably the luck of the draw. There were too many names beginning with "S" in our section. I doubt that much effort was put into the initial placement of personnel, especially in an infantry division. The names that I remember are too many to list here but in Kirkman's section I was privileged to count among my close friends Bob Stoll, Walt Snyder and Henry Thurner. It required two men to pool their equipment to create a pup tent. This fact alone fostered friendships that would not have come about otherwise. Early on, most of us in the Detail platoon did not have jobs requiring a close working relationship with the howitzer crews, so it took a while for the entire battery personnel to become acquainted.

The primary responsibilities of my Instruments Section were to support the battery commander in the field, conduct topographic surveys of targets and gun positions, and function as forward observers. As a surveyor, I trained in a lot of algebra, trigonometry, and calculus. While all soldiers carried a carbine, I also carried a slide rule and trigonometric tables for surveying. I spent a lot of time on field exercises surveying.

A great deal of emphasis was put on this survey activity while in training, but once the unit went into action in Europe the box containing all this equipment was never even opened. Registration fire was "observed" in all situations and concentrations of multiple batteries and unobserved fire at night were coordinated through Fire Direction Centers from measurements directly on maps or air photos. The communication was via telephone and/or radio between the observer and the firing batteries. (In retrospect, I can see no reason for the topographical survey for the artillery, since the time required implies a static situation and a battle can only be won when the enemy is being attacked and pursued.)

We accomplished our basic training and practiced division-scale maneuvers at Fort Jackson, S.C. during the remainder of 1943.

Our division was referred to as motorized but we walked everywhere. When we finally began to use the vehicles, dust respirators and goggles had to be issued. The dry dirt roads throughout the maneuvering area sent up clouds of dust that infiltrated everything and made it impossible to breathe or see ahead. At the end of the day we were mud balls from the dust and the sweat. All of that summer and fall the division was active in the field practicing those skills required to defeat the enemy.

We had been issued the Carbine M-1 and taught everything about it: how to take it apart, and keep it clean, and to love it, and never be without it. It was to become a living part of us. When the day finally came to actually load it with live ammunition we were as excited as being on a first date with a real live girl. The temperature at the firing range must have been at least 100°F. The targets were placed across a bare, sandy field at 100, 200 and 300 yards. As we tried to zero in on our targets, the hot air shimmering off the sand seemed to make the bull's eye perform like a belly dancer. Nobody qualified, so the firing for record was postponed for another day. When the time came, I made "Expert" with the carbine. On occasion, in later days, I have heard disparaging remarks made about this weapon, but I never had any problems with mine, then or later. And, among others, it was made by the Rockola Juke Box Company; Wurlitzer made them and some were even stamped as being made by the Singer Sewing Machine Company. In those times some very unlikely industries were put to work manufacturing the tools of war.

One day the battalion was in the field conducting war games and our survey team was measuring a base leg for plotting the targets and gun positions for unobserved fire. Two men had a 100-foot-long tape, which is used by having the front man shove a steel pin that has an "eye" in the ground, threading the tape through the eye, and proceeding another 100 feet. When the man bringing up the rear approaches the pin, he shouts out to the front man to stop and the front man marks another 100 feet and threads another pin. It is also the responsibility of the man at the rear to collect the pins before proceeding toward the next pin marking another 100 feet. This day, when the lead tape-man had exhausted his supply of pins, he called out, "Hey Milt, bring me the pins!" Milt replied, "What pins?" The result was that they had to retrace 1,000 feet of their work to recover the pins. Sergeant Kirkman took a dim view of the whole operation.

We were learning to live in the field and there was much practice in placing the howitzers in combat situations. A Battery became very proficient and there was much unit spirit among the men. We knew that we were the best. At one point in the training we were subjected to the "infiltration course." Everyone was expected to advance across rugged ground on their bellies, with dynamite charges exploding next to and all around them, and with machine guns firing live ammunition just inches over their heads. Barbed wire was also strung across the ground making progress all the more difficult.

There were very few interruptions to our training schedule, but whenever one came along I was ready. There was to be a concert given in Columbia that summer featuring operatic soprano Gladys Swarthout, Gregor Piatigorsky, Eleanor Steber, and Julius Huehn, all well-known artists. The director of the program apparently asked the post commander to supply him with a number of GIs to make up a "Soldiers' Chorus." The word went out for volunteer singers to fill the request. This sounded pretty good to me so, although I couldn't carry a tune in a bucket, I volunteered. As it turned out, all we needed was a clean uniform and we qualified. When the day came around a hundred or so of us were transported to Columbia and the theater. We rehearsed some military songs of the day and some back-up sounds for a couple of other numbers, and by show time that evening we were ready. Of course there were rave reviews. Oh, I almost forgot, Gladys received a mention too.

On another occasion I was called into the first sergeant's office and told that I was to be assigned to travel to Nashville to bring back one of our men who had "overstayed his leave." He had been tracked down and arrested by the MPs and was being held for return to the unit for disciplinary action. I was given an MP arm brassard, white MP leggings, a loaded .45, official orders and travel arrangements. I was very apprehensive about the whole thing, but I put on a stiff upper lip and took off for my prisoner. As it turned out, he was very docile and gave me no problem at all. When I returned him to the Battery HQ and released him to the Battery Commander that was the last I ever saw of him.

We were given short passes to leave the post occasionally. There were buses to take you into Columbia or other nearby, smaller towns, but when you arrived there you would find everything closed after five o'clock, and "the sidewalks rolled up." As I remember it, there was one movie house in Columbia, and a couple of fraternal service clubs that offered some very quiet recreation. I did manage to come home once on a seven-day furlough while we were at Ft. Jackson. When passes were issued I frequently teamed with Bob Stoll to get away from the post to seek out some diversion. We would hop on a bus and visit a town within traveling distance and, if lucky, even meet local folks to spend time with. The two of us got a weekend pass once and Bob said that he knew some folks who had a summer home at Cedar Mountain, N.C. and asked if I would like to go visit them. Sure, why not?

We departed Jackson on a Friday evening for Columbia. From Columbia we caught a bus to Greensboro, N.C. Now came the hard part. We were still a long way from our destination and there was no public transportation for the rest of the way. The time was getting away from us, but we had passed the point of no return. The only way now was to use the good old thumb. In those days a man in uniform usually had no trouble hitch-hiking, not like today. We were picked up several times for short distances and were not making very good time. Finally we got a lift with a young fellow who was to report for induction on Monday and was out celebrating his last weekend of freedom. He insisted that he knew where we were going and would eventually get us there if we would only stick with him. The problem was he wanted a drink in every bar and honky-tonk in that end of the state before getting us where we wanted to go. So, it was up and around the mountain with a driver getting drunker by the minute. By now, we didn't have any idea where we were. At last, very late at night, we entered a "joint" where some folks knew this fellow. We explained to them about the fix we were in, so one of them offered to accommodate us with a ride. When we finally arrived at Cedar Mountain the sun was rising in the sky. Bob and I had a bit of breakfast with his friends and then we got a few hours' sleep. The only thing that I remember doing at Cedar Mountain was watching a baptism in a cold mountain stream and being glad that it wasn't me being baptized. That day, Sunday, one of the folks there drove us back to Greensboro and we caught a bus back to Columbia and then another to Jackson, arriving back on the post with no time remaining on our pass.

The artillerymen called themselves Red Legs, a throwback to the Civil War when a red stripe down the side of their pants identified the artillerymen. U.S. batteries during World War II were organized into highly trained teams around a set of four cannons, or howitzers, called pieces, led by the Battery Executive and his assistant. Next in line was the Chief of the Piece Section, whose duty was to control the service and operation of the piece. Even the location of the chief was dictated: two yards from the end of the trail on the side opposite the executive. The Ammunition Sergeant was in charge of the ammunition dump, and tracked every shell and charge in the battery. The telephone operator took the commands coming from the Fire Direction Center, or FDC, and relayed them to the battery executive. To support the operator, the lineman made sure the phones were operating, and the recorder took down every command and message.

Everything was scripted and practiced and each soldier had a specific task. They marched in specific positions around the piece. When they emplaced the piece, they executed specific duties in specific orders. One unlimbered a leg, another put in a bolt. One opened the breach, another used the ramrod to clean the barrel. The artillerymen could set up their piece in five minutes and begin sending rounds down-range.

John Gatens, Battery A, 589th Field Artillery Battalion

I, along with a whole train load of 19-year-old draftees, joined the 106th Infantry Division at Ft. Jackson, S.C. in March 1943. I was assigned to A Battery, 589th Field Artillery Battalion and placed in the gun section under Sgt. Johnnie B. Jordan. There were no assigned positions at this time. After about three weeks of orientation about chain of command, close order drill, making a GI bed and physical fitness, we received the four 105 howitzers that make up a firing battery. A section is made up of nine men. A sergeant is in charge of the section. Next is the gunner (most important position when firing): his job is to set all firing commands, on a high-power sight and traverse the barrel to correct direction to be fired. This is the procedure when the firing command comes down from the observation post. This is called indirect firing. In direct firing (when the target is in view) the gunner's responsibility is to set the elevation, then track the target and give the order to fire. The Number 1 man's responsibility is to set the elevation for indirect firing. The Number 2 man's responsibility is to put the shell into the barrel. The other four men prepare the shell for firing—the type of shell to be used as given from the observation post. We had three types: armor piercing, high explosive and time fuse. Each shell had seven powder bags. These powder bags determined how far the shell would travel. You could use all seven or as little as one. If one was used, the target was way too close. The last man is the truck driver.

During our early training period, each man was being observed by the officers. Ten men were chosen to take the test to be gunners. Only four made it and I was one of them. This carried the rank of corporal.

We now had four complete gun sections under the command of Lt. Graham Cassibry. His responsibility was to make us an efficient, accurate and fast-firing unit. This he accomplished because he won the hearts of every man and they would do anything for him. Under his command we won the title of the best firing battery in the battalion.

We were the youngest group of men ever drafted into the U.S. Army. Now they had to find out how much these kids could take. I don't think they missed one torture test available. Most of our time was spent camped in the woods. We had day and night firing missions. Twenty-five-mile forced marches. Dry and muddy infiltration courses. We lived on bag lunches, so much so that we became known as "The Bag Lunch Division." Lo and behold! after many months of really grueling training we passed with flying colors. We were now ready for the next phase of our training.

After New Year's holiday the division then moved from the comparatively comfortable Fort Jackson to the Tennessee Maneuver Area for the period of January, February and March 1944 where we became accustomed to living in the "field." The cold and wet weather during those three months was extremely difficult, with some 30 inches of rain setting a record of some kind for the area. We spent a great deal of time just extricating the howitzers and vehicles from the mud. Everybody was wet and cold most of the time. We learned to exist with these conditions and I can't recall that anyone even caught a cold. On one particular day we were occupying a farmer's pasture that was about eight inches in snow when one of his cows gave birth to a calf. That was a "first" for most of us "city guys" on the scene. When the maneuvers were finally over we were confident that we could handle anything. Before the division had completed this phase of our training we heard of quite a few casualties. During a crossing attempt of the Cumberland River at flood stage, a raft loaded with a truck and a group of infantry GIs upset in mid-stream. We heard that there were no survivors. In our battery one night we had a man run over by a 2½-ton GMC backing to hitch on to a howitzer. We heard later that he recovered, but he never re-joined the outfit.

One of our simulated battles required that we cross the raging waters of the Cumberland River. To get us across was the responsibility of our engineers. What they had was a pontoon-type raft. It was large enough to carry a 2½-ton truck. In the rear and on one side was an outboard motor. When it was our turn to cross there was a group of old-time farmers gathered around watching what was going on. They kept shaking their heads and telling us we would never make it. They convinced me, and I would have waited for the river to stop raging. However, when the Army says "GO," you go. The gun and its crew had to go first. The thinking was that if we didn't make it, a truck, alone on the bank, would not win the battle either. So off we went. There were two engineers on board. One worked the engine and the one up front give directions. I must say, they were very good. We headed upstream against the current. The engine roared full blast. While headed upstream he [the engineer manning the engine] was also moving across at the same time. When we were approximately two-thirds of the way across he started heading downstream. Now I really got scared. It took us a quarter of the time to go down as it did to go up. Now, while traveling at this rate of speed. he had to slow it down so we could get in to the dock. It took a few tries but he did get us in safely. Now he had to go back and get our truck. Lucky him.

We did have some fun times during all this serious training. I remember one of our early morning missions when we had to move positions. When we arrived at the new position my gun was placed in the front yard of a farmhouse. The occupants of the house were all sleeping because there were no lights on. When we were set up and a fire mission came down all four guns fired. On these missions we fired blank shells. They made the same noise as a real shell, except no projectile was in flight. All of a sudden all of the lights in the house went on and the farmer came running out with his shotgun, ready to kill us all. After he calmed down his wife came out and asked us if we would give her fifty cents a man she would make us coffee, eggs, bacon and hot biscuits. We all accepted and, believe me, after what we had been eating, we hoped that we would never leave this position.

The weekly routine while on this phase of training was that every Monday morning we started out on a new battle problem. One week you would be the attacker and the next you would be the defender. The battle lasted for five days, until Friday. Everything was realistic. One of the judges would come around and if he pinned a tag on you "wounded" you had to call a medic. The tag would specify what kind of wound you had. The medic would treat the wound and if it was serious, off in the ambulance you would go to the Aid Station. You now stayed there until the battle was over for that week. I tried to bribe the judge many times for a serious wound, but I never got one. On one of the missions the battery was judged to be captured. This gave us two days off.

On Friday the problem was over. Every Saturday we spent cleaning up our equipment. This was a hopeless job. Everything was covered with mud. Even after you got it somewhat clean it didn't stay that way for long. Saturday evening and Sunday passes were given out on an alternating basis. It was great to go to town, find a place where you could take a good hot shower and then sit down in a restaurant and have a good hot meal. Some of the time we were close to Nashville. Many of the southern guys would line up and go to the Grand Ole Opry. Us city guys thought they were nuts.

One of the many stories that I could tell relates to my good friend Lt. Cassibry. He came from a very wealthy family. He was a brilliant young man. He was not a military man. Being young and rich he was more of a playboy type. He treated his men more like friends than subordinates. He had one bad fault: he was an alcoholic. He never let it interfere with his duties, but on his time off he would come to the barracks and share his bottle with the men that were drinkers. I was not a drinker, which made him trust me and I became one of his favorites. Every time he had to go someplace he would order a Jeep and I would have to drive him. Officers were not permitted to drive and I didn't even have a GI driver's license. With that background we are now back to Tennessee. One Saturday night a bunch of us were sitting around a fire and along comes my favorite lieutenant. He calls out my name and says, "Follow me." We go down to the motor pool and he requisitions a Jeep and off we go to town. He tells me to pull over and stop by a taxi stand. He went into the office, came out with another man, they get into a cab and leave. Half an hour later they return. The lieutenant gets out with a big bag in his hands. Into the Jeep and back to the guys still sitting around the fire. Out come two bottles of Vat 69 Scotch. Tennessee is a dry state. I don't know where they went or how much it cost him, but I bet it was plenty.

On April 2, 1944, the division moved again, from Tennessee to Camp Atterbury, Indiana, near Indianapolis. We traveled in the division vehicles across the mountainous areas of Tennessee using the unimproved back roads. In some places on the switchback curves it was necessary to unhitch the howitzers from the trucks in order to make it round the bend. The howitzers were then manhandled by their crews who struggled to get the pieces hooked up again so they could proceed. The division made it to Camp Oglethorpe to spend that night. As we dismounted the vehicles and were assigned barracks for the night, the officers informed us that this post was the WAC [Women's Army Corps] training facility and anyone found outside our restricted area was subject to be hung or worse.

Here again my favorite, Lt. Cassibry, came along and asked me and a few others if we wanted to go to the PX for a beer. The only problem with this was that the PX he wanted to go to was in the WAC area. Not being brave enough to refuse an officer, we went. We met some very nice WACs. I must say here that after coming *from the muddy fields of Tennessee we looked like we had come from a war. They indeed must have felt sorry for us. They had also been told not to entertain these overnight-staying GIs. Before we could finish one bottle of beer the MPs came in. Now my playboy lieutenant took over. He took the MPs over to a corner and with his charm talked them out of turning us in. They did, however, escort us back to our area with a warning that if they caught us again we would be turned in.*

Newly promoted Lieutenant Colonel Thomas Kelly, his wife Jean, and their new daughter Carla Jean drove down to Fort Jackson, South Carolina to join the 106th Infantry Division. As S-3, Division Artillery, Kelly was responsible for training the four new battalions of artillery. Of course, he had plenty of help. Army Ground Forces Headquarters in Washington prescribed the schedules, regimens, courses, tests, and field exercises that kept the units busy from reveille to retreat, and the officers busy from retreat to taps. Kelly never wanted to be a professional soldier, he wanted to be a lawyer like his father. When the Florida real estate boom collapsed, and the depression hit, his only real choice was to attend the University of Florida or none at all. Being a state institution the university made ROTC mandatory for the first two years. When his four years of education were complete, he became a second lieutenant in the 116th Field Artillery Regiment, Florida National Guard. The fact was that he made more cash as a reserve officer than the monthly $35 salary he made as an associate at his father's law firm. He eventually joined the 106th as an S-3 Plans and Training Officer, before committing to the 589th Field Artillery Battalion full time, in what was at that time considered to be the one of the worst disciplined outfits in the division but all that was about to change.

Lieutenant Colonel Thomas Kelly, 589th Field Artillery Battalion
Three of the battalion commanders were Academy graduates who were rapidly promoted from lieutenant to lieutenant colonel in the two and half years since Pearl Harbor. By the end of the summer, it was apparent that two of the four battalion commanders were letting their battalions fall behind in performance and responsiveness. The 590th Field Artillery Battalion failed in early tests, and the 589th Field Artillery Battalion not only failed tests, but also its commander was frequently hard to find.

I felt compelled to ask Colonel Craig for command of the 589th. My argument must have been persuasive, because in a matter of days, I had command of what I felt was the worst battalion in the division, if not the Army, so I got right to work. At 1900 hours the following night, I called a meeting of the battalion staff and only half arrived on time. By 1920 hours, when the rest of them straggled in, I opened the meeting.

"Lax discipline will no longer be tolerated," I said. "Anyone who is late for any scheduled event will be confined to post for one week."

It was drastic punishment, particularly for the married officers living off post, but it worked. I began to notice a difference in the demeanor of the officers and the enlisted men. A week or so later the division was on a three-day field exercise when I received notice of a 1500 hours meeting of battalion commanders at Division Artillery HQ. I was late, and although none of my staff knew I was late, I restricted myself to post and slept in the barracks. Strangely, this self-imposed disciplinary action did more to unite my men than any other measure I could have possibly adopted.

In October, the division was ready for field maneuvers under simulated battlefield conditions. For four months, the 106th Infantry Division did well, tearing up the roads and fields of Chester and York counties in central South Carolina.

One particular member of the new division hailed from a rather privileged background. Eric Fisher Wood's father, General Eric Fisher Wood Sr., was a member of Eisenhower's staff and a renowned World War I veteran. Eric Jr. graduated from Valley Forge Military Academy & School as a member of the Class of 1937. He was an outstanding cadet who graduated first of his class *summa cum laude* and was a Gold-star student for his four years at the Academy. Thereafter, Eric Wood Jr. went to Princeton, where his achievements were equally distinguished. He graduated in 1942. After his time at Princeton University, Eric served in the Pennsylvania National Guard and was called to active duty on April 19, 1943. Later on that year he completed the basic artillery officers' course at Fort Sill and was assigned as first lieutenant to the 589th Field Artillery Battalion, 106th Infantry Division for further training at Fort Jackson. This man would become the warrior incarnate.

Following Basic and Advanced Infantry Training, on March 28, 1944 the Division moved to Tennessee to take part in maneuvers with the Second Army. The story of Camp Atterbury was rumored to go back to 1902 when three traveling ministers preaching fire and brimstone came to the little town of Mt. Pisgah, Indiana. One member of the congregation recorded the following excerpt from a sermon:

"The time will come when not a house or farm shall be left standing in these parts and your lands shall be a place of desolation."

Forty years later, Mt. Pisgah was the center of Camp Atterbury. The Army's announcement that a training camp for 30,000 men would be built, came from Washington DC on January 6, 1942, less than a month after the United States officially got into World War II. The Army moved swiftly to start construction of the camp, and by April 1942, more than 15,000 civilian workers were employed. The camp was built on the northern part of 40,000 acres of land purchased from farmers in the three surrounding counties. Throughout the spring of 1942 it rained almost continuously and a sea of mud confronted the builders.

Colonel Welton Modisette, the new Post Commander, arrived shortly after construction began and was impressed by the mud. When he arrived his car sank to its axles and he had to walk to the outskirts of his new camp. The new post was named for Hoosier Brigadier General William Wallace Atterbury, the famed World War I military transportation expert, and later President of the Pennsylvania Railroad. Later the soldiers took the cue and nicknamed it Mud-Berry.

John Gatens, Battery A, 589th Field Artillery Battalion

The next morning was clear and cold when we loaded up to continue the move to Camp Atterbury. Again we had to travel on the small, lightly traveled roads. The scenery was very nice, but no girls to whistle at.

Our next night stop was at Ft. Knox, Kentucky. For me this was a blessing. My brother Jim was stationed there. We were escorted to our bivouac area. This was an open area on the outskirts of the camp. No barracks this time. I spotted a chapel not far from our area. I took off and entered the chapel. There was a chaplain in the office. He didn't know what to think of me. This was an armored camp and muddy artillerymen didn't show up here. I told him who I was and that I had a brother on this base, and could he find out where he was and get me to him.

He located him and called a taxi for me. Jim was in a heavy tank corps. They had their own group that was self-contained. I went into the office and a soldier asked what I wanted. I told him that I wanted to see my brother. He said, "Wait here." When Jim came around the corner and saw this cruddy-looking GI he almost didn't recognize me.

When he introduced me to his friend, the first sergeant, he told Jim to take me down to the barracks and clean me up. Being their own group, they had all kinds of supplies. Jim asked me for sizes and while I was showering he went and got me a complete new set of clothes. I think they burned mine.

In Ft. Knox a first sergeant had his own home supplied. He was kind enough to invite Jim and me to supper and to stay the night. What a joy, a real home-cooked meal and a real bed. Heavenly.

After supper he drove me over to where the outfit was staying. I had left so fast that I never asked what time we were leaving the next morning. My gun crew was all around a fire trying to keep warm. I, in my new uniform, walked up to them. Being dark, and with only the light of the fire to go by, I told them to put out the fire: it was not allowed on this post. Not recognizing me, you can guess where they told me to go. The look on their faces when they did recognize me was of complete surprise. When I left to go to my nice warm bed, they all wished me a pleasant good night. Ha! ha! ha! that will be the day!

No one in that outfit ate until the first sergeant was seated. With all the men seated, we walked in. They were used to the Sergeant and Jim, but all eyes were on me. Who was this special corporal who could sit at the head table? It felt very good. Then it was time to say goodbye. I didn't see Jim again for over a year, until the war was over and we were all home again. We then left for Camp Atterbury, Indiana.

The civilians in Indiana treated the GIs with open arms whenever we were on pass. The hospitality was unlimited, even invitations to private homes for Sunday dinner, if you could get a pass into town. Invitations were posted in the service clubs for anyone desiring to take advantage of them. This is the way that I remember Indianapolis, Indiana. It was what we called a "GIs' town."

We were toughened to the task ahead, training was becoming routine, and everybody just wanted to get at whatever was laid before us. At this time the

106th was considered to be one of the best trained divisions in the Army. There was a great deal of pride and esprit de corps among the men. In the parlance of the day, we were a "crack outfit."

I was lucky again. One of the fellows in my crew lived in Chicago. His name was Phillip Diasio. We called him "Nippy." Every time we could get a three-day pass we would go up to his home. His mother and father were very nice people. He also had two sisters. On Saturday night Nippy, his girlfriend, Margie (his sister), her girlfriend, George Sparks and I, would go to The Loop. In Chicago, The Loop is like our Times Square. It was a sailors' town, what with Great Lakes Naval Base being there. This made it nice for us: not too many soldiers.

This is where I got my first taste of bars. The first one we went into was very embarrassing for me. When asked what I wanted to drink, I didn't know what or how to order a drink. Lucky for me one of the girls asked for a rum and Coke, so, liking Coke, I said, "I'll have one too."

On Sunday we would all go to church. After church Nippy's mother would cook a typical Italian Sunday dinner. This took us about four hours to finish. Just in time to run for the Greyhound Bus back to Indianapolis. This is the only time that we would get a bad deal. The only way back to camp in the early morning hours was by cab but there were lots of GIs all waiting for one. It was a long wait and many times we would only get an hour of sleep before reveille. But being young and needing something other than army life, it was worth it.

During May and June a large number of 106th Division men were transferred to overseas units and were replaced by men from Replacement Centers at Ft. Bragg N.C. and Camp Roberts, Cal. Training had to start all over again. These new men were mostly from units no longer considered necessary to the war effort: ASTP [Army Specialized Training Program] programs, pilot training, anti-aircraft and coast artillery, etc. The need now was for infantry. Casualty numbers in Europe and the Pacific were climbing and it still required the Infantry to take and occupy territory.

Not long after we arrived at Camp Atterbury came a sad day for me. My pal Lt. Cassibry was a big thorn in the side of all the brass in A Battery. He was a superior artilleryman, but in their eyes not a good leader. His drinking and lack of discipline was cause for a change. In our eyes he was the best. They transferred him to C Battery. This broke his spirit. He had taken us from green young civilians to the best firing battery in the Division. He then applied for Liaison

Pilot Training. I wrote to him many times while at training base. He loved it there. I don't know the circumstances, but he cracked up a plane so they washed him out. I really think our Battalion Commander had a little to do with that. Knowing how good an artilleryman he was, Lt. Cassibry was transferred back to Battalion Headquarters. I never did see him much after. His pilot's training probably saved his life. At the height of the Bulge an order came down to burn the artillery planes because some of the pilots were not around. Lt. Cassibry volunteered to fly one out. He did and survived the war.

We now in turn received as our Battery Exec., a Lt. Kiendl from C Battery. We knew of him and his reputation. He was a real GI and a very strict, to-the-book guy. After losing our best friend, this guy didn't set too well. We spent many months under his leadership. I guess it was all for the better. We had to train a group of new men in a short period of time. The training was as usual, with very little let-up and grueling.

According to most military men, a base is born on the day its headquarters is set up and the first numbered order written. Camp Atterbury's first special order rolled off a mimeograph machine on June 2, 1942, in a headquarters set up in a red brick house formerly the home of a farmer. Six months after construction began, soldiers poured into the camp. No official dedication took place to mark the opening of the $86-million camp, but, on August 15, 1942, the 83d Infantry Division was activated, and Camp Atterbury was thrown open to visitors. 25,000 Hoosiers watched the colorful ceremonies and inspected the camp and its facilities. It was a biting cold morning when John Schaffner and the 589th Field Artillery Battalion loaded up and headed for Camp Atterbury.

John Schaffner, Scout, Battery A, 589th Field Artillery Battalion

The division moved again, from Tennessee to Camp Atterbury, Indiana, near Indianapolis. After hearing all the songs written about Indiana, I expected the weather to be balmy. Not so. When we arrived on the post the temperature was freezing and the wind was enough to blow your mustache off.

Henry Thurner and I had girlfriends in Indianapolis and we frequently dou-ble-dated. These girls were next-door neighbors and if we were there on Sunday it was often for a mid-day dinner at the Stewarts' house. We would take in a movie or go to the Indiana Roof for dancing. I was never a good dancer, but I liked to hold the girls while they did. It was often in the wee hours of the morning when we caught the bus back to Camp Atterbury. If you were lucky enough to be one of the first ones to board the bus you could swing up into the overhead luggage rack and grab a nap on the way home. No problem for somebody six feet tall and only about a 145 pounds. This is the way that I remember Indianapolis, Indiana.

On one occasion at Camp Atterbury the battalion was performing maneuvers in the field, and I was assigned with another GI to take a message from one place to another. This was summer time and the weather was hot and dry. We were driving along a dirt road, just inside the military reservation, when we passed a decrepit farmhouse not 40 feet from the roadside. As we went by I glanced to the side, and there, at the side of the house, was a woman standing in a galvanized washtub, taking a bath, right out there in the bright sun in front of God and everybody. Of course, she wasn't expecting us, and I suppose God didn't count. My driver stood on the brakes and turned our jeep around in a cloud of dust and we went back for another peek, but, there was only an empty tub there by that time.

Another time, during a field exercise at Atterbury, I was assigned to man an observation post with a radio operator. Just the two of us, until recalled. When we arrived at the location given on the map we found ourselves in the midst of a peach orchard, with the fruit at its peak. All day long we ate peaches and when we couldn't eat any more, we picked, and loaded the jeep until they ran out on the ground. On returning to the bivouac area that evening, we distributed peaches to everybody in the battery and the mess sergeant got what was left. What a shame it was to see all that fruit wasted, but when the U.S. Government needed land on which to train the troops I'm sure that was not a consideration.

I learned how to handle bitter-cold nights on solo guard duty. When I was dropped off I figured that meant the night so I asked the driver to bring back my bedroll. I was in the middle of nowhere, had no idea where he was, where the battery was, no food, no map, no compass, no telephone, no radio, and no nothing, except orders to stay put. That night I learned to gather pine needles and take it easy while bedding down in them. To my surprise, I slept pretty well and when the driver showed up in the morning I greeted him with a special unprintable name.

Just prior to leaving Camp Atterbury, our battery C.O., Captain Elliot Goldstein, was promoted and transferred to Battalion HQ, and we were assigned a new battery commander. I will not elaborate, but I will say that this new officer did not have my respect as a leader. So much so, that I, with some of the other guys

in our section, went over the chain of command and requested a
Airborne Division to escape the intolerable situation that we were .... g
Trying to effect a transfer without going through proper channels is a big "no-no"
in the military and the Battalion C.O., Lt. Col. Kelly, even got into the act. He
found it necessary to have me demoted to buck private and transferred to Battery
B and my good buddy Bob Stoll (who was with me a hundred percent) busted
also and transferred to Battery C. This made all of us happy. I wasn't pleased to
be separated from Bob, but at least my situation with Captain M. was relieved.

So, it was with Battery B, 589th Field Artillery Battalion that I went into
action in Europe. Captain Arthur C. Brown was the C.O. and a leader who
was easy to follow, an officer and a gentleman par excellence. I quickly became
acquainted with the guys in Battery B and although assigned in my MOS 761
as scout, it wasn't until the actual German offensive beginning on December 16,
1944 that I functioned as one.

As the spring of 1943 approached and graduation loomed, young
Kenneth Raymond Johnson, took the standard army exams to see if
he was qualified to join the new Army Specialized Training Program
(ASTP). This was a military training program instituted by the United
States Army during World War II to accommodate wartime demands
for both junior officers and soldiers with technical skills. Conducted at
a number of American universities, it offered training in such fields as
engineering, foreign languages, and even medicine. Kenneth passed the
exam. On graduating he enrolled in the Army Reserves because he was
not yet 18, and started studying at the R.C.A Institute in New York
City, exactly as he had planned.

On Friday morning, August 7, 1943, two weeks before his 18th
birthday, he was off for his first assignment at Syracuse University.
Syracuse University welcomed the ASTP'ers warmly because many
of its students had been called up for active duty with the passage of
the Selective Service Act in November 1942. Once Johnson settled
into his studies at Syracuse, his parents made plans for the eight-hour
drive from Tappan to Syracuse in their '37 Plymouth, and that meant
saving their weekly four-gallon ration of gasoline for several weeks and
taking it with them. By New Year's Eve, 1943, Johnson found himself

at Fort Benning, Georgia, where he was to do his basic training with 10th Company, 3d Battalion, 5th Training Regiment before returning to Syracuse University. With the cancellation of ASTP in February 1944, Johnson found himself at Fort Benning, Georgia for basic training. From there he got what he thought was a good racket as driver for a detachment of special troops from Second Army HQ. He got to stay at the detachment HQ and drove dignitaries and officers around camp and town. For Johnson this was a lot better than drilling with his company.

Like most soldiers, his stay at Benning was short and he was transferred to B Company, 506th MP Battalion at Fort Jackson for training to become a military policeman. Then, in mid–June, word got around that many of them were transferring out. His orders and those of several hundred others with the 506th came when they saw the list on the bulletin board with the names of those headed for the 106th Infantry Division at Camp Atterbury, Indiana. It would be another month before he could tell his parents where his going and that he was now a rifleman with A Company, 424th Infantry, 106th Infantry Division.

John (Jack) M. Roberts, 592d Field Artillery Battalion

Our arrival at Camp Atterbury was the signal that we were to get ready to go overseas. Whether our departure would be to Europe or to the South Pacific was still unknown. Our training at Camp Atterbury was quite intensive. The reason for the grueling training was due to the mass exit of many officers and enlisted personnel being sent overseas and the arrival of replacements that needed accelerated field training. Just when we thought we had a solidly trained Division, the shifting in personnel would take place.

The day we arrived at Camp Atterbury, we unloaded our equipment and were assigned our barracks. This was a nice camp, newer, but much like Fort Jackson in many respects, with the same facilities, barber shops, PXs, chapels, movie houses, training grounds, artillery range, parade grounds, etc. On June 3, 1944 our Division was up to full strength and we went to the field in full combat gear. We were visited and observed by Under Secretary of War, Robert P. Patterson. He called it a "great performance." A Division parade was to be held the weekend of June 15th. This review included everyone in the Division, with all our combat gear and equipment. This meant the vehicles, half-tracks, howitzers, cannons, etc. had to be in tiptop condition and either cleaned or painted.

There appeared on the bulletin board a notice that I had dreaded, but knew it had to happen. We were scheduled to take a survivor training exercise which consisted of jumping off a tower into a lake. On campsite there was a small lake where a tower was built over the water itself and had a steep ramp running from the tower top platform to the ground level. Each soldier, dressed in full combat gear with back pack, carbine, etc., was required to climb the ramp to the top of the tower, then jump some twenty feet into the water below and swim to shore. Did I ever luck out! The day before the survival exercise, I was summoned to the first sergeant's office and told that I would be on special assignment the next day. The special assignment I received, along with a few other guys, was to go to a special building near Divisional Artillery Headquarters to assist in indoor training exercises for the artillery officers. This large building was built specifically to house a simulated artillery firing range. Inside, and to one side, was a high platform where the artillery officers stood to overlook a large 3-D miniature landscape. The landscape contained miniature houses, trucks, tanks, personnel, roads, etc. It was very well done. The structure beneath the landscape to hold all of it in place was wood support beams. The landscape itself was mounted on rigid mesh burlap.

Everything, the trees, grass, hills, houses, tanks, personnel, vehicles were all painted and built to scale. A marvelous piece of craftsmanship that looked very authentic. The underside of the landscape was anywhere from one foot to several feet over our heads, depending upon the terrain of the landscape and marked with coordinates, just like an artillery terrain map. Our job was to work beneath the landscape and to receive our commands from the artillery officer by field telephone, which was simulating firing howitzer shells at a particular target over our heads. The officer gave his commands to us in the sequence of Fire Command Orders, such as Battery Adjust, Shell HE, Fuse Quick, etc. We listened to the officer's commands as if we were at the gun position. We then mathematically transposed his commands so that we could go to the proper coordinates where the shell was supposed to hit. We used a gadget that sent out a puff of white smoke (powder) through the mesh landscape to simulate an impact "burst." The officer observing the "smoke" knew exactly where the shell landed. If the officer missed the target, he would then telephone additional commands for us to adjust his firing. We would then follow his commands until he accomplished his mission. We never knew which officer was doing the firing because we could not see him.

On July 4th, there was an Independence Day parade in Indianapolis. The 589th Field Artillery was asked to represent the artillery and we in the 592d did not have to participate, nor did the 590th and 591st. About this time a notice appeared on the bulletin board stating that all units of the 106th were to have a group picture taken and the Divisional booklet would be published.

Since receiving his commission as a second lieutenant from the U.S. Military Academy at West Point in June 1943, Alan W. Jones had wanted to command an infantry platoon that was actually going to Europe. A rumor had been circulated that his old unit, the 42d Infantry Division, wasn't actually going and this was the reason he'd requested a transfer to the 106th Infantry Division. However, he wasn't sure if the Commanding General of the 106th was going to acquiesce to this request. Moreover it was highly irregular for a division commander such as Major General Jones to request a meeting with a newly arrived lieutenant. Especially one who'd transferred in just a week ago when the entire division would be preparing to leave the States for Europe in less than three months.

In fact the Major General had never heard of it happening unless there was discipline involved, and even then, it was rare. When the lieutenant arrived at Division Headquarters, the General's staff promptly let him in the office. With his cover under his arm he walked through the door, snapped a salute, and, standing at attention, formally introduced himself, even if it was surplus to requirements: "Lieutenant Alan W. Jones reporting, sir," he said, to a man he'd know all his life, his father, Major General Alan W. Jones, Commander, 106th Infantry Division. The discussion between father and son had hints of familiarity behind the formality of rank. Jones's father wanted to know why his son had requested a transfer. Certainly he understood his son's desire for a combat position, but wasn't too keen on his son serving in his division. It wasn't that he didn't respect his son's capability, but things could get complicated. The younger Jones put it in simple terms: when he learned that the 106th Infantry Division was on alert status for deployment to Europe, and that the 42d Infantry Division he'd trained with since graduation from West Point the year before was going to become a training unit, he'd applied for the transfer. Jones was proud of his father. Ever since he was a young boy, his goal had been to follow his father's example as an officer.

Rumors of overseas deployment were now rampant throughout the camp. The 106th knew they were going but when was reduced to fervent speculation at that time. In early October, a week before leaving Camp Atterbury, the division review was staged in which all of the units in the division passed before an assorted group of generals. In preparation, they stood around for hours while 13,000 men and heavy equipment including their trucks, jeeps, artillery pieces and armored vehicles, lined up and prepared to march. The 423d I&R Platoon knew they were headed overseas and felt therefore compelled to have a "Farewell to the States" party suitable for their departure. This was going to be the big adventure. Many of these young men hadn't seen outside their own state let alone another country until they'd been inducted into the armed forces. For some of them it would be a one-way journey.

At eight o'clock sharp, October 5, 1944, in the little town of Columbus, Indiana, a rumbling six-by-six rolled to a screeching stop in front of the local armory. Upstairs in the drill hall everything was laid out, including the two bartenders. The band was set up, the floor was waxed, the bar was open, and there was food on the tables. Everything was perfect, except that GIs hated dancing without female partners, and at that time, there weren't any. Someone had goofed. Recon units were dispatched, and in a surprisingly short time they returned with their objective: girls! The band played, they danced, the liquor flowed, and they sang. Fortunately, the night ended without major incident. Men were stacked in the trucks under supervision of the loading crew and the first sergeant, and their thoughts returned to leaving the States. Over the next several days the division turned in old equipment and clothing for new. The men made what might be their last phone calls home, still largely oblivious to the timing and destination of their next move.

John Gatens, Battery A, 589th Field Artillery Battalion
A very surprising thing happened just before leaving Camp Atterbury. Lt. Kiendl was transferred to B Battery and we in turn got as our Battery Exec Lt. Eric Wood. To this day even Lt. Kiendl doesn't know the reason for the change. Lt.

Wood was more of the Cassibry type, except he was from a military family and very professional. His father was a general on General Eisenhower's staff. At the same time, our Battery C.O., Captain Elliot Goldstein was promoted and transferred to Battalion Headquarters. We then got Captain Aloysius Menke. The division was alerted for movement overseas in September 1944 and moved by train to Camp Myles Standish, Mass. on 9 and 10 October. The following month was spent awaiting transportation during which time the equipment was packed and training was continued.

Major General Alan W. Jones addressed his assembled troops:

Be proud of your assignment, of the fact that you have been selected for a combat division, that upon your shoulders rests the responsibility for the victory we have to win. Never forget that your individual part is of first importance to the success of the division.

CHAPTER 2

THE GOLDEN LIONS GO
TO WAR

Camp Myles Standish served as the main staging area for the Boston Port of Embarkation (BPOE). It was one of six on the Atlantic seaboard, ranked third after New York and San Francisco for the amount of men and materiel shipped overseas to the Allied armies. The camp had opened there on October 7, 1942. Records state that the base covered 1,620 acres and was traversed by 35 miles of paved roads and almost ten miles of railroad track connected to the main lines that reached every corner of the United States. Its mission was to receive military personnel from all over the United States and make certain that they and their equipment were ready for immediate shipment to the European Theater of Operations (ETO).

John Gatens, Battery A, 589th Field Artillery Battalion
During our train movement the train stopped at Trenton, N.J. We opened the door to look around. A couple of civilians got on the train. We told them they were welcome to come along, that we were headed for overseas. When they saw nothing but GIs it didn't take them very long to back off. We had many Southerners and Western people in our outfit. Our next stop was in Grand Central Station in New York and they couldn't believe that we had gone under the Hudson River and now were under the ground in New York City.

As usual in the station in New York there were people out to make money. Men were carrying big baskets filled with sandwiches and candy bars. Others had sodas and juice. Needless to say they made lots of money on our gang.

Camp Myles Standish, Mass. was a staging area for the troops awaiting shipment overseas from the port of Boston. All of our equipment had been packed up and was on its way overseas. We spent most of our time with physical fitness and classes on abandoning ship. Glad we didn't have to do that. Nightly passes were given for a strict 50 miles radius. Also, no telling anyone that you were waiting for a ship for overseas.

Here is where I (one of the few times I disobeyed orders), along with two others, took off for home. We hitchhiked to Providence, Rhode Island, and then took the train to New York, raced to the bus depot for a bus to Paterson, N.J., then another bus to my house. Of course my parents were very glad to see me. Spent a few hours with them and a few hours with Ann, my future wife. At around 2300 hours my father would drive us to New York to catch the train back to Providence. It was only later on that I realized what I was doing to my father. This meant that he didn't get home until around 0030 hours. He had to be up again at 0530 hours to get ready for work. Many mornings we almost didn't make it back in time. One morning we didn't make reveille. In a Port of Embarkation this is like desertion. When we got in the men were already gone for the day's workout. Lucky for us our first sergeant was from New York. All he said was, "I know where you were. I won't report you this time, but don't let it happen again."

I went home about four times. Each time I would tell them, "When I don't come home anymore you will know that I am gone." I'm sure that when I was a POW, with what they had to go through, they were glad that I did make it home when I did.

November 10 the battalion moved to the Port of Embarkation at Boston on special trains from Camp Myles Standish. It rained hard most of the day and the troops were soaking wet by the time they boarded the train. You know how it is with the Army, hurry up and wait. After a short ride we de-trained directly on a covered pier and were served hot coffee and stale donuts by the Red Cross. Couldn't have tasted better. Everyone was kept moving, leading immediately onto the troop transport SS Wakefield, the former luxury liner SS Manhattan, sister ship to the SS Washington and one of the largest ships ever built in America. The battalion occupied D and E decks forward, sharing the ship with the 590th, 591st, 592d Field Artillery battalions, Headquarters Battery, Division Artillery, and the division Special Troops. The ship was crowded, there being five canvas bunks on pipe racks between the deck and the ceiling with precious little space left for passageways. We kept our packs and duffel bags in the bunk with us. Very few men were on deck at about 1630 hours when the ship slipped out of the harbor in the fog and driving rain.

The average stay at Standish lasted three to five days during which GIs received physicals, inoculations, dental exams and last-minute training. Meanwhile, their equipment that included everything from office stationary to howitzers was given a last thorough check before being loaded onto trains bound for the ships waiting in Boston harbor. To accomplish all this, the camp had a permanent military complement of more than 2,500 personnel, including segregated African-American GIs who worked in service companies and women who served as nurses or members of the Women's Army Corps. The camp also employed approximately 750 civilian workers, most living within a 30-mile radius of the base. Thousands of GIs passed through Standish every week. In fact, by the first week of September 1944, BPOE records show that a half million Allied personnel had been processed through the camp. This included not only Americans but also several thousand British, Canadian and Australian soldiers who were in the States for training or on special assignment. It was now the turn of the 106th Infantry Division to join the ranks of those participating in the European Theatre of Operations.

John Schaffner, Scout, Battery B, 589th Field Artillery Battalion
The division was alerted for movement overseas in September 1944 and moved by train to Camp Myles Standish, Mass. on 9 and 10 October. The following month was spent awaiting transportation during which time the equipment was packed and training was continued. I was bored stiff at this place, and one day when a request for a volunteer who could read blueprints was made, I responded. What the hell, didn't I have a course in mechanical drawing in high school? Seems a construction crew was erecting a Quonset building and the engineer didn't show up on that day. When I reported to the job and was put in charge I quickly let the men know that I had no idea what they were doing and simply stayed out of their way so they could get on with it.

On one of the days at Standish just about everyone in the camp came down with a case of the "GIs." There was a line-up at every latrine that day and another line at the dispensary to get something for relief. We were in bad shape for any duty that day, except maybe laundering underwear. Later on word got around that a bar of GI soap was found in a coffee urn at the mess hall. The camp was staffed with Italian and German POWs so we all suspected one of them. Who knows?

While we were at Standish I received short passes to visit Taunton, Mass. and also went as far as Providence, R.I. The area had U.S.O. clubs that we took advantage of and I even learned to dance in GI boots while there. There were a lot of sweet things there, including the native maple sugar candy.

Moving a whole division from the United States to Europe was a gargantuan task and one that had to be undertaken with the utmost gravity. Everyone had a part to play from the lowliest private to the highest commanding officer and no one was left wanting. The logistics for organizing this mass departure were simply staggering. It took skill, timing, intelligence and expert coordination to achieve the goal of getting everyone across the sea safely. It was the fall of 1944 when various troopships were employed to take the Golden Lions to war, among them the RMS *Queen Elizabeth* (October 8, 1944) that made her first voyage with elements of the 106th plus advance parties, including Colonel Thomas J. Riggs, CO of 81st Engineer Combat Battalion. On the ship's second perilous journey for the 106th she carried the 423d Infantry Regiment and 2d Battalion of the 424th Infantry Regiment. The troopship USS *Wakefield* left Boston harbor (October 11, 1944) with remaining 81st Engineer Combat Battalion soldiers, 589th, 590th, 591st, 592d Field Artillery battalions, Division Artillery, Division Artillery Headquarters Battery, Special Troops (including 106th Reconnaissance Troop) and a battalion of African-American quartermaster troops. The RMS *Aquitania* left New York harbor (October 20, 1944) with 422d Infantry Regiment and the 424th Infantry Regiment minus its 2d Battalion. They all set sail into the grey, spuming North Atlantic to run the gauntlet of inclement weather, German U-boats and numerous other obstacles that could potentially impede their progress. Between October and November 1944, 106th troops were transferred from Camp Myles Standish, Massachusetts overseas to Liverpool and Greenock, then to Batsford Park in the South Midlands, England.

Sergeant John P. Kline, M Company, 423d Infantry Regiment

Left New York early morning. Did not see Statue of Liberty. The trip was peaceful. I ate mostly Spam sandwiches and Malo Cups, for I could not stand the greasy English sausage and potatoes. Would like to bring wife and family on the "Queen" after the war. Were told that the "Queen" was chased by two submarines. I understand that the she had a record of out-running fifty subs on one mission.

10/22/44: Arrived Glasgow, Scotland, Firth of Clyde. This was the only time in crossing the Atlantic that we were placed on alert. We were instructed to stand on the outside deck with our lifebelts on. They told us this is standard practice going into a harbor, where the subs could be lying in wait.

10/24/44: Left Glasgow by train late evening. Rode all night. Breakfast was coffee, chips and meat pie on the train.

10/25/44: Arrived Cheltenham, England. The 423d Regiment was billeted on the grounds of the Cheltenham Steeple Chase track about ½ mile from town. My squad was billeted in the press building.

For those relatives who were left behind news of the war was highly censored and hard to come by. They would watch the newsreels at the theater and pick up maps the Esso Company published showing where the fighting was taking place. They got a kick out of the Disney cartoon depicting Mussolini, Tojo, and Hitler as a goofy German oompah band and its accompanying song, "der Führer's Face," in which the singer blew a raspberry every time he sang *Heil!* Most nights families simply sat around the radio in the living room and listened to Lowell Thomas reporting the news on the fighting in the Pacific and Africa. Voices were reverently hushed and ears alerted when Thomas would begin every broadcast with "Good evening, everybody," and sign off with "So long, until tomorrow." For many Americans he became the household voice of the war along with others such as Edward R. Murrow.

Soon after the RMS *Aquitania* set sail, Captain David Ormiston, Commander, I Company, 422d Infantry, called his men to the smoking lounge. Ormiston laid out the rules. "Men," he said, "you will have two meals day. You'll get your mess schedule shortly. If you're late, you miss your chow. Right now, there are two important things to remember on this trip. First, water is extremely scarce, use only what you absolutely need. Second, fire and panic are more of a danger to us than German submarines. Smoke only in designated areas, and I caution you snuff out your cigarettes completely. And whatever happens, stay calm."

What Ormiston did not tell them was that if the ship did sink, there were lifeboats for only 3,000 men. The next day the men of I Company stood in the chow line amid the deafening clatter of hundreds of trays slamming against the trashcans. Unaware of the potential consequences, Private Littell decided to have something done about the noise and beckoned the mess sergeant.

"Sergeant," he said politely, "would it be possible to have the garbage cans placed a little farther away from the chow line?"

"Gee fella," responded the sergeant with a smile, "if it please Your Highness, I'll be happy to have nice white lacey doilies placed under the garbage cans so you'll feel more comfortable dining here." Then, with a jerk, he moved right up close, sticking his chin in Littell's face. "Listen, soldier, this is wartime. This is a troopship. Who the fuck told you that you were being booked into the Waldorf-Astoria?" By then the sergeant's face was beet red. He turned, and disappeared into the galley. Littell's humiliation in front of his buddies was total.

In 1939 young American Joseph Littell was attending St. Andrew's in Middletown, Delaware when he was called into the headmaster's office and told of his selection to represent the school as an exchange student to Germany. Within a month, Littell was physically in Germany wearing a khaki uniform, black leather belt and shoulder strap with the crimson-red swastika armband of the Hitler Youth. He was one of hundreds of young men exchanged between 30 American and 30 German schools by the American Schoolboy Fellowship to promote a better understanding between the two countries. In his case, it was the Nationalpolitische Erziehunganstalt, (National Political Reformatory) or NPEA, one of ten boarding schools set up to indoctrinate the cream of the German crop for leadership in the Third Reich. Littell was still in Germany participating in Nazi-sponsored war games with 14-year-old schoolmates when war broke out on September 1, 1939. He and a couple of other students stole Nazi wristbands and escaped to the French border only to find it completely sealed off. After that he hopped on a train to Basel, Switzerland, and made straight for the American consulate where those good people arranged passage to Le Havre, France and back to New York on the SS *Manhattan*.

Four years later, he was going back to Europe but this time with a possibility that he might even end up fighting against some of the kids he had gone to school with during that summer in 1939.

John Schaffner, Scout, Battery B, 589th Field Artillery Battalion
November 11, 12, 13, 14 & 15—The North Atlantic was violently rough and few of us (including me) escaped becoming seasick. Two meals a day were served to those able to eat. To get the meals necessitated standing in an hour-long chow line that started in the compartment, wound up the stairs to the next deck and ran along about half the length of the ship to the "mess hall." There was nothing else to do anyway, so it was a welcome break in the monotony and it got us away from the bunk area for a while. And, it didn't smell very good down there either. Chow was served on a stainless steel tray without regard for any niceties. You could have your ice cream on top the mashed potatoes or, if you preferred, in the beans. As one received his food, he would proceed to the "stand-up-height" steel tables to eat. You had to hang on to both the tray and the table to eat. The ship was rolling, so that if you didn't hold on to something you could end up in your neighbor's chow tray. Nobody could go out on deck in this weather.

About the third day out the weather became better and the seas smoothed out some. It was now possible to get outside for a breath of fresh air once in a while without being swept overboard. Our course must have carried us farther south. The ship moved along fast and alone. The possibility of an encounter with a German sub was on everyone's mind, but nobody dwelled upon it. The ship was considerably faster than any German sub, though don't know about German torpedoes. Nothing but the cold winter ocean was in sight for about six days.

On the afternoon of November 16 another transport was sighted as we were nearing the British Isles. A destroyer escort also appeared to guide the ships through the minefields at the entrance to The St. George's Channel and protect against possible sub attack. The water became extremely rough again and the destroyer escorting us completely disappeared in the troughs as it made way off the beam. This actually was a comfort since it made a torpedo attack highly unlikely. Our ship literally plowed through the giant waves that crashed over the deck. The sailors on the "can" must have been taking a real beating. We must have been getting close to England because K-rations were issued that day for our first meal on shore.

James (JD) Forsythe, D Company, 424th Infantry Regiment
As a mid-westerner, I hoped that I might see the Statue of Liberty as the troop ship Aquitania departed from New York City harbor. I positioned myself on the fantail for a good view. However, this could only happen to a landlubber: as the

ship began to roll so did my stomach, and I suffered my first bout of seasickness and the viewing of the Statue of Liberty did not occur for many years.

On the same voyage, when we were more than half way to our destination on a day that was inclement and most of the soldiers were on the decks below, the ship's crew fired the artillery gun on the fore part of the ship. This was an alarming sound. Everyone grabbed a life preserver and headed for the open deck. The pouring out was similar to ants pouring out of an ant hole after a liquid is poured into the opening. This was a frightening situation until it was announced that the gun fired was due to a ship in close vicinity that did not show its colors. All was well when it was announced the ship was a friendly Dutch ship and not an enemy ship.

Frank S. Trautman, A Company, 422d Infantry Regiment

When I was 18 years old I volunteered before being drafted to go into military service. I was sent to Blytheville, Arkansas to the Camp Joseph T. Robinson Induction Center north of Little Rock. After exams I was sent to Camp Polk, Louisiana, and selected service in the Army Air Forces and was shipped off to Sheppard Field in Wichita Falls, Texas. I was sent to the University of Nebraska for math and science enhancement and basic flight training. There was apparently little need for more air crew and my class received a polite notice from our Government, "For the convenience of the Government and without prejudice you are ordered to report to Camp Atterbury, Indiana, to be assigned to the 97th Infantry Division. While there I transferred to the 106th Infantry Division. Later we crossed the Atlantic on the RMS Aquitania.

Slowly but surely the 106th Division began to arrive on British shores. One of the first was the 423d I&R Platoon. They had become exceedingly proficient at loading and unloading hundreds of barracks bags on and off the trains and ships, and in quick order they were seated in the coaches of what they thought was a miniature train. As they left Glasgow they gazed out the windows and marveled at the majestic splendor of gentle rolling hills and picturesque Scottish crofts with white plastered walls and thatched roofs. They saw herds of sheep and cattle grazing peacefully in these broad, lush green valleys. The train passed through dozens of small villages that were immaculately clean and neat. Children and adults alike appeared sporadically along the tracks, proudly holding up a V for Victory. It was difficult to reconcile their apparent happiness with the fact that they were at war.

Sometime around 1800 hours, the train stopped for coffee and donuts at Carlisle. Behind blackout curtains, the troops played cards and gambled their last American currency. Soon, the sleepy GIs stretched out on the card tables, the lights dimmed, and they slept. It was 0100 hours when they reached their destination. A large sign on the platform said Cheltenham. Then the barracks bags routine began again, but this time they were handled by a baggage detail. The trucks took them through the darkened streets of a good-sized town, and, ultimately, to a small concentration of Quonset huts that were to be their home for the next month.

For the newly arrived GIs life in Cheltenham was surprisingly pleasant. The huts accommodated 16 men. In the center of each stood a small potbellied stove, flanked on either side by a row of double-decker bunks. These facilities were new to the men, and actually, the most uncomfortable garrison life they had experienced. Before long, however, it had become their new home. They had lights, tables, chairs, and a public address system that played the latest American jazz.

This was also their first serious look at the British people and their country. The GIs found British mornings depressingly cold and consistently foggy but on most days, by 1000 hours, the fog had dissipated, making way for a milky fall sun. Most afternoons they got passes and took advantage of these from the seats of Red Cross bicycles that enabled them to explore the local shops in search of souvenirs and whatever else might be on offer at the time.

They would have seen camouflaged munitions factories with anti-aircraft guns pointing skyward, interrupting the rural beauty of the English countryside. Such sights would remind the soldiers that Britain was a country that had already endured five years of war, and it was far from over.

Duties were lax at the 106th base. There were occasional classes where they learned to identify German uniforms, German aircraft and armor and polish up a few phrases in the German language. They also brushed up on radio procedures and security. Life was good and the most demanding task at the time was having to go for coal late at night and clean out the barrack stove.

One duty the men did everything to avoid was cleaning the latrines. They could easily stretch it to three times longer than it should have taken, and in doing so stay out of sight for even more unpleasant duties. The company latrine was in an open field 75 yards behind the huts. It was a trench pit and wooden box with six holes surrounded by a tarp. Every morning they would remove the box they called the throne, pour gasoline down the pit, and toss a match to create a spectacular burn-off. When it was all over, they would cover what was left with lime and put it all back together for the next occupant.

One sunny morning they gathered at the site on time, removed the throne, and poured the gasoline. The igniting of the waste was interrupted by a frantic voice hollering, "Wait a minute! Wait a minute!" It was a GI suffering from some serious digestive maladies. Since the latrine duty guys hadn't finished with their work, they took pity, placed the throne back over the hole, and stepped aside to allow the GI to attend to his pressing problem. On finishing, and thanking them profusely, the GI inadvertently reached into his pocket, pulled out a cigarette, and without a second though tossed the match down the adjacent hole. The result was predictable and within seconds the poor man was shuffling at speed back to the barracks with his pants around his knees. The I&R Platoon never knew if that cured his problem, but for the next several days they did notice he ate all his meals standing up.

The most enjoyable aspect of life in England was the evenings spent meeting the locals over a pint of beer at the local pubs. At these establishments they would meet WAAFs and RAF pilots, and local characters who corresponded with most of the pre-informed idiosyncrasies, as the men expected. Despite their peculiarities, an obvious friendship put them at ease and they discovered soon enough that they were, as Winston Churchill aptly described, "two nations divided by a common language," but that didn't deter them from making friends; they were after all Allies against a common foe. On the whole the significance of American soldiers arriving in the United Kingdom was immense. They were very popular with the British ladies, probably because they looked considerably smarter than the poor weather-beaten old Tommies.

On some occasions this led to a great deal of tension that could erupt into fistfights. But the majority welcomed these young Americans with open arms. They attended dances, participated in numerous social activities and countless British families gratefully welcomed what most considered polite young men into their homes. British civilian women were regularly overawed by their generosity and "Hollywood" smiles. During a time of frugality and strict rationing the GIs appeared to have plenty of everything. British men were not quite as easily impressed and most just regarded the GIs as loud-mouthed, brassy and arrogant—in other words, serious competition. Moreover there was some consternation among the British military, some of who considered the Americans as poorly disciplined soldiers that didn't apply military doctrines stringently enough. For their part the Americans regarded the British as intransigent and lacking personal initiative. It appeared to all American soldiers that the British soldier was incapable of performing any allocated task without applying regular tea breaks.

John Gatens, Battery A, 589th Field Artillery Battalion

Many things in the U.S.A. were rationed. Almost everything in England was rationed. The reason for this was because almost everything was sent to the military. Food, of course, was one of the biggest items. This leads to my first trip to the mess hall. There was a big sign on the wall that read, "Take all you want, but eat all you take." Going through the line, I came upon a pot of what I thought was mashed potatoes. Being hungry, I told the guy to let me have a lot of this. He did just that. Further down the line, I came upon another pot, but this one did have mashed potatoes in it. I then asked him what this other thing was. When he said, "Parsnips" my appetite suddenly left me. I don't like parsnips. Remember the sign? MPs were at the garbage cans making sure you didn't waste food. Now I found out who my friends were. No one would take any from me. I was the last person out of the mess hall that night. I had to eat all of it. I learned to ask first when in doubt.

Because of my experience in Camp Myles Standish, I didn't go over the fence. Another reason was that the first sergeant had promised me that if any three-day passes were given I would be first on the list. The reason being, he knew, was that I came from Glasgow and I would be very happy to see my relatives. No passes were given, so I didn't get to Scotland. Many times as a POW, I wished that I had gone anyway.

On December 1 we loaded our equipment onto the vehicles and departed the Gloucestershire Barracks in convoy at about 0530 hours. We drove to what was known as a casual camp, which was just outside Weymouth (Portland harbor), and arrived at about dusk. C-rations were issued for supper that night and we were given cots to sleep on in some temporary barracks on the site. This was the last time for a long while that we would be afforded this kind of comfort.

A lot of the Americans who went to the United Kingdom were generally summed up by the tongue-in-cheek British adage "Over-sexed, over paid and over here." Unlike the Canadians the GIs didn't have any of their money held back, and were given their entire pay packet; of course they blew it on girls, gambling, and generally having fun. A lot of British people only saw the GIs indulging in recreational activities, on leave, having a night out, and of course on these occasions they could indeed be raucous and quite rowdy. The British government initiated various massive public relations exercises to get the British to accept the GIs, because ultimately they were going to have to fight together and maybe even die together.

Most the men in the I&R Platoon managed a three-day pass to London where they did their best to immerse themselves in British culture by attending concerts at the Royal Albert Hall, or going to the Odeon Theater, and George Bernard Shaw's *Strike it again* at Piccadilly Circus. They also had to contend with terrifying V2 buzz bombs falling in the suburbs a few blocks from their hotels. They also witnessed the devastation that five years of war had inflicted on the homes and buildings of the British capital.

John Schaffner, Scout, Battery B, 589th Field Artillery Battalion

November 17 found us traveling St. George's Channel with the mountainous green coast of Wales on the right and in the far distant left the east coast of Ireland. Plenty of traffic was passed that morning in the channel and the troops on deck were straining to get their first glimpse of England. The haze and fog pretty much prevented any sightseeing on this leg of the trip. In the afternoon our ship proceeded north up St. George's Channel for Liverpool. The weather was deteriorating as the day grew late and the ship, being in the channel with heavy traffic both ways, had to proceed slowly. When we were approaching the harbor at Liverpool the visibility was down to zero. I don't know how the pilot ever found a place to tie up.

We docked at about 1600 hours. It was already dark and a drizzling rain and fog enveloped everything at the blacked-out city. The 589th was the first outfit off the ship at about 2000 hours. As we left the ship it was to the music of a band on the pier. Music or not, we were all happy to be on land, even if it wasn't dry. The troops came off the ship marching in a file of twos, with full packs and toting duffel bags on the shoulders, from the dock area to the rail station, maybe three blocks away, and the scene was like something straight out of a Sherlock Holmes movie. Fog, wet cobblestones, the city blacked out and quiet except for the sound of the troops walking uphill through the narrow streets. No talking much, nobody out on the street to watch as we marched by, just apprehension as to what was coming next. We made it to the rail station after the short march and after another Red Cross coffee and donut welcome, boarded the train. When the train was fully loaded, the doors slammed and with a shrill whistle, we were off to Gloucester.

The battalion arrived at Gloucester at 0400 hours on the morning of the 18th and, after departing the train, was met by the "advance party" which had left Atterbury about three weeks ahead of us. We were led to the camp situated at the edge of the town. It was small, and had previously housed the British Gloucestershire Regiment. The battalion was housed in individual barracks of about 20 men each. The double-decked bunks were equipped with straw-stuffed mattresses. We had to displace all of the mouse families that had taken up residence in the straw since the last group had occupied the place. There was one small potbellied stove, burning soft coal, to ward off the chill, and the "ablutions" were in a separate building at the end of a concrete walkway about 150 feet away. At night, in fog and blackout conditions, you could not see your hand in front of your nose. No exaggeration, it really was that dark. To get to the ablutions, one had to inch along the walkway until one bumped into the door of the other building. It was best to take care of business while there was still some daylight. The 589th and 590th Field Artillery battalions shared one large mess hall.

The period from the 18th to 30th November was spent in re-equipping the division with all of the necessary implements of war. Vehicles, weapons, ammunition, rations, clothing, and whatever else was necessary, was drawn from depots all over the area. Some limited training was carried on and a few "short time" passes were issued, (and some guys went "over the fence"), but there was really no place for us to go except into Gloucester, a "one movie town." The town was blacked out and all businesses were closed by 2000 hours. We began to appreciate the difficulties of living in a war zone.

Soon it would be time to cross the English Channel and take part in World War II. For the men of I&R Platoon that day finally came on

November 29, 1944. The situation in the European theater at the end of November was considered relatively stable. The Allies had made good progress since the fighting in Normandy but there had been general disagreement at ETO on how to progress. The Allies had crossed the Siegfried Line in September and were now fighting on German soil. Despite this the general misinformed assumption that the German army was a spent force had been completely overturned during November, which had witnessed a terrible slogging match in an area known as the Hürtgen Forest, east of Aachen. As freezing November rain and sleet descended into bitter debilitating cold and snow, the Allied offensive slowed in preparation for a harsh winter. No one on the Allied side had any preconceptions about Germany's next move, but the 106th had been earmarked to occupy a quiet, stable area just over the German border in proximity to the Belgian Ardennes.

Sergeant John P. Kline, M Company, 423d Infantry Regiment

12/01/44: Arrived at Field J-40 (a staging area) near Rouen, France. We joined other M Company members who brought along our squad jeeps. We used our pup tents for sleeping. The weather was wet and miserable. We could hardly keep the tent stakes in. As a consolation the food was good. The terrain was flat and open, with a few small woods. It reminded me of Indiana farm land. We had little to do.

One afternoon, a couple of us walked down the road and bought a bottle of wine from a farmer. He got our money, and we got his bad wine. We went across the road into some woods, where we found an old wooden building. We finished our sour wine then went back to camp. We bivouacked in our two-man pup tents for the six days we were at J-40. It rained at least once a day. We were never able to get completely dry and comfortable.

12/07/44: Left J-40 combat loaded with jeep, driver and 1st gunner early morning. It was getting colder. We had the jeep top up and the side curtains on. We kept warm by using our new liquid fuel cooking stove. It was a small stove, enclosed in an aluminum canister about the size of a large thermos bottle. Some men used a can filled with sand and gasoline to keep warm. As we traveled along the French road towards Belgium, we came across miles and miles of German vehicles that had been strafed and burned. They were lying in the ditches, either completely burned or stripped.

In early November, at Bletchley Park in England, Ultra cryptanalysts succeeded in deciphering Reichsbahn (German railroad) codes which clearly indicated that around 800 trains were being used to move men and equipment to the west. They also intercepted messages concerning significant relocation of Luftwaffe forces to the Western Front. This information was sent to ETO but at that time there were only two officers in the Allied command who believed that the Germans were planning a major offensive, namely, Major General Kenneth Strong, Eisenhower's personal G-2, and Colonel Benjamin Dickson, G-2 of the First Army. Dickson had recently analyzed reports that had arrived from the Ardennes region of Belgium and on the basis of these he expressed his consternation at a purported build-up of enemy forces to the east of the Ardennes. Unfortunately his colleagues didn't take Dickson seriously and he was subsequently ordered to kick back and take some overdue furlough to Paris.

General Strong had received intelligence concerning significant enemy movement that was in progress. According to his information during the first week of December, nine panzer divisions had been removed from the eastern front and relocated to the west. He sent out his summary to the senior Allied commanders, stating his belief that the attack would come through the Ardennes. Eisenhower expressed some concern and sent Strong to Bradley's headquarters to discuss the possibility of an attack in the Ardennes. Bradley, brushed the warning aside and said, "Let them come."

Meanwhile three German armies were surreptitiously massing to the east of the Ardennes for an offensive that would take the Allies almost completely by surprise.

CHAPTER 3

MAN FOR MAN AND GUN FOR GUN

Shortly after Major General Jones and the 106th Infantry Division arrived in France, they were assigned to VIII Corps, First Army, 12th Army Group.

During the war, a corps consisted of two or more divisions, at least one of which was an armored division. Divisions were attached rather than assigned to a corps, and were frequently moved from corps to corps as a situation evolved or changed. In theory, a corps was a tactical headquarters that carried out combat missions with whatever units were attached to it at the time. In practice, attachments often became assignments. Like the triangular organization of the 106th Infantry Division, most corps had at least three divisions and kept the doctrine of "two up, one back," always maintaining one division in reserve.

Three corps constituted an army, usually commanded by a lieutenant general, and, because there were so many divisions, corps, and armies in the European Theater at the time, armies were grouped into army groups.

By December, Eisenhower's forces had been arranged in three army groups: the 21st under British Field Marshal Bernard Montgomery in the Netherlands to the north, the 12th under General Omar Bradley in Belgium and Luxembourg in the center, and the 6th under General Jacob Devers in southern France and the German Saar region. Eisenhower, who was responsible for all operations in Western Europe, not only commanded the army groups but the naval and air components supporting them.

The chain of command at the front line meant that Major General Jones reported to his immediate superior Major General Troy Middleton,

Commander, VIII Corps who in turn reported to Lieutenant General Courtney Hodges, Commander, First Army. Hodges' immediate superior was General Omar Bradley, Commander, 12th Army Group who kept his good friend General Eisenhower, Commander, Supreme Headquarters Allied Expeditionary Force (SHAEF) informed of all developments. It did not end there because Ike reported to General George Marshall back in Washington DC who was ultimately responsible for the war in Europe and Pacific. All this meant little to the men who were going to do the actual fighting as opposed to moving pieces around on a map comfortably well behind the lines and out of harm's reach. In total there were almost two million Allied soldiers in Western Europe and at the time the 106th Infantry Division would have had no preconception of the struggle they were about to endure.

John Schaffner, Scout, Battery B, 589th Field Artillery Battalion

At dawn the next morning, December 2, we loaded up again, and in convoy, moved down to the harbor where we were issued donuts, coffee and seasick pills for breakfast. Life preservers were passed out for good measure. They were a rubber tube that belted around the waist and could be inflated using two small CO$_2$ bottles (or by blowing into a tube). I can't imagine that they would have done much good should we have had to go into that cold sea. That morning the battalion loaded onto two LSTs and spent the day at anchor in the harbor. Accommodations on these ships were far better than those on the transport. There weren't enough bunks to go around but the men slept in shifts and some made "beds" in the trucks. I recall hanging around the ship's galley and "bumming" a piece of sheet-cake or whatever else the "chef" was willing to hand out. Again, I avoided becoming seasick.

On December 3, the LST left Portland harbor and, crossing the English Channel, arrived at the mouth of the River Seine in the evening. The water was very rough but only a few of the men became seasick this time. Anxiety was taking over. The ship would ride up on the huge waves and then come crashing down, throwing the cold salty spray everywhere. If one could stand at one end of the "tank deck" and watch the overhead, you could see the ship bend and twist with the force of the beating that the sea was giving it. The ship anchored about five or so miles off Le Havre and tossed violently in the rough water all night.

Next day, the 4th, we cruised back and forth off the mouth of the Seine all day, waiting to merge into an endless column of LSTs, Liberty ships and merchantmen waiting their turn to enter the river. We started up the Seine in late afternoon, one ship following another, in an endless column reminding me of circus elephants walking along, each holding the tail of the one in front. Sometime after dark we anchored upstream for the night. By this time in the war, the Allied air forces had rendered the Luftwaffe ineffective, otherwise an operation like this would have been in extreme jeopardy. On the way we saw for the first time some of the destruction that the war had brought to France. Destroyed harbor facilities, bomb-pocked concrete gun emplacements, sunken ships, etc. I couldn't help but think, "What am I getting into?" It wasn't over yet.

It was simply a matter of fate that the 106th Infantry Division was ordered to the Ardennes to replace the 2d Infantry Division. The 106th was new to the ETO and, like all new units, needed time to adjust and familiarize with how things were done. When the generals decided the 2d Infantry Division, then occupying a position along the Siegfried Line in the Ardennes, was needed elsewhere, moving the new kids on the block to replace them was the logical thing to do. The orders to the 106th were simple: *Replace the 2d Division, man for man and gun for gun!*

John Schaffner, Scout, Battery B, 589th Field Artillery Battalion

December 6, we arrived in the area of Rouen and waited our turn to beach the ship and unload. At about 1500 hours we drove off the ship directly onto the muddy beach and proceeded to a bivouac area in the field a few miles from town. The weather was cold and not at all pleasant. I was driving a jeep with no side curtains and a manual windshield wiper. The driver had to employ the wiper by twisting a handle on the inside end of the wiper where the shaft was installed at the top of the windshield. A minor inconvenience. That night I bundled up and slept at the wheel of the jeep. It was not the first time that I had done that. Nor would it be the last.

On the 6th, Headquarters, A and B batteries waited in the bivouac area all day while the remainder of the battalion (on another LST) unloaded at Rouen and joined us in the afternoon. The remainder of the 422d Combat Team lined up in the prescribed order of march on the road ahead and behind us, to spend the night.

We broke camp early on the morning of December 7 and proceeded to a bivouac area near Roselle, Belgium, arriving late in the evening. The route was via Amiens, Cambrai and Maubeuge. There were many bomb craters and much wrecked German war material along the route, evidence of a difficult retreat from France the previous summer. Driving the jeep was numbing cold. At times I couldn't feel my feet and would have to push down on my knees to operate the accelerator and clutch. No, the jeeps didn't come with heaters either, or even side curtains on this one.

December 8 we marched (drove) from Roselle to St. Vith, Belgium, arriving early in the afternoon. Parked on a hill, just east of town, we ate lunch and soon got orders to move into a bivouac area near Wallerode. It seemed to be very peaceful with only the occasional sound of an artillery round exploding somewhere way off in the distance. It was very cold and the snow was quite deep.

Our initial task was to relieve the 2d Division on the Schnee Eifel, a "quiet" front about 27 miles wide. Pretty thin for one division, but then nothing was happening here (they told us). It was to be easy to trade places with the 2d Division units.

By the end of November General Courtney Hodges' First Army was covering almost 120 miles of front from the German town of Aachen in the north to the border of Luxembourg and France in the south. On his left, Major General "Lightning" Joe Collins's VII Corps held 20 miles of the line from Aachen to the Hürtgen Forest in the Hohes Venn (high fens) region. In his center was Major General Gerow's V Corps holding the next 20 miles that stretched all the way to Losheim. On his right was Middleton's VIII Corps that held almost 85 miles of front from Losheim to the boundary with General Patton's Third Army in the south. Hodges wasn't completely impervious to the risk he was taking by expanding the line beyond the capacity of the units in the field and he had voiced his reservations to General Omar Bradley and General Eisenhower. Bradley furrowed his brow while Hodges spoke and interrupted him to say, "First, when anyone attacks, he does it for one of two reasons. Either he's out to destroy the hostile forces or he's going after a terrain objective. If it's terrain he's after then he feels he must either have it himself or deny it to the other fellow."

Hodges pointed to the topographic map laid out on the table before the generals and indicated the terrain features before saying, "If they come through here we can fall back and fight a delaying action to the Meuse. Certainly we can slow them down until you hit them on the flanks." This appeared to pacify all present and the meeting drew to an amicable close.

ETO was aware that a normal U.S. Army division front at that time was considered to be approximately five and half miles. This was the area that a full division could effectively cover both offensively and defensively. The 106th Division front was seriously overstretched, covering almost 26 miles and reaching eight miles into Germany. Two of the divisions in General Troy Middleton's VIII Corps situated in the quiet Ardennes region, namely the 4th and the 28th, were licking their wounds after the attritional battles in the Hürtgen Forest. To the north the 106th and the 99th hadn't fired a shot in anger. They may have been considered "battle ready" but they were most definitely not "battle hardened."

Some months earlier Generaloberst Alfred Jodl, the head of the Oberkommando der Wehrmacht (OKW), and his staff had been ordered by Adolf Hitler to formulate plans for an offensive in the west. The Führer stipulated that the objective was to retake the port of Antwerp and divide the Allies piecemeal. Jodl submitted five plans at the time. The first one, named Operation Holland, entailed a single attack from the Venlo area, maintaining Antwerp as the primary objective. Operation Liège–Aachen was a two-pronged envelopment attack that would be launched simultaneously from northern Luxembourg and northwest of Aachen culminating at Liège and completely isolating the whole First U.S. Army. Operation Luxembourg was a variation on the same theme, attacking west from central Luxembourg and Metz in northern France with the purpose of converging on the Luxembourg village of Longwy and confining Patton's Third Army. Operation Lorraine focused from Metz and Baccarat simultaneously and closing the pincer at the town of Nancy. Lastly, Operation Alsace again proposed a two-pronged attack from Epinal and Montbeliard, converging on Vesoul.

Hitler considered all the plans and decided that he would combine the first and second plans, thereby maintaining his initial objective of taking Antwerp. This plan, called "Wacht am Rhein" ("Rhine Guard"), was comprehensively worked out and submitted to the Führer on October 11. The purpose of the title was to deceive the Allies into thinking that this was a defensive plan. Hitler compared his military prowess to that of Frederick the Great when he told his generals:

Our enemies are the greatest opposites which exist on earth, ultra-capitalist states on one side; ultra-Marxist states on the other; on one side a dying empire and on the other side a colony, the United States, waiting to claim its inheritance. Deal a heavy blow and bring down this artificial coalition with a mighty thunderclap.

Generalfeldmarschall Gerd von Rundstedt and Generalfeldmarschall Walter Model were far from convinced by Hitler's plan. On the basis of this they consulted with other German generals and formulated alternative plans to present to their Führer who was in no mood for discussion at the time, and remained adamant that his plan to divide the Allies was irrevocable.

When the 106th Infantry Division's Commanding General assumed responsibility for the defense of his allocated sector in compliance with a VIII Corps order to relieve the 2d Infantry Division, he and the rest of his division would have had scant prior knowledge of how incredibly vulnerable their strategic situation now was. The major units attached to the division at this time were 14th Cavalry Group, 820th Tank Destroyer Battalion, and the 634th Anti-Aircraft Artillery Air Weapons Battalion.

The 14th Cavalry Group alone was committed to holding a front of roughly 9,000 yards, which was the equivalent of the frontage normally allocated to an entire infantry division. The 2d Battalion, 423d Infantry and the 1st Battalion, 424th Infantry were held out as a division reserve. In addition to the four division artillery battalions, VIII Corps had designated eight field artillery battalions to be available to the 106th if and when required. While the firepower provided by these artillery battalions may have been more than adequate to support a division in a normal defensive position, the 106th was dispersed far too widely along the lengthy sector it would be called upon to defend.

John Schaffner, Scout, Battery B, 589th Field Artillery Battalion

December 9, 1944, the battalion moved into the line east of the town of Laudesfeld and about one and a half miles west of Auw, Germany. The 589th Field Artillery Battalion took over the positions of the 15th Field Artillery Battalion.

The battalion command post was set up in the kitchen of a substantial German house. The firing batteries took over the dugouts and log huts vacated by the men of the 15th Field Artillery Battalion. The howitzers were put into the same emplacements dug by the 15th and in some cases they were simply swapped since it was easier than trying to extricate the pieces already in place. A Battery was placed on the south side of the road to Auw and B and C Batteries on the north side. There was much snow here and the drivers were having big problems once they left the hard road. Service Battery was sent into a position a few miles to the rear, about four miles south of Schoenberg [also Schönberg], Belgium. The veterans of the 2d Division assured their successors that they were in a very quiet sector where nothing ever happened. They hated to leave and when the 589th men saw what relatively comfortable quarters the 2d's men were leaving they could understand that. We had been prepared to pitch pup tents. I shared a dugout that was roofed over with heavy logs and had a jerry can stove. Just like up-town. Things were looking up. By 1630 registration was completed by A Battery and the battalion fired harassing fire that night. We were feeling rather secure. After all, our infantry was between us and the Germans. It sounded good to me.

Because of all the work that the men of the 15th Field Artillery Battalion had done and placing our gun in the exact spot that they had used, we had very little work to do. We used the same foxholes that they had dug. They had also built a small log cabin. This we used to get warm and sleep in. In a position like this, every member of the gun crew had to stand guard duty at night. This included me and the sergeant. I will tell you, that first night was very nerve racking. Not knowing very much about the situation or from what direction the enemy might come from, every sound was a cause for concern. Two hours felt like eight. The severe cold made it even more difficult.

By December 12, the 106th Infantry Division had occupied 2d Infantry Division's former sector and had begun evaluating their mission and means. Of the Allied divisions of varying types and nationalities up and down the 400-mile front, Jones's 106th was one of the few physically on German soil. His mission was to defend that 26-mile-wide salient in the German lines and prepare the 106th for their next mission, whatever that was going to be.

When Jones arrived in theater, VIII Corps attached the 14th Cavalry Group to his division. Jones deployed his 14th Cavalry Group, reinforced, and 422d, 423d, and 424th Infantry Regiments in a line from north to south along the Siegfried Line. His nearest supply depot was over 40 miles west at the small town of Noville.

The northern five miles of their flank were defended by the 14th Cavalry Group, which tied in to the 99th Infantry Division then defending the Losheim Gap on their north. To the south of the 106th Infantry Division, the 424th Infantry Regiment tied in to the 112th Infantry Regiment, 28th Infantry Division.

The area was home to numerous little villages of half a dozen houses here, 30 houses there, connected by barely traversable roads and dirt tracks a mile or two long that followed a ridgeline or river valley. The villages often sat in a ravine or by a river and were aptly named by the rank and file as "sugar bowls." From any of the tree-covered hilltops in between they had eyeballs on church steeples and roofs of half a dozen small villages in proximity.

John Schaffner, Scout, Battery B, 589th Field Artillery Battalion

December 10 to 15: The 422d Infantry Regiment, which the 589th Field Artillery Battalion was supporting, was occupying the first belt of pillboxes of the Siegfried Line, which had been cracked at this point the previous fall. The Germans were well dug in opposite the 422d in pillboxes and held other defensive positions in the area of the Schnee Eifel, a wooded ridge about three miles to the front. The enemy communications center for this area was Prüm, which was at maximum range (12,000 yards) for A Battery.

During this period there was little activity other than a few patrol actions. Few observed missions were fired due to the poor visibility. The battalion did, however, have a substantial unobserved, harassing program that was fired every night. The forward observer adjusted by sound, using high-angle fire, which made it necessary to re-dig the gun pits. Alternate positions were selected and surveyed by the survey officer and his party. There were some reports of enemy activity but nothing, apparently, more than routine truck and troop movements. Headquarters Battery crews reported being fired upon on the 15th and that night an enemy recon plane circled the area for an hour or more. Numerous flares were seen to the flanks of the battalion and an enemy patrol was reported to be in the area. During this period most of my time was spent at various outposts near the battery position. There was nothing to report. At night, watching across the snow-covered fields, one's eyes tended to play tricks. On more than one occasion an outpost guard would fire away at some movement out in front of him, only to find out in the morning that he had "killed" a tree stump or boulder.

The Eifel had a commanding view of German territory and the Siegfried Line to the east but visibility was only good when the clouds and fog were not clinging to the hilltops and riverbeds. On the western side of the Eifel from the Losheim Gap in the north, past the 106th Infantry Division area, and on into 28th Infantry Division ran the Our River. There were several tributaries: the Alf and the Ihren ran east–west and fed the Our River as they dropped from the heights of the Eifel. The general consensus of opinion among the 106th was that this would be a good place to sit out the winter.

The Eifel plateau was the location of three divergent areas accentuated by prominent ridges. The central area was known as the Schnee Eifel. At the western foot of the Schnee Eifel there's a long narrow valley notched into what is known as the Losheim Gap, a five-mile-long, narrow valley at the western foot of the Schnee Eifel, on the border between Belgium and the Germany. On this western side of the gap courses the Our River, and beyond the river to the west the plateau is more heavily wooded. The Losheim Gap area is home to steep hills and sizeable ravines. Some of the hills are exposed and bare while pine trees and thick undergrowth cover some of the others. The Losheim Gap was occupied on December 16 by a reinforced squadron of the 14th Cavalry Group.

Sergeant John P. Kline, M Company, 423d C Infantry Regiment
12/09/44: As we entered St. Vith, Belgium, older, established troops gave us the normal "new kid on the block" salutations. They yelled at us, "You'll be sorry" and other similar phrases, some not so nice. We set up bivouac in woods on the edge of town. The large pines, looking like huge Christmas trees made the woods quiet, warm and very beautiful. The silence and peaceful surroundings of the pines and snow was a pleasant experience. Particularly after the week near Rouen, France with rain beating on the pup tents and the hustle and noise of the motor march to St. Vith.

12/11/44: We left the woods near St. Vith for front-line positions. Our destination was a defense line in the Ardennes forest atop the Schnee Eifel

(Snow Mountain). The positions were 12 miles east of St. Vith and were in Germany. A name we would learn to remember, Schoenberg, was nine miles east of St. Vith and three miles west of our positions. We were facing the German troops from emplacements on the eastern slopes [reverse slopes] of the German Siegfried Line, known as "The German West Wall."

We took over positions held by the 2d Infantry Division and exchanged much of our new equipment for their old. The exchange was to be made as quickly and quietly as possible. The 2d Division was being transferred to Aachen to participate in an attack on the Roer Dam area. My machine-gun position was a log bunker with field of fire obstructed by dense forest. Conditions were quiet. Excellent chow was served twice a day.

The Headquarters Battery, 589th Field Artillery Battalion arrived in the area outside St. Vith in the early afternoon, parked on a bleak-looking road, and had lunch. By that time it was getting progressively colder, and the snow was getting deeper. Late in the afternoon, they moved into a bivouac area near Wallerode to camp for the night. It was a heavily wooded area with tall pines that was enveloped in pitch darkness when night set in. The ground in the dense forest was a combination of slush, snow, and half-frozen water. None of the soldiers had been issued with rubber Pac winter overshoes that they were supposed to have. That first night was bitterly cold, the ominous silence only interrupted at brief intervals by the occasional rogue enemy artillery shell resonating from somewhere off in the distance.

Lieutenant Colonel Thomas Kelly had no problem finding his new command post (CP). Kelly's predecessor was busy with his battalion's displacement so he was briefed by the executive officer, a major with many months of combat experience. Over a cup of coffee, which was welcome after the frigid ride from France, the major did his best to impress the inherent danger that Kelly's battalion faced in their new positions.

First, he said, the 26-mile front was four to five times the length of a normal front for a division in a defensive posture. Second, Kelly's batteries were exposed to an enemy advance from the northeast through the Losheim Gap defended by nothing except a reinforced squadron of cavalry. When they reviewed the maps, the major told Kelly that the division's infantry were all west and south, and that he couldn't count on them coming to his rescue if the Germans came through the gap.

Over the next few days, Kelly took the time to familiarize himself with the front-line positions and terrain around the 422d Infantry. The escarpment forming the slope of the southern Eifel was almost certainly impenetrable to a frontal attack. What gave him serious concern was the disposition of the cavalrymen in the Losheim Gap. Kelly didn't consider himself an infantry tactician, but he wondered by whose design so much confidence and responsibility was placed on a few hundred cavalrymen in the Gap. When he put his question to Colonel Descheneaux, Commander, 422d Regimental Combat Team, he didn't like the answer.

"They," responded Descheneaux, shrugging his shoulders, "won't let us do anything about it."

In his summary dated December 12, Omar Bradley, expressed this opinion that

It is now certain that attrition is steadily sapping the strength of the German forces on the Western front and that the crust of defenses is thinner, more brittle and more vulnerable than it appears on our G-2 map or to the troops in the line.

Even Field Marshal Sir Bernard Montgomery, the sometimes over-cautious commander of 21st Army Group, said,

The enemy is at present fighting a defensive campaign on all fronts; his situation is such that he cannot stage major offensive operations. Furthermore, at all costs he has to prevent the war from entering on a mobile phase; he has not the transport or the petrol that would be necessary for mobile operations. The enemy is in a bad way.

ETO were so confident that the Germans weren't planning any immediate offensive actions that a memo was sent to VIII Corps intended for the 106th, stating that the division was scheduled to participate in field exercises and maneuvers along with other combat training from December 13 through January 3. The Ardennes region had long been regarded as impenetrable and strategically negligible terrain that should be avoided or when possible completely circumnavigated. Two thousand years previously Roman legions had described the Arduenna Silva as "a frightful place, full of terrors."

Precisely how terrifying would soon become apparent but in early December, just like the 106th units, the 2d Infantry Division's 15th Field

Artillery Battalion was oblivious to any potential danger, and at that time vociferously reluctant to relinquish their positions to Battery A, 589th Field Artillery Battalion, when they occupied the dugouts and gun emplacements built over the previous two months. There were many soldiers there who were quite content to take up these newly vacated positions. Granted it was bitterly cold and there was already a good layer of snow on the ground but all in all things could have been substantially worse. At least they managed to get warm food regularly and were well provided for, all things considered.

Despite the fact that their location rendered the division extremely vulnerable, being so deep into Germany out on the Schnee Eifel at that time doesn't appear to have raised any questions at ETO. The most ill-informed military observer would have accurately deduced that their position formed a salient that could potentially expose their flanks to enemy attack or infiltration. Moreover they were far too thinly spread to provide any serious deterrent and German intelligence was well informed of this at the time. The 106th were largely oblivious to the fact that their position was at best indefensible, at worst exposed and downright precarious. Through no fault of their own the last infantry division ever to be formed in World War II was blindly staring into the jaws of potential obliteration. It is often said that it is always calm before a storm, but the severity and magnitude of the storm soon to be unleashed would shake ETO to its very foundations.

Sergeant John P. Kline, M Company, 423d Infantry Regiment

We slept in rough, but warm dugouts and enjoyed solid gun bunkers. Built by the 2d Division, they were built of logs, with a log and earth roof. We completed our changeover with the 2d Division as darkness came. We had no time to become acquainted with the territory around our new positions. Because of that, and since we were fresh and inexperienced troops, our first night was unforgettable. We were facing, for the first time, an enemy that we only knew from newsreels and training films. It was a sleepless and anxiety-filled night.

I can personally confirm that a snow-covered tree stump will actually move. That is, if you stare at it long enough—and if you are a young, nineteen-year-old machine-gun squad leader peering into the darkness towards the enemy through a slit in a machine-gun bunker.

Every sound is amplified, every bush could be an enemy crawling towards you. Your eyes grow bleary from staring into the darkness. You are happy when the relief crew shows up. The next day, you take a good long look at the stump that moved during the night. You take note of all unusual objects, and then things start to settle down.

There were two gun emplacements (bunkers) for my machine-gun squad. One was higher on the hill, and the other a couple of hundred yards down the slope. When we first moved in our gun position was in the lower bunker. After the first night we were asked to move back up the slope to the alternate bunker. For what reason, I don't know. We did appreciate the move, for the alternate bunker was much warmer and drier. As in the lower bunker, there were "trip lines" running from the bunker down into the forest and through the barbed wire. The lines were attached to hand grenades and flares that were placed in their shipping containers attached to the trees. If we detected movement in the area beyond the barbed wire we could pull a trip line. This would cause a grenade to explode after it was pulled from its container. A flare could be ignited to light up the area in the same manner.

Our field of fire was good, but very limited. The 2d Division had cut down a lot of trees and cleaned out the brush. However, the forest still offered the enemy excellent cover.

I remember one day being convinced that I could see a vehicle in the woods several hundred yards down the hill. The contours of the hill and the thick forest were playing games with my imagination. When I looked at it from another vantage point, the illusion disappeared. There was one rifleman to the left of my bunker. He was entrenched in a log-covered foxhole. According to members of the patrols, this rifleman was the last person between my machine-gun emplacement and the 422d Regiment. The 422d Regiment was reported to be five miles across a valley. The two regiments sent alternate patrols across the unoccupied space each half hour. They reported very little German activity.

The first days passed without incident. The most excitement we had in my bunker area was when a nearby .50-caliber machine gun started blasting away. The gunner had become bored and decided to kill a deer. We left the bunker area twice daily to eat our meals in a mess tent. It was back of us, to the west, on the opposite side of the hill. To get to it we had to walk along a trail, through a clearing, and down the other side. The Germans had the clearing zeroed in. As we crossed the clearing, we had to be prepared to hit the ground in case they decided to harass us. The 2d Division's squad leader that I relieved said two men had been killed crossing the clearing a few days ago. Our daily trips to the mess tent were something to look forward to. The food was good and the Mess Sergeant seemed to be friendlier since we moved up to the front lines. I did enjoy those meals, there were generous portions and we could chat with the others and get brought up to date on the local news.

Between December 10 and 15, the 422d Infantry Regiment, supported by the 589th Field Artillery Battalion, was occupying the first belt of reinforced concrete pillboxes along the infamous Siegfried Line that had been penetrated by U.S. forces during the previous fall. The Germans were well dug in opposite the 422d, also in bunkers and pillboxes, along with other defensive positions in the area of the Schnee Eifel.

Meanwhile Private Schaffner was going to share a dugout with a roof and an improvised jerry can stove near the village of Herzfenn, about a mile and half south of Auw.

The 589th had moved into these positions on December 9 and in some cases it had been easier to swap some of their howitzers rather than trying to extricate the pieces already in place. By this time so much snow had fallen that drivers found their progress impeded once they left the hard roads. These age-old lanes and dirt tracks were quickly churned up by the wheels of deuce and a halves and other military vehicles. Battery A was on the south side of the road to Auw. Batteries B and C took the north side of the road. The Service Battery was a few miles to the rear, about four miles south of Schönberg.

To the professional artillerymen, everything was distances and locations. They had excellent maps and surveys of the terrain they covered, and knew, for instance, that the enemy communications center in the village of Prüm was 12,000 yards from Battery A. They also knew that the 3,000 infantrymen of the 422d were on the top and front side of the Schnee Eifel three miles east of them. By 1630 hours on December 9, Battery A completed its registration and spent the rest of the night harassing the Germans on the other side of the Siegfried Line with sporadic rounds.

The battalion CP had been set up in the kitchen of a sizeable German house near the Auw–Bleialf road just outside Schönberg. The fire control section was in the adjacent farmhouse, 150 yards in front of the CP, and the mess hall was in a large barn-type building roughly 75 yards behind the CP. Their new home was allocated as the communication barracks because it housed the radio, wire, and fire control sections. Their quarters were situated in a big 12-x-15-foot room that had eight double bunks and relatively comfortable improvised chicken-wire mattresses. Compared to the tents and rain they had endured throughout the previous week, the men considered themselves lucky.

Over at OKW General der Panzertruppen Baron Hasso von Manteuffel, an experienced and highly decorated officer, had been selected to lead the German Fifth Panzer Army, one of the three armies scheduled to participate in Hitler's planned offensive. From the offset Manteuffel had regarded these plans as unfeasible and militarily unsustainable but he deferred from making his objections known, no doubt influenced by Hitler's volatile and erratic state of mind at the time. To fellow officers Manteuffel voiced further concerns regarding the low-caliber replacements that some of his units had received prior to the offensive. Nevertheless he was a dedicated soldier and he had a job to do. One of his primary objectives was to capture and hold the road network servicing the Ardennes towns of Malmedy, Houffalize, Bastogne and St. Vith as soon as possible and then advance towards St. Vith, which would have to be taken by the second day of the planned attack.

This plan envisaged the complete encirclement and isolation of the 106th Infantry Division by the LXVI Armeekorps commanded by General der Artillerie Walther Lucht. This corps consisted of the 18th Volksgrenadier Division (VGD) and the 62d VGD, each numbering around 20,000 men supported by corps artillery and 42 assault guns. Manteuffel had already voiced his consternation regarding the dubious quality of some of the men in this corps but this wouldn't detract from the attack going ahead as scheduled. The main assault would be orchestrated by the 294th and 295th, regiments, 18th VGD who would effectively orbit the Schnee Eifel on the right flank while the 293d Regiment, 18th VGD would attack on the left and link up with the other two regiments at the town of St. Vith on the second day of the offensive. The 18th VGD was a mobile battalion consisting of a 100-man bicycle-mounted reconnaissance company and one company of engineers in horse-drawn wagons. This force was attached to a tank destroyer battalion that had 12 self-propelled 76mm tracked vehicles.

Volksgrenadier was the name attributed to German Army divisions assembled during the fall of 1944. The name itself, literally "people's grenadiers," was intended to build morale and embrace Germany's old military traditions, while appealing to the patriotism of its citizens. Germany formed 78 VGDs during the war. Volksgrenadier divisions arose due to the desperate need to replace shattered units such as Army Group Center and the Fifth Panzer Army that had been obliterated by the Soviets on the Eastern Front. The Volksgrenadiers had a higher proportion of sub-machine guns and light automatic weapons and thus relied more on short-range firepower than other existing German Army infantry units. Automatic weapons like the Sturmgewehr 44 and anti-tank weaponry such as the single-shot panzerfaust were widely used by Volksgrenadier units.

They were organized around small squads of seasoned war veterans, NCOs and officers, and then fleshed out with whatever they could find from depleted Kriegsmarine and Luftwaffe personnel. They even incorporated wounded soldiers returning to duty from hospitals, older men who would have been considered too old or too unfit for the peacetime army, and even teenagers were recruited into the ranks. This gave rise to the Allied misconception that these units were comprised of young boys and pensioners.

Back in 1944 St. Vith was home to around 2,000 inhabitants whose loyalties lay most decidedly with Germany. Before 1918 the town of St. Vith was part of Germany but since the Treaty of Versailles it had been the property of the Belgian state. The reception the U.S. troops got there was considerably different to the one they received from the French-speaking Belgians because many of the residents of St. Vith had relatives serving in the German armed forces. To the rest of Belgium the Allies were liberators but there in the heart of the region known as East Belgium they were generally regarded as an army of occupation. St. Vith and surrounding German-speaking areas had been briefly repatriated between 1940 and 1944 during the German occupation but now they were all in Allied territory. The town is situated on a low hill surrounded by gently rolling pastures. About a mile and a half to the east there's the

Prümerberg, a sizeable forested hill bisected by the road to Schönberg that veers to the left at the base of the hill and leads to the Our valley.

Not far from here is the village of Auw that before the war had a population of about six hundred. By late 1944 most of them had either been evacuated or had simply left. The village sat near the apex of a hill looking down into a valley toward the front line roughly three miles away. Between there and the front were the riflemen of the 422d Infantry dug in just below the ridge of the Eifel. Despite the bitter cold, morale among the ranks was high. The 3d Platoon, A Company, 81st Engineers had set up shop in a schoolhouse in Auw that was situated beside the main road that ran to Schönberg. A German family living there ensured that the soldiers received clean bedding but they weren't in any hurry to make friends with these Americans and remained distinctly aloof for the duration.

Staff Sergeant John Collins, 3d Platoon, A Company, 81st Engineers

On Thursday, December 7, I made my way to the supply depot at Rouen to get firewood for the camps. Thirty feet high, for as far as I could see, were piles and piles of equipment and supplies; soup to nuts, trucks coming and going bumper to bumper. There was so much stuff even the corporal tried to trade his jeep for a truck. Once we arrived at our new position in Auw, it was down to business. I thought that in any other movie it would have been a beautiful place. My squad was billeted in a schoolhouse with Lieutenant Woerner, Smitty the jeep driver, and Stanley the tool keeper. In addition to the men, the school housed a German family of eight: four girls of ages 18, 20, 22, and 22, one young lad of 12, and a little girl age 4, with their uncle and mother.

I found them aloof. That could have been because of the language difference, or it could have been because shelling a few weeks earlier had killed one of their young tots. One thing I noticed about the German people was they attended church every day. As far as I could tell, it was simply to swap stories about the Americans occupying their homes.

My squad started clearing, repairing, and building roads for Company K, 422d Infantry. Lieutenant Woerner swapped days, one up front, one back at the CP in Auw cleaning and repairing our equipment. Typically, the one that stayed behind kept a small crew of three men. The weather was sloppy during the day when the foot or more of snow began to melt, and at night, the ground froze solid, making it extremely difficult to do what we usually did—dig.

I kept myself busy with tasks such as trying to procure a stove for the company cook shack at the other end of Auw. For that detail I rounded up a few of the engineers and headed to the village of Bleialf. Along the way, we noticed the signs telling us that we were under enemy observation so we did our best to be sneaky about the trip. We stopped at a beautiful church, but we didn't manage to get the stove because our own infantrymen in the village ran us off. Along the way we stopped and inspected the pillboxes originally built by the Germans, and now occupied by our own men, about 400 yards from the front. Those walls must have been five feet thick and reinforced with braces holding them.

Most of my squad didn't carry their ammo belts while working. It was just too intrusive. However, a few of the men not only made sure they carried their belts but specifically asked me for permission to shoot a deer if they spotted one. I told them it was OK as long as it was close to the road. To my surprise, and dismay, they did not get a deer, but a big old black and white Holstein cow. I couldn't believe they were that stupid because it was against regulations to take domestic animals from the populace. I think we ate it for dinner that night but I'm not sure.

By the end of the second week of December the 106th Infantry Division was deployed along an uneven line running roughly northeast to southwest. Colonel George L. Descheneaux, Jr's 422d Infantry Regiment occupied the most forward positions that extended 2,000 yards to the west of the Siegfried Line on the crest of the western slopes and covered the mid-section of the Schnee Eifel. This regiment and the 14th Cavalry were mutually responsible for the defense of the salient in this sector. The 14th Cavalry consisted of the 18th and 32d Cavalry Reconnaissance squadrons. Their task was to maintain and improve the defensive positions in the Losheim Gap. The Group Headquarters was located just over the Belgian border in the village of Manderfeld. December 11, shortly after assuming control of the sector, Colonel Devine placed the 32d squadron in reserve near Vielsalm, 20 miles west of Manderfeld. Devine had planned to keep the 18th CRS in Manderfeld while the 32d refitted in Vielsalm. After refitting, the 32d would replace the 18th on line allowing the 18th to rotate into Vielsalm so they could also benefit from the repair and replacement process.

Lieutenant Alan Jones, 423d Infantry Regiment

We were led to believe that this was a quiet area. We thought of it as a place where we would have combat training, learn to use patrols and become accustomed to a combat zone. We used much of our time to calibrate our radios and check all of our guns.

Our major concern was to readjust some of our defensive positions. While the switch with the 2d Division was on a man for man, gun for gun basis [at dug-in emplacements for everything from machine guns to artillery pieces, the newly arrived troops swapped their equipment for that of the units they relieved], the 2d Division was a battle-seasoned outfit. They had accumulated many weapons not formally listed in the table of organization. As a result, they had a helluva lot more machine guns than we did. With fewer guns, our weapons did not conform to the kind of defensive arrangement that the 38th Regiment had.

We were aware of some enemy activity. We could hear trains in the vicinity of Prüm. Our patrols reported one or two sightings of isolated tanks but we did not notice any increase in enemy patrols. We reckoned that there was some unusual activity on the other side, but we had no concern for any massive attack.

We could see the enemy in the distance and they could see us. Actually, they occupied other parts of the Siegfried line. There was a little bit of fire, sporadic rounds of artillery. We knew this was now serious business and you felt you had to sort of tiptoe around.

Still, the word was this was a quiet area. It was our first experience on the line. People were a little uptight. We didn't know what it was going to be like.

The line occupied by the 423d Infantry (Colonel Charles C. Cavender) continued to the south of 422d's position on the Schnee Eifel. Below the 423d was a gap screened by the division reconnaissance troop. The 424th Infantry was situated in the vicinity of Grosskampenberg and north of Luetzkampen with A and B Companies located between Lommersweiler and Steinebrück, while C Company was way out in Germany on the Schnee Eifel at Winterscheid. The 424th Infantry perimeter bordered on that of the Pennsylvania National Guard, the 28th Infantry Division whom they encountered occasionally while on patrol to the north of Lützkampen.

One particularly debilitating factor for the 106th was that they didn't have any attached armored units in their ranks or even in close proximity to their current position. Precisely how problematic this was would soon become apparent.

James H. Cooley, D Company, 1st Battalion, 423d Infantry Regiment

I was one of the advanced guard, and we drove through France into Belgium. It was cold, cold, cold. I did everything I could to keep warm, but when you're in the back of a jeep and you have that wind blowing at you for hours at a time, you get past feeling numb. I took my boots off and put my feet in a sleeping bag.

I did everything, and I still couldn't get warm. Anyway on December 10, 1944, I went into the battle line. This was about on the extreme eastern part of Belgium and I was really in Germany, but not very far. The Division HQ was in St. Vith. If you go straight east of St. Vith you come to a town on the border of Germany called Schönberg. I imagine two miles straight east of there is where I was in a foxhole. I was in heavy weapons. I was in 81-millimeter mortars, which is a shell that you lob over that explodes when it hits the ground. I told my Mom in a letter home that I would be the first GI to cross the Rhine, or at least one of the first and I wasn't wrong.

Mildred Gillars, known to the Allies as "Axis Sally" was an American radio personality employed by the Third Reich to broadcast propaganda. Many in the 106th had heard her disconcerting welcome as she identified all the units by name and number when they arrived. So much for secrecy. If Axis Sally knew then the whole German Army knew who 106th Infantry Division was.

Sometime before dawn December 16, sentries out on the Schnee Eifel heard footsteps crunching through the snow as specially trained German *Stoßtruppen* shock troops emerged menacingly from the dense mist to infiltrate U.S. Army lines. In the distance numerous pointillisms of light appeared to dissect the black sky as 2,000 guns, ranging from 3-inch mortars to giant 16-inch railway guns erupted simultaneously and began to impact against the entire American front line. The fight was on.

GERMANS EVERYWHERE!

Well before dawn December 16, out on the Schnee Eifel two 423d Regiment GIs were idly chatting in front of an abandoned Siegfried Line bunker. They smoked, talked about home, complained about the bitter cold and having to pull lookout duty at such an ungodly hour of the morning. One of the GIs looked up as massive searchlights eerily pierced the misty gloom illuminating heavy clouds above their heads,

"What the hell is that?" he asked.

Suddenly there was a whizzing sound, followed by a blinding flash of light as he exploded into thousands of pieces. A mortar shell had impacted his body and in a split second reduced it to unidentifiable flying chunks of bloody flesh that slapped down on the cold hard snow like fresh meat on a butcher's block. The other GI dived for cover, pressing one hand on his helmet and muttering inanely as he burrowed frantically, shells bursting around him. They'd been hit by the dreaded "Nebelwerfers," five-barreled mortars, known to more experienced soldiers as "Screaming Meemies." Officers and ranks in the line were momentarily stunned by the ferocity of the barrage. The first ones to encounter this furious deluge of German shells were the men of the 106th Infantry Division.

It was 0530 hours, December 16, 1944. A date and time that would be forever etched into the minds and hearts of those who were there. A few days previous Major Elliott Goldstein, 589th Field Artillery Battalion, had been given a tour of the region around their position near Herzfenn by his old friend from Atlanta, Lieutenant Franklin De Jongh, an officer with the 14th Cavalry Group on the northern side of Auw. Franklin told him the 14th Cavalry was spread so thin that if anything did happen, all he could do was report and run. Goldstein considered himself warned. He already suspected something was going on to the east of his position but regardless of the information he provided to his superiors, it was considered worthless. Instead of asking questions, the division artillery S-2 told him:

This is the route the Germans took through Belgium in 1870, and taken in every war since. It's in their tactics manual and a training exercise for all German officers. I've told them that, and they don't believe me. They're convinced the attack is coming well to the north of us.

Things had been calm the previous days on Goldstein's night shifts. This predawn morning, though, something was different. All of his forward observers reported a traffic jam near Auw, convoys with headlights, flares overhead and German patrols apparently permeating the American front line.

Hugh Colbert, B Company, 422d Regiment

I was at the 422d Battalion Command Post at 5:30 a.m. I started hearing incoming artillery shells. I was ordered to take messages from Battalion Headquarters to company commanders. On December 19th I was surrendered to the Germans with other members of Company A and Company B, 422d Regt. We were in a valley and we were attempting to cross Skyline Drive when German tanks opened up on us with their 88s. We were in a valley, and they, the tanks, were at the top of a hill firing down on us. We had no chance with our rifles to combat the tanks. We were among the first ones who got caught going to Schoenberg. I believe only Joe Massey and about eight others made it across Skyline Drive and were not captured at that time.

One GI of the 106th was taking care of business at the latrine before he reported to the Fire Direction Center for the day shift. With his pants around his ankles, squatting over the slit trench in the frigid morning air, he was one of the first to see hundreds of tiny flashes on the horizon and hear the first terrifying, guttural booms of artillery fire.

His personal business was rudely interrupted by the menacing *whoosh* of incoming artillery landing in close proximity. The GI did his best to correct his predicament and pull up his pants before falling face first on the snow-covered ground. Explosions caused chunks of frozen mud to spray his dangerously exposed backside and fill his ears with the sound of murderous fragments zipping overhead. In his hand was an intact copy of *Stars and Stripes*, which had been intended for both reading matter and necessary ablutions. Lying there with his trousers still around his knees, here was at least one GI who was "going commando" that morning.

Meanwhile John Schaffner was in his dugout when all hell broke loose. He'd weighed up the odds and decided that being in a dugout was probably better than being back with the rest of Battery B.

John Schaffner, Scout, Battery B, 589th Field Artillery Battalion
Early in the morning, before dawn, at 0605, on 16 December our position came under a barrage of German artillery fire. I was on guard at one of our outposts, and though I did not realize it at the time, was probably better off there than with the rest of the battery. We had a dug-in .50 cal. MG so, it being somewhat protected, I got down in the lowest possible place and "crawled into my helmet." Trying to get down as far as possible, I found my buttons to be in the way. During the shelling, many rounds exploded real close and showered dirt and tree limbs about, but also there were quite a few duds that only smacked into the ground. Those were the "good" ones as far as I was concerned. After about 30 minutes the shelling ceased and before any of the enemy came into sight I was summoned to return to the battery position. We apparently did not suffer any casualties, even with all the shells that fell around the battery position. I did not have the foggiest notion what was going on except that we were under attack and things were becoming serious. (Frank Aspinwall reported in his book that from an inspection of the fragments, somebody determined that the enemy was using 88mm, 105mm and 155mm guns. I can't imagine that anyone was actually concerned about that bit of trivia at the time.) Wire crews were sent out to repair the phone lines that were out. At about 0800 the battery positions again came under heavy artillery fire, and again no casualties were reported.

As those first explosions resonated, the 423d I&R Platoon scrambled frantically out of their sleeping bags, grabbed their weapons, and assembled on the first floor. Emanating from outside their billets was a cacophony of different noises, powerful mounted 88s, artillery shells primed to burst at treetop level and sever the treetops, mortars, and most terrifying of all, the "Screaming Meemies," the five-barreled German mortars that detonated simultaneously and pierced the skies like banshees. Lieutenant Ike Long immediately organized the men. Lines to their outposts were still operational, so he ordered those manning them to return to the schoolhouse, while he dispatched a runner to Regimental HQ to find out what the hell was going on.

Outside flares of red, green, amber and white irradiated the night sky. Powerful enemy searchlights reflecting off the low hanging clouds added to the spookiness of that bitterly cold morning. Within minutes, wire communications were being disrupted and radio frequencies were getting jammed. Some buildings that had been hit were on fire. The incessant noise was accompanied by ground-shuddering explosions that shook buildings to their foundations. The I&R Platoon wouldn't be served breakfast that morning. Someone at ETO HQ had referred to this sector as the "Honeymoon Place"—well the honeymoon was well and truly over now.

Shells had been falling on the provisional battalion, 423d Infantry Regiment at Bleialf since 0530 hours. By 0600, wire communication between Lieutenant Alan Jones, S-3, 1st Battalion, and Bleialf was out. The only way to communicate with Captain Charles Reid, commander of the provisional battalion, was by radio. What Jones did know was that particularly heavy fire around Service Company and the regimental ammunition supply point at Halenfeld had destroyed a large number of vehicles and much of the regiment's stocks of reserve ammunition.

When the German preparatory barrage lifted, a battalion of German infantry, under their artificial moonlight, struck Bleialf, driving the Anti-Tank Company back in house-by-house fighting. Simultaneously, another enemy group moved up the railroad tracks on the regimental right toward Mützenich, quickly driving a wedge between the Anti-Tank Company and Troop B, 18th Cavalry Reconnaissance Squadron in Winterscheid. Yet another group hit B Company from the Sellerich road.

At 0615 hours, the bombardment suddenly ceased. For most the silence was almost as scary as the shelling. Small patrols sent across the 1,000-yard gap that separated the I&R Platoon from the Anti-Tank Company in Bleialf, reported the village was under attack from masses of tanks and infantry dressed in white winter camouflage suits screaming at the top of their lungs.

John Gatens, A Battery, 589th Field Artillery Battalion

I was at breakfast in a quite nice log cabin. I had a good plate of pancakes and strawberry jam. The shells were hitting the trees. Shell fragments and tree limbs were falling all over the place. The official thing to do under these conditions was to get back to the gun. It wasn't easy, trying not to get hit with anything that would wound or kill you. Little did I know at that time that that breakfast would be the last standard meal I would have to eat for four and one half months.

At about 0900 communication was again established with Division and with the 422d Infantry Regiment. However, the lines were soon shot out again by the enemy artillery and after 1300, the battalion was, for all practical purposes, isolated from its supported regiment.

The Battalion Communications Officer and his assistant Comm. O. went forward to the Infantry Regimental CP after 0900 and while returning were fired upon and the Comm. O. was wounded. He was brought in and later evacuated.

At 0915 a report was received of enemy patrols in Auw. An observer from C Battery went forward to a position commanding a view of Auw and from there directed effective fire on the town until he was pinned down by small-arms fire. C Battery was unable to bring guns to bear on Auw due to a high mask of trees between it and the target.

At about 1030 a patrol was sent out, as additional security, to man defensive positions along the road from Auw. Since it was now apparent that the enemy held Auw, an attack from that direction was expected. This patrol soon reported small-arms fire from enemy infantry moving out of Auw. An OP was set up in the attic of a building being used as quarters for part of Headquarters Battery. At about 1500 three enemy tanks were seen coming along the road from Auw toward the battalion command post. At about 400 yards range the lead tank opened fire on one of our outposts, damaging three machine guns. Small-arms fire was directed against the tank, but it just "buttoned up" and kept coming.

WARRIORS OF THE 106TH

The lead tank now came into view of A Battery. With the way that the battery was situated, my gun crew was the only one that could get a shot at it. The tank was riding on the road from Auw to Bleialf. We were located about 50 yards lower than he was and on his left. Before we could get a shot at him there were four GIs running down the hill towards our position. I had to get in front of our gun and signal them to lay down which they did. I now tracked the tank and missed with my first shot. Immediately reloading and firing, I hit it this time. I fired and hit him again and it burst into flames. The enemy crew bailed out and was killed by small-arms fire. The second and third tanks also took hits but were able to withdraw to defiladed positions. One of the tanks kept up harassing fire from a hull-down position but counter fire was directed at it, and it is believed that it too was knocked out. The effective work of a patrol and our firing batteries kept the whole battalion position from being overrun that afternoon.

The 2d Battalion of the 423d Regiment, in division reserve, was ordered to hold positions in front of the 589th while it withdrew to the rear ("Strategic Withdrawal" they call it). Meanwhile, the 589th held on in the face of heavy small-arms and machine-gun fire until the infantry was able to move into position shortly after midnight. Anticipating a move, a recon party had been sent to select positions for a relocation about three miles south of Schönberg, near Service Battery's position on the Belgian–German border.

Now that the initial barrage had begun to abate, the noise was replaced by the ominous throaty grumble of motor and track sounds of German tanks and vehicles that were beginning to permeate the freezing air. Many American units found themselves in danger of becoming completely isolated, and in some cases heavy shelling had destroyed hastily laid phone lines, rendering necessary communications useless. In the ensuing confusion ongoing efforts were made to contact regimental and divisional headquarters in an attempt to get a clearer picture of the situation. Despite the fact that some units managed to maintain basic communications with headquarters, most were now attempting to check and respond to the situation and repel or delay the German attack as best they could. Lack of communication led to lack of coordination and this would induce potentially fatal consequences.

From the crest of a hill some men from the I&R CP saw a column of German tanks that had bypassed Bleialf and was heading towards Schönberg.

Beside the column stood the wreckages of smoldering American vehicles. It took a moment before the Germans spotted their observers but as soon as they did they began peppering them with small-arms fire. The men at the I&R CP didn't have to go to the hill: they could see Bleialf directly. The fighting there was house to house. Outside the village, hordes of German tanks, self-propelled 88s, and infantry approached on the three roads from the south and east. On the American side, one of the artillery batteries with Captain Reid's small provisional battalion fired away. Back at the schoolhouse the men had already assembled a radio. Members of the platoon took turns cranking the generator while radio operators tried desperately to contact adjacent outfits, but all to no avail.

1st Platoon, B Company, Engineers was immediately overrun at 0600 hours when, the first German wave hit Bleialf. By 0800 hours the village was in enemy hands. Colonel Cavender reported the situation to Division and requested the return of his 2d Battalion from division reserve. General Jones vehemently denied the request claiming that it was too early to release them but he did make a few small concessions. He dispatched B Company, 81st Engineers to assist Cavender. In addition to the 70 engineers, Cavender committed every available man to take up arms, about 100, from Headquarters, Service and Cannon companies. If the Germans took Bleialf, they would have free access to the Schönberg road and Skyline Drive.

The name "Skyline Drive" was attributed to various locations in the Ardennes. In the case of the 106th it referred to the road that ran along the backbone of the Schnee Eifel. One stretch, about three-quarters of a mile long, was completely open to viewing and shelling by the Germans, and known as "Eighty-eight Corner." The sign on the side of the road said to "Drive as fast as hell until you were under cover of the trees on the other side." It was apparent to all the 106th GIs that they were on German soil, consequently every road and strongpoint had its coordinates marked on German maps. The previous occupants of the area had made a corduroy road through the woods that started and ended on either end of Eighty-eight Corner. They called it the "Engineer's Cut-Off," and it would play a vital role in the survival of many men of the 106th Infantry Division over the coming days.

Lieutenant Hans Joachim Neutmann, 18th Volksgrenadier Division (VGD)

We received official notice that we were about to embark on a great offensive; the objective of the offensive was Antwerp. We then heard the daily order of the Oberbefehlshaber (OB) West, General Field Marshal Gerd von Rundstedt, whose headquarters were located in Vallendar. It read, "Advance to the Our, over the Our to Antwerp."

In the early morning hours on 16 December 1944, before the break of dawn, we entered our preparatory (rendezvous) positions. It was cold and deep snow covered the countryside. Our first objectives for the attack were Kobscheid and Roth, northwest of Prüm. Americans had already occupied these villages since September 1944. After we assembled for the attack, we waited for our designated artillery support. However, the artillery was employed too late. Located too far back, the artillery fire hit our own men from the regimental 6th and 7th companies. Moreover, the Americans recognized the situation and subjected the regiment to heavy fire. At this point, the battalion commander, Captain Lorenz, was seriously wounded. I was able to pull him out of the killing zone behind a small wall. Later, along with other severally wounded men, I had him brought to a field medical aid station. Unfortunately, Captain Lorenz succumbed to his wounds. Command of the battalion was given to First Lieutenant Kaufmann, the commander of the regimental 5th Company.

Major General Troy Middleton's U.S. VIII Corps hadn't expected an attack of this magnitude from the Germans. He hadn't sufficiently established an organic system of mutually supporting dug-in defensive positions in depth to cover the occupied ground. The current organization relied on fragmented points of defense astride rivers such as the Our. His four divisions, the 4th, 28th, and 106th, along with the 9th Armored, 14th Mechanized Cavalry Group and a reconnaissance regiment were covering a front that extended almost 90 miles from north to south. Being so thinly dispersed rendered all these units vulnerable to any potential enemy attack and now they were realizing precisely what that entailed and how dangerous the situation was. In some cases there were substantial gaps in the division perimeters that the Germans were going to slice through like a hot knife through butter.

At the time this problem was exacerbated rather than helped by the U.S. Army's capacity for fast mobility and powerfully supported, improvised attacks rather than concerted defense. Patton said, "Fixed fortifications are monuments to man's stupidity." He believed that static defenses were completely useless, but a defensive line without an effective cohesive support network was equally superfluous. This had never been a strong point of the U.S. forces in World War II and now it was going to invoke serious consequences.

Many fateful decisions were taken on that first day that would directly affect the 106th Infantry Division's situation. Just to the south of Losheimergraben (the Losheim Gap), Colonel Mark A. Devine Jr., commander of the 14th Cavalry that incorporated the 32d Cavalry Reconnaissance Squadron, 12 75mm towed guns and two reconnaissance platoons, was feeling the full force of a barrage delivered by the German Sixth Army. Colonel Devine's peers and subordinates regarded him as a "hard-nosed, blunt-talking, spit and polish" officer. Commissioned too late to participate in the First World War, he spent the inter-war years undergoing the normal series of military schooling and assignments. It took ten years for him to attain the rank of captain. Another nine years passed before he became a major. After about 20 years of service, in 1940, he was promoted to lieutenant colonel. This was just three years after pinning on the gold oak leaves of a major. He was promoted to the rank of full colonel in January of 1941. Three years later, at age 48, Devine assumed command of the 14th Cavalry Group. It was his first combat assignment and he vigorously began honing the unit to his personal specifications. By the time they reached France, Devine's leadership methods caused many to believe that he would earn his general stars.

To the north of his position seasoned SS units were pouring through the almost six-mile-wide gap between the 106th and the 99th divisions, and directly in front forward elements of Manteufell's Fifth Panzer Army were hitting hard across the 106th Infantry Division front. The 14th Cavalry had established some static defensive positions in and around small isolated villages in proximity to the Schnee Eifel. Two platoons managed to hold at the village of Kobscheid as the fighting ebbed and flowed throughout the course of that first day but their position was becoming untenable and something had to be done to redress this. A few light tanks were dispatched from Manderfeld to provide assistance to the 14th Cavalry but these were brought to a halt en route in the village of Auw, which had already fallen to the Germans. Colonel Devine contacted General Jones to request infantry support from the 106th but was reliably informed that this wasn't going to be an option at the time. Earlier that day Devine had reported that he was having difficulty contacting some of his units due to the poor radio communications. This was partially due to the Germans jamming U.S. radio frequencies with music. Other 106th units were experiencing the same difficulties.

Lieutenant Hans Joachim Neutmann, 18th Volksgrenadier Division (VGD)

Command of the battalion was given to First Lieutenant Kaufmann, the commander of the regimental 5th Company. Around midday we captured Kobscheid and continued further towards the distant objective of St. Vith. According to the timetable of the offensive, the capture of St. Vith was estimated for 19 December. Due to severe vehicular congestion on the roads and, in some cases, heavy enemy counterattacks, this important logistical point could not be captured. Attacking spearheads from the 18th VGD, units from the Führerbegleit Brigade [Hitler's Escort Brigade], and the 62d VGD that attacked out from the area of Winterspelt, then met in Schönberg.

Things had been incredibly tough for young soldier Pfc Ken Johnson and his rifle squad since they dug in earlier that afternoon. They'd been shelled from the moment they dismounted and found whatever cover they could. He'd survived those first critical minutes of combat that either broke a man or hardened him. When evening came the Germans renewed their attack and committed all three regiments of the 62d Volksgrenadier Division to the task of penetrating and taking Winterspelt. Thousands of German infantry, heavy weapons, and artillery pieces moved up the road from Pronsfeld through Eigelscheid toward Winterspelt both directly and around the flanks. Little by little, they advanced, first laying down artillery fire, and then moving their infantry forward, taking American defensive positions one by one. German losses were high and mounting, starting in the tens, then hundreds, then many hundreds. Johnson and A Company had put a crimp in the 62d Volksgrenadier plans to take Winterspelt quickly. American losses were also high: almost three quarters of the 200 riflemen in A Company were dead or captured as midnight approached. Still, at 2030 hours on the night of the 16th, Johnson's platoon sergeant looked over at his foxhole and saw

Johnson fighting. By 2330 hours, the Germans broke through the lines and it was time for the platoon to withdraw. As the sergeant went from foxhole to foxhole to round up his men, he looked over to Johnson's foxhole—two Germans armed with machine guns occupied it. Ken Johnson was not going to withdraw with A Company that night. In fact, it would be almost 70 years before anyone knew the full details of what had happened to him.

The Germans were attempting to orchestrate a double envelopment. In the U.S. Army's northern sector they had identified a relatively unde-fended gap running between Weckerath to Kobscheid; in the south their movement around the right flank of U.S. positions out on the Schnee Eifel through Bleialf to Schonberg, had the potential to subsequently isolate GIs out on the Schnee Eifel ridge.

Beside the village of Roth that lay in the trajectory of the German advance to the Our River, a lone platoon of Cavalry equipped with only two 75mm artillery pieces found themselves in a rapidly deterio-rating situation as they began to succumb to the force of the attack now underway. Devine attempted to dispatch a few light tanks to provide some assistance to the besieged platoon but they found their progress blocked by German grenadiers who had managed to bypass the village. Further reports reached Devine from other units that were suffering the same fate.

In the village of Weckerath a little farther north a few soldiers of Troop C, 14th Cavalry Group, 18th Cavalry Squadron witnessed the main attack of the 18th VGD and opened fire along with other U.S. artillery in proximity on a ridge behind their position. In doing so they exposed their position to the enemy and even though a few tanks had arrived to assist, they were now in an extremely precarious situation. Despite this the cavalry troops continued to offer significant resistance to the enemy for the time being.

In front of the small villages of Krewinkel and Aft First Lieutenant Kenneth Ferrens and other soldiers from Troop C were well dug in and heroically repelling all attempts by German soldiers of the 3d Parachute Division to infiltrate their position. For a moment the firing abated and a voice with a distinct German accent shouted, "Take a ten-minute break, soldier. We'll be back." Ferrens cupped his hands to his mouth and defiantly responded with, "And we'll be waiting for you, you son of a bitch!" The two platoons were able to hold the villages and in the process only sustained three casualties. On the frozen ground before them were the dead bodies of around 150 German soldiers. Ferrens's bold riposte was just as inspiring as General Tony McAuliffe's "Nuts" was to the Germans who would attack Bastogne sometime later.

Realizing the mounting seriousness of his situation, at 0930 hours, Colonel Devine decided to give the order to all of his units to pull to the south to a line that ran from Manderfeld to Verscheid. This fateful decision to pull back the 14th Cavalry could have exposed the northern flank of the 422d Regiment, thus allowing the German advance to accelerate and surround the 422d and 423d regiments stranded out on the Schnee Eifel. Consequently it made little difference to the overall strategic situation at the time because the German Army had already penetrated so deeply that the 422d flank was vulnerable anyway. The division reserve, 2d Battalion, 423d Infantry, was ordered to fill the gap between the 14th Cavalry and the 422d Infantry in an attempt to prevent the Germans from advancing around that dangerously exposed flank. Later that afternoon the 14th Cavalry Group executive officer called 106th Division HQ to request further permission to withdraw to the Andler–Holzheim line along a series of ridges. Permission was granted.

When Devine arrived at 106th HQ in St. Vith that evening to explain the situation to General Jones he was requested to wait at the CP. Jones was too preoccupied with plans for a counter-offensive and by the evening December 16 he had committed all his available reserves.

Sergeant John P. Kline, M Company, 423d Infantry Regiment
Our company commander set up his headquarters in one of the enormous Siegfried Line bunkers. The bunker was not completely demolished, as they usually were. The underground rooms were intact and accessible. He had taken a room several flights down. The command bunker was on a crest of a hill. The firing apertures faced west towards Belgium, the backside towards the present German lines. There were steep slopes on either side, with signs and white caution tape warning of "Mine Fields." There was a pistol belt and canteen hanging in one of the trees on the slope. Apparently, some GI had wandered into the minefield.

When the shelling started Lieutenant Colonel Thomas Riggs put his staff on alert and headed for the 106th Division HQ. By the time Riggs arrived, German shells were raining down on the town and causing havoc. At the G-2 section, they told him the entire front was under attack and from the phone lines that were still operable, numerous reports of enemy infantry, tanks, and artillery were pouring in. Riggs was reliably informed that attempts were being made to convey the reports back to VIII Corps, but at the time Corps didn't respond accordingly because they considered the reports exaggerated and vague.

By the time Riggs left, the G-3 told him he should prepare his engineers for their secondary mission as infantry reserve. It was a quick trip back to his HQ at Heuem. By 0800 hours, he found most of his line companies already committed as infantry reserves by their regiments. All he had left to work with were his own Headquarters and Service companies. Riggs instinctively deduced that it was going to be a long day.

C Company, 424th Infantry Regiment was rudely awakened by the steady pounding of incoming artillery. This was the fifth morning that the men had assembled in the chow line but on this occasion there were a few disconcerting comments about the heavy enemy barrage. Standing in line Private Royce Lapp looked forward to the al fresco hot breakfast of hotcakes, doughnuts, and coffee. All seemed well until Sergeant Gribbin interrupted the breakfast proceedings and yelled, "They've broken through Cannon Company, and Company C is going up to plug the hole." Suddenly mess kits clattered to the ground as the men anxiously grabbed the coffee and doughnuts, and then ran to grab their gear. Each man was promptly issued two cans of C-rations, two hand grenades, and two boxes of .30-caliber ammunition. This would be their first action and nobody was looking forward to it. As the men assembled, eyes widened as enemy shells began falling around them in relatively close proximity. Lapp attempted to suppress the gnawing feeling of trepidation that increased by the minute in the pit of his stomach and almost caused him to regurgitate his breakfast. They climbed into their trucks and headed out to meet the enemy as fast as they could go.

Private First Class Royce E. Lapp, Weapons Pit, C Company, 424th Regiment

If everything went right we would go up and meet this bunch that had broken through, push them back, regain Canon Co's old positions and set up to hold.

Our packs and overcoats would soon be brought up to us in trucks. As it turned out I never saw my pack, overcoat or any other of my equipment again. There were plenty of uniforms in those duffel bags and the Jerries weren't slow to take advantage of them. We learned later that, dressed in our uniforms, they had a merry time disrupting communications, traffic flow and supply lines.

The front line was fluid and we didn't know how far the Krauts had come already. Our trucks were open and we were ready to jump out at any time. It was a mad dash for a couple of miles up the road to Winterspelt before we were fired on and piled out. We hadn't gotten our mortar ammo yet and had to wait for our jeep to catch us. It was a scramble tearing down the clover leaves. We threw 16 rounds apiece into our ammo bags and slipped them over our shoulders. I stepped back inside a barn and tore my rounds clear out of their cases while a little boy stood nervously in the other end watching me. I was briefly overcome with sadness, sensing that the whole village—and everyone left in it—was doomed and I was unable to stop it. No sooner did we get out than artillery started tearing it up from one end to the other.

Our section was broken up and each mortar squad was attached to one of the rifle platoons. We were assigned to the 1st Platoon and moved out with them as one of the attacking platoons. Three days later we joined remaining remnants of the company and found that we were the only squad to survive those first few days of hell intact. The 1st Platoon quickly moved out of the town in column across open country and soon into some heavy woods where we spread into a skirmish line. The terrain was rough and the load of ammo grew heavier with every slippery step. We soon began to see what was waiting for us up ahead. We saw that a fellow can be a beat-up bloody mess and still walk. These boys making their way back to the aid station were not a pretty sight. All we could do was stare at them as they passed and wonder when it would be our turn. It was a trickle going back then compared to what must have been on the road after the barrage that was soon to come. Some of the men that we met were not wounded—they were dazed, disoriented, disorganized, wandering aimlessly looking for buddies. We got a blurry picture from those men of what had happened so far that morning. It had truly been a breakthrough—the line hadn't given and bent or fallen back—it had been chewed up right where it was with massive artillery fire and overwhelming infantry assault.

We still hadn't met their riflemen when their artillery caught us there in the woods as we were getting organized. It was a baptism of fire to be long remembered. They [the shells] first whistled in off to one side—I had to think what to do. It soon *became instinct to hit the ground with the first whistle, find the lowest depression possible and hug it close. It seemed as if they were bursting right at your side or just over your head and you lived years waiting for that hot shrapnel to tear through you. We had changed loads earlier and I was carrying the mortar instead of ammo. I leaned it up against me hoping it was some protection. You would think that nothing in all the world could pry you loose from that earth, but when the fellow in front of you moves out you've got to move too or you're alone and lost. At every little let-up or pause in the bombardment we moved ahead. They had those woods boxed in as perfectly as if they knew in advance exactly where we would be going. It appeared to us that they were throwing everything they had in there at once to catch us before we could reach them—and they did succeed in getting well over half the company in those first few hours. If I ever did any honest to goodness praying, I did it lying there with my face in the slush. Time had ceased to exist and the cold was no longer your primary concern.*

We were still pushing ahead to get out from under the artillery when we made contact with their infantry. They were taking chances then—practically dropping their shells on their own men. I heard the rip of a burp gun, a very rapid-fire German machine gun, for the first time and everyone instinctively scooted back to lower ground as chips flew from the trees above. One of our boys got that first gun with a rifle grenade.

Once the 14th Cavalry had withdrawn the 18th and 32d squadrons from their positions, the way was clear for the 18th VGD to occupy the rear flank of the 422d Regiment; by midday the German grenadiers were starting to take advantage of the situation and move through the gap toward the pivotal village of Auw, where A Company, 81st Engineer Combat Battalion was billeted. The engineers were busy working on the roads when the Germans began to approach. They immediately threw down their picks and shovels and raced back to the village to set up their machine guns and engage the approaching German column that was supported by self-propelled assault guns. Outgunned and outmanned, A Company was compelled to abandon their positions but they had held long enough for U.S. artillery units to zero the position and bring the German advance to a stuttering halt. At this juncture it was all about buying time for whatever reserves were available to push forward and provide support to some of the stranded 106th units currently receiving a hard pounding from the Germans, but time was running out.

Colonel Descheneaux of the 422d Regiment had effectively recognized that the village of Auw was crucial for the protection of his rear flank so it was he who ordered a small task force comprised of L Company (the cannon company) and part of an anti-tank company to counterattack towards the village to support the engineers there. Shortly after they left contact was made with the Germans attacking Auw, but a fierce blizzard hit and further orders were given to immediately return to the regimental command post at Schlausenbach, which was now also under threat. Further attempts were made to establish cohesion during an extremely fractious situation that appeared to be deteriorating by the hour.

Just behind the tiny village of Schlausenbach on the northwestern slopes of the Schnee Eifel, Battery A, 589th Field Artillery Battalion, 106th Infantry Division, was supporting the 422d Infantry. First Lieutenant Eric F. Wood, Jr., was executive officer of the battery. Wood had attempted to contact his immediate superior officer, Captain Aloysius J. Menke, up at a forward OP, but Menke was ominously silent. Wood was then acting battery commander. Realizing that he was probably surrounded, Wood decided to extricate his men from a very precarious situation. Whether they would make it out remained to be seen.

By the early afternoon December 16, Eisenhower was still largely oblivious to the events unfolding in the Ardennes and out on the Schnee Eifel. He'd occupied most of the afternoon at SHAEF HQ, a villa previously occupied by von Rundstedt, taking care of business before sitting down to read a letter from Montgomery requesting permission to spend Christmas in England with his son. In the letter Montgomery reminded Eisenhower that he'd won a bet made 14 months earlier wherein Eisenhower predicted the war would be over by Christmas. Eisenhower penned a response, noting his envy at Montgomery's opportunity to visit his family with the addendum that there were still nine days until Christmas.

Eisenhower was expecting General Bradley for dinner. Steve Early, President Roosevelt's press secretary, managed to airfreight a bushel of oysters that day as a present to Ike for receiving his fifth star. Bradley arrived shortly after dusk. Instead of discussing ETO, the two were exchanging their concerns over the scores of infantry replacements being sent to the Pacific when suddenly Major General Kenneth Strong, Eisenhower's G-2, interrupted them, spread out a map on the table and indicated in no uncertain terms the five points on the VIII Corps front that the Germans had penetrated.

As they studied the map, there were some present who suggested it was probably just a German spoiling attack to detract the Allied advances north and south of the Ardennes. What concerned Eisenhower was the obvious German penetration through the V and VIII Corps boundary in the Losheim Gap. The calculated risk the Allies had taken in the Ardennes was based on their ability to counterattack in the event of trouble; now it looked like the trouble had arrived.

"That's no spoiling attack," declared Eisenhower.

As the discussion progressed, Bradley and Eisenhower agreed that VIII Corps needed help. While SHAEF had the 82d and 101st Airborne divisions in reserve, Bradley's reserves, already assigned to his army commanders, could not be used without his consent. Their final decision was to send Lieutenant General George Patton's 10th Armored Division and Lieutenant General William Simpson's 7th Armored Division to Hodges' First Army, which was clearly in the middle of the German attack. Bradley reminded his boss that Patton would be irate.

"Tell him that Ike is running this damned war," replied Eisenhower.

Bradley quickly got Patton on the phone and told him to send the 10th Armored Division to Middleton's VIII Corps: he wanted to stab the German's southern flank if they broke through Middleton's front. Patton was not at all happy, but agreed to comply. Bradley then called Major General Leven Allen at Eagle Tac, his HQ in Luxembourg City, to tell him of his orders to Patton, and have Allen order Simpson to turn over 7th Armored Division to General Courtney Hodges' First Army immediately. Simpson would be far more cooperative than Patton was. Now, Bradley had enlisted the assistance of two armored divisions to hit von Rundstedt's flank but would they get there in time?

Hanging up the phone, Eisenhower's aide, Lieutenant General Walter Bedell Smith reminded the affable Bradley of the times he'd wished the Germans would come out and fight in the open. "Well, Brad, you've been wishing for a counterattack. Now it looks like you've got one," said Smith.

"A counterattack, yes, but I'll be damned if I wanted one this big," replied Bradley. As for the dinner, Bradley was allergic to oysters and had scrambled eggs instead while they debated the situation in the Ardennes well into the night.

Lieutenant Colonel Joseph F. Puett, 2d Battalion, 423d Infantry Regiment December 16, 1944 the battalion was billeted with G, H, and HQ Co. at Born, Belgium and E and F Co. at Medell, Belgium in division reserve. At approximately 0700, the battalion was alerted for immediate movement, upon receipt of 30 2½-ton trucks furnished by Division Headquarters. Upon receipt of 28 trucks the battalion was ordered to an assembly area one mile north of St. Vith, Belgium. I proceeded to Division Headquarters. At 1215 hours I was ordered by the Commanding General to proceed at once to Schönberg, Germany with one platoon of TDs attached to secure the roads leading north and east from Schönberg. This was done and the advance elements of the battalion arrived at Schönberg at 1315, and immediately began digging in. The defensive set-up of the roads and Schönberg was completed at 1730. Telephone communications with Division had been established at 1345. At 1400 reconnaissance patrols both foot and motorized had been put out, and reported each half hour. Contact with front line friendly units was established on all roads to the north and east.

At approximately 0830 the battalion was ordered by the Commanding General to proceed to the high ground just south of Auw, Belgium and to extricate the 589th Field Artillery Battalion and to release the trucks upon arrival at this point.

Just before receipt of this order, 2d Battalion patrols had reported the fast withdrawal of Cavalry and Engineer units from their positions between Andler and Auw. This was reported to Division. Two of my patrols had skirmishes with German patrols about 1½ miles to the north of our positions at Schönberg, with our receiving two casualties. This was reported. At 0845 the Cavalry and Engineer units came streaming from the north through Schönberg, retreating towards St. Vith. At 0900 hours I stopped the Commanding Officer of the Cavalry Troop and ask him if he were going to make a stand. He informed me that he was, and that they were laying a minefield at Andler. I informed him of my orders to move and also told him if he let Schönberg fall into enemy hands that two regiments would be cut off.

He said that he could hold till late the next morning. However, this officer proceeded on toward St. Vith. Those facts and conversation were reported to Division, and I asked if there were any change of orders. There were none.

The 2d Battalion was withdrawn from its dug-in positions defending Schönberg and entrucked and proceeded to the high ground just south of Auw at 2200 hours.

During this time there had been no let-up of the vehicles and men of the Cavalry and Engineer units retreating toward St. Vith. This was reported to Division as late as 2200 as telephone communications were broken for the move. The move was made in complete blackout with a drizzly rain and without loss of a vehicle.

From the offset General Jones had voiced reservations concerning the disposition of his inexperienced division into a potentially dangerous salient along the First Army front. He had raised the matter with some urgency at a VIII Corps staff meeting. Hodges, Bradley and Eisenhower remained intransigent regarding the defense the Schnee Eifel and the Losheim Gap. Eisenhower was aware of the dangers and later wrote, "The risk of a large German penetration in that area was mine alone." Jones had argued vociferously that too many of his units were situated in vulnerable areas out in the valleys where they could easily become isolated and surrounded. Since he had arrived, Jones hadn't referred to the matter with General Middleton. It was a decision he would come to regret.

Since occupying the 2d Infantry Division's positions, the 106th had inherited an intricate wire line system that had been devised by the 2d Infantry Division. According to Captain Alan Jones Jr. the general's son who was with the HQ Company, 1st Battalion, 423d Infantry Regiment, the 106th had been issued radios in England that hadn't been calibrated or tested before arriving in the ETO. By the time they needed to establish communications radio silence had been imposed across the board. This was a similar situation that the British 1st Parachute Regiment had experienced at Arnhem some months earlier. In both cases the radios should have been tried and tested before being distributed to the ranks. Communication for any unit on the front line was an imperative and the lack of adequate radio equipment would cost the 106th dearly.

Placing an untested division in such a vulnerable forward position emphasizes the glaring lack of coherent military planning at ETO at the time. It was argued that the 28th or the 4th divisions would have fared better but both of these were still reeling from a previous military blunder, the battle of the Hürtgen Forest, that had effectively deprived the U.S. forces there of almost all previous tactical advantages that they had benefitted from until that stage in the war. Some parallels could be drawn with the predicament experienced by the 106th on December 16.

Albert C. Reed, Construction Platoon, 106th Signal Company

The first day I remember coming under fire was before the 16th of December (the day of the beginning of the Bulge). A few members of the team went up to Grosslangenfeld to check on the Recon Troop. We checked their switchboard and the way that the field wire entered the location for future reference. When we were finished we asked if they had seen any of the enemy. One of them handed me the glasses and said if you want to see some Germans, look at that village across the valley. Sure enough a few could be seen walking in the street of the town. We asked if any shots had been fired and were told that a few mortar barrages had occurred, but recently they only fired a return shot if one was sent over at them. One of them said, "Wanna see?" and someone said, "Yeah." A mortar shot was fired, and we watched it explode in their territory. Nothing happened for quite a while. One of the men said, "Guess they are all asleep." "Don't count on that," someone answered. Suddenly we heard the flatter sound of the fins of a mortar shell overhead. We all hit the ground except for the gunnery crew who dove in the foxholes beside their weapon. The shell exploded about 75 yards away doing no damage. We waited, still on the ground, for a second shell to arrive. Someone said, "I guess we woke the bastards up." Moments later a member of the team said, "Let's get the hell out of here!" and we did.

I had come under mortar attack along the road. I was very near to 424th HQ dugout. I knew that mortars had a short range and that the German troops that were firing them could not be any more than 500 yards away. Many vehicles had been stopped as the barrages became more intense. So I stopped and got away from the road by running to a house and flopping on the opposite side from which the mortars were coming. I heard another GI arrive behind me. A few minutes after the barrage had stopped the GI behind me said, "What are you doing lying on the ground?" Without looking I replied, "What the hell do you think, stupid?

Taking a nap? I'm smart enough to know that the barrage might start again any second. And I don't want my fucking ass blown off!" As I followed that GI walking back to his jeep, I discovered he was a two-star general. Fortunately, he didn't ask for my name, rank and serial number.

At 0830 hours the 106th Division Signal Officer, Lieutenant Colonel Earle Williams, relayed some worrying news when he sent out the message that German tanks were approaching from Andler and that he intended to destroy his switchboard. Around the same time it was acknowledged that Germans were approaching from Bleialf and Radscheid and converging on Schönberg. Manteuffel's' Fifth Panzer Army had effectively trapped two regiments on the Schnee Eifel. With still no word from Combat Command B (CCB), 7th Armored Division, at 0945 General Jones sent an update to his 422d and 423d Infantry Regiments: "Expect to clear out area west of you this afternoon with reinforcements. Withdraw from present positions if they become untenable."

General Middleton called General Jones with some welcome news: "I'm sending you a big friend, 'Workshop.' It should reach you by 0700 tomorrow." Jones knew that "Workshop" meant the 7th Armored Division. Things were looking up for Jones and the 106th but the 7th Armored Division had only recently been withdrawn from the Ninth Army, and at that juncture was somewhere en route to VIII Corps in the vicinity of Vielsalm, roughly 12 miles northwest of St. Vith, and six or seven miles west of Schönberg. Middleton may have been a little overconfident with his prediction regarding the 7th Armored. It wasn't going to be easy to move that kind of force along muddy roads, over the rugged and snow-bedecked terrain of the Ardennes at night. The move could be further exacerbated by the confusion that was surfacing as some forces attempted to hold their positions while others were perfectly happy to leave the area.

As night approached Lieutenant Donald Beseler and his small band of survivors from A Company, 424th Infantry took refuge in a small stone shed. It wasn't much given that it had only three sides and was open on the fourth. The Germans were everywhere. They marched by in an endless stream of tanks and carriers. Hundreds and hundreds of infantry passed within feet of the shed throughout the night. Yet, none of them looked inside. Beseler had a hard time believing they weren't discovered. Maybe it was the continuous noise of German and American artillery shells pounding down around them. Maybe it was the continuous screams and bright fiery tails of German Nebelwerfer overhead. One German soldier spent the better part of the night within a few dozen feet of the open shed. Beseler thought about taking the man out, but knew it would be their death warrant. Between moments of sheer terror believing they'd be found, Beseler began plotting an escape. His fight was far from over.

After action report: 81st Engineer Combat Battalion
16 DC 44 HQs and H&S Co. received 5 rounds enemy artillery fire estimated as 380mm. from the SE at around 1230–1300. The Co. formed a defensive position around the C.P. The battalion heavy equipment was evacuated to vicinity of Rodt, Belgium. Co. A received enemy shell fire during period 0600 to 0655. At 0600 all three platoons commenced work on roads in regimental area. At approximately 1030 the enemy were reported moving into Auw. The Co. C.O., Capt. Harold M. Harmon, one platoon leader, Lt. Purtell, and about two squads evacuated Auw and returned to battalion. Seven men of the first platoon later returned to battalion and rejoined their Co. All of Co. A present left at 1230 for Andler to assist 422 Inf. Regt. in counterattack on Auw. The Co. HQs, under Lt. Rutledge, were reported resisting the enemy from a hilltop near Auw, and later rejoined company. Co. at 1535 reported holding Wisscheid. In the evacuation of Auw, the 20 T trailer was hit by artillery and the D-6 dozer and trailer were abandoned. The 6 T prime mover pulled a trailer and D-7 dozer from the 168th Engr. Combat Battalion to safety to the rear. Co. B received continuous artillery fire estimated at 380mm during the morning starting at 0600. The company was attached to 423 Inf. Regt. and moved from C.P. at 0930. On the morning of the 16th a patrol led by Lt. Gordon entered Bleialf with mission to drive large enemy patrol from town. The German patrol was pushed out of town and artillery fire from TD laid on them. All heavy equipment was evacuated to the rear. Co. C was alerted to act as infantry in regimental reserve and formed a defensive position along the ridge running W and S through Hechalenfeld.

CHAPTER 5

GOLDEN LIONS FIGHTING LIKE TIGERS

The early morning December 17 found the 106th dealing with a serious predicament. Their situation was deteriorating rapidly and Colonel Reid, commander of the 424th Infantry, had every reason to believe that his group was becoming surrounded. He'd been aware that his exposed left flank was becoming increasingly vulnerable, but to what extent he wasn't entirely sure; to make the situation worse he had lost all communications with his right flank. By now the attacking enemy had introduced tanks during the night and were hitting the 424th in considerable force. Reid instinctively knew that his regiment had its back to the Our River and if the 62d VG Division captured the bridge at Steinebrück and moved along the west bank, it would be tough going to retreat to the west.

The most powerful attack came from farther north and was orchestrated by the 62d VGD. In the course of the night elements of the 62d VGD had captured and occupied almost half of the small town of Winterspelt. They had incurred heavy casualties in the process but were planning to take the rest of the town and drive out the 1st Battalion, 424th Infantry when expected reinforcements arrived at dawn. There had been some vicious hand-to-hand fighting as both sides struggled to dominate the position. The 62d VGD had been unpleasantly surprised by the ferocity and determination of these fresh young "Ami's" which is how they referred to the American forces in general. The battle for possession of Winterspelt ebbed back and forth quite erratically and despite the appearance of enemy reserves, the 1st Battalion was able to benefit from the unexpected arrival of Combat Command B (CCB)

9th Armored Division, who came across the Steinebrück bridge, checked the German advance and helped to push them back to Elcherath, which they took around 1530 hours. Despite the increasingly overwhelming odds, those "Golden Lions" of the 106th were fighting like tigers out in the valleys and on the snow-covered hills.

Lieutenant Donald Beseler looked at the case of hand grenades in the corner of the shed. If they had any hope of escaping the German stranglehold on Winterspelt, it was now or never. Beseler handed two grenades to each of the four men who had survived the night in the shed with him. At the signal, they pulled the pins on all ten grenades and charged out of the shed, throwing them left, right, and anywhere they thought there might be a German. The shock tactic worked. Germans scattered everywhere. Fifty yards further, approaching another barn, they stopped, caught their breath, and took stock of their situation. Nobody was wounded so they dashed from the barn into the woods. It didn't take long to find other stragglers from the battle for Winterspelt. Beseler did his best to count the survivors of A Company. There were 15, maybe twenty.

Meanwhile First Lieutenant Eric Fisher Wood was handling the rapidly changing situation to the best of his ability. He gave an order to his men to disengage from their original positions, and relocate to a new position in the vicinity of the village of Schönberg. At this juncture the attacking Germans were in dangerously close proximity to Wood's unit and streaming down every road, path and dirt track heading west. Most of Wood's battery managed to attach their artillery pieces and hit the road, except one gun that remained immovable. Wood didn't think twice about staying to assist the men. After several tense minutes they extracted the gun and immediately sped towards the village. Suddenly, as they made their way down the road toward the spire of Schönberg church, German shells began exploding around them and they had to run the gauntlet and press on. That spire was enticingly close.

They were unaware that Schönberg was by now almost entirely in German hands. By the time they realized this, it was too late to do anything about it. Wood told his driver to step on the gas and try to drive straight through the middle of the town. Suddenly he saw a tank blocking the road out to St. Vith. Wood and his men got out of the truck to attack it. One of the GIs, Pfc Campagna, had a bazooka, the others carried M1 carbines. The tank reversed back across the bridge and disappeared into the town with Wood and his men in hot pursuit. They crossed the bridge going west down Schönberg's one street. With snipers pecking at them, Campagna and Sergeant Scannapico ran ahead to see where the tank had gone. As he was about to climb into the truck Campagna managed to fire at the tank with his bazooka as it rolled past into view but the shot didn't have the desired effect. The truck slowed to let Scannapico catch up, but a sniper got him cold. So the section rolled on. They gathered speed as they left the village but just over a rise in the road, another German tank blocked their way and began firing.

Wood reflexively pitched his men and himself out of the truck into a ditch by the side of the road before the tank reduced their vehicle to scrap iron. Suddenly German bullets started impacting the snow around the ditch. Fire appeared to be coming from three directions. The GIs raised their hands to surrender but Eric Fisher Wood leapt out of the ditch and ran as fast as his legs could carry him, northwards toward the tree line before disappearing from sight into the shelter of the forest.

John Gatens, Battery A, 589th Field Artillery Battalion

Our new position was a field on the right side of the road that runs north from Bleialf to Schönberg. We were about a mile and a quarter from Schönberg itself. We arrived with only three guns and went into our positions. During the night Sgt. Alford's truck had run into the barrel of one of the howitzers and caused the radiator to start leaking. With the truck overheating, they had to lag behind. When they finally arrived Lt. Wood held him on the road to act as anti-tank defense.

Lt. Wood then gave the order, which in artillery terms is "March order." He also made it clear that he meant "right now." Having been in this position for only about one and one half hours, we knew that the enemy was very close. I was waiting for our Sgt. to give the order, but I couldn't find him. Being second in command, I gave my men the order to pack up and be ready to move. I looked all over the area and just couldn't find my Sgt. Shook. The two other crews started to move, so I jumped in the truck and gave the order to go. I was now in command.

Never knowing when something that bugs you turns out to be a good thing. Before we left the first position they asked that one of our men be assigned to the group that was leaving to search out the next position. This bugged me because that left me a man short for the tough job that we had in front of us. This turned out to be a blessing. He told me not to go out the way we came in. He knew an easy way out because he had used it in checking out the position.

One of the other crews followed us. We got out on the road and started racing for Schönberg. Our destination was as ordered: St. Vith. Sgt. Alford, who was already on the road, ditched his truck and hooked up to a supply truck and was right on our heels. At this time artillery and small-arms fire could be heard all over the place.

Sgt. Scannapico, who was in charge of the fourth gun, started to leave the area the same way that we came in. Before they reached the road, the truck got stuck. Lt. Wood, knowing this, stayed with that crew. They pushed and shoved like crazy until they got on the road.

Our three guns got through Schönberg just in time. The Germans were now all over the place. Sgt. Scannapico along with Lt. Wood had lost precious time. When they got to Schönberg they were met in the middle of the road by a German tank. Sgt. Scannapico jumped out of the truck and started firing at the tank. He was killed on the spot. The tank opened fire and had a direct hit on the truck, killing the driver. Lt. Wood and the rest of the crew bailed out of the truck and ran for the cover of a brook. With the infantry firing at them, the crew put their hands up and surrendered. Lt. Wood, leaping the ditch, ran, dodging bullets all the way, reached a tree line and disappeared. The remainder of the battalion assembled again west of St. Vith where they were joined by Service Battery of the 590th Field Artillery Battalion. They were ordered into position north of St. Vith to establish a roadblock to protect the town. Later, that night, they were withdrawn to a bivouac area in the vicinity of St. Vith.

Early on December 17, batteries A and B of the 589th Battalion were almost in position approximately one mile east of Schönberg on the Schönberg–Bleialf road. Although they had managed to pull back to fresh positions, just before dawn, units of the 18th VGD had captured Bleialf and consequently the Schönberg–Bleialf road was clear for the enemy to advance on Schönberg, which was at that time considered the only feasible exit for the 589th. As the first hesitant rays of daylight filtered through the dawn mist a deuce-and-half truck from the battalion's Service Battery charged down the road from the direction of Bleialf wanting to warn batteries that the Germans were right on his tail. Communications had been lost with battalion commander Lieutenant Colonel Thomas P. Kelly Jr., who was still trying to save Battery C, and so battalion executive Major Arthur C. Parker III took command and in a spate of clear, coherent thinking he immediately ordered the remaining units of the 589th to evacuate once again to new positions west of St. Vith.

The 333d Field Artillery Battalion (155mm), like most African-American artillery battalions in the segregated U.S. Army, was a non-divisional unit under the command of VIII Corps that had nine African-American Field Artillery battalions in its ranks. Four of the seven Corps Artillery units supporting the 106th Infantry Division, the 333d, 559th 578th and 740th, were black. Previously, most African-American soldiers in the European theater had been assigned to service units such as the famed convoy system, the "Red Ball Express." Now these troops were permitted to volunteer for duty as combat infantrymen, with the understanding that after the necessary training they would be committed to front-line service. Eventually, some 2,200 were organized into 53 platoons and assigned to all-white rifle companies in the two U.S. army groups. The exigencies of combat had temporarily forced the Army to discard its policy of segregating white and black soldiers.

Situated along the Andler–Schönberg Road, east of St. Vith, the 333d Field Artillery Battalion had been in position since early October. After the departure of the 2d Infantry Division the first week of December, it became attached to the 106th Infantry Division. A liaison officer, Captain John P. Horn, had been assigned to the neighboring 590th Field Artillery of the 106th Infantry Division.

Unlike other 106th units in the area, the 333d did have combat experience. Commanded by Lieutenant Colonel Harmon Kelsey, a white officer, the battalion had been in action since coming ashore at Utah Beach on June 29, 1944. Typical of most segregated units in World War II, it had white officers and black enlisted men. After the Normandy campaign the unit arrived on the German border in late September. It was attached to the 2d Infantry Division as it moved into the Ardennes in the early fall.

Down at Bleialf, the two forward observer groups from the 333d Field Artillery Battalion had their outposts on the edge of the village and held their ground. Lieutenant Reginald Gibson was in charge of one of these groups and Lieutenant Elmer King the other.

Their job was to identify targets for any artillery battery that would respond. Both groups managed to stay at their posts until 0600 hours the next day. On the early morning of December 17, before dawn, the men of C Battery tried to have some breakfast while the sound of tanks and small-arms fire appeared to resonate all around them. Fog obscured observation. Their radios were filled with frantic calls from the infantry. The Germans seemed to be everywhere. Still the men were waiting on word from Corps to displace. It was too late. At 1000 hours German armor appeared along the Andler road in front of C Battery and German infantry began pouring out of the woods. Most had no time to escape. A few groups managed to make it into the woods. Roaming around the dark woods of the Ardennes with its muddy paths and steep, slippery hills slowed them down considerably.

A small band headed south toward Schönberg, but the Germans were there already and waiting for any Americans trying to cross the bridge. The 333d survivors had aimed for the east bank of the Our River and made their way out of the village. As they trekked up the road, they encountered a convoy from the 589th Field Artillery and warned the drivers that there were Germans all over the village. They were ignored. As the Americans crossed the bridge, a German tank opened fire. Two trucks were hit and several men killed. The men tried to scatter but were forced to surrender soon after.

A few other survivors kept moving east, deciding to link up with the 106th's infantry regiments scattered in the hills. In the early evening the 11 333d survivors made it to the tiny village of Wereth, just northeast of St. Vith where two Belgian civilians, Mathias and Maria Langer, took the extremely dangerous risk of bringing them into their home. According to the Langer story, a German sympathizer in the village informed on them. Sometime later, around 1600 hours, a four-man German patrol of the 1st SS Panzer Division Leibstandarte SS Adolf Hitler belonging to Kampfgruppe Peiper, arrived in Wereth in their Schwimmwagen.

At the time Langer took in the African-Americans in he was hiding two Belgian deserters from the German Army and had recently sent a

COMPANY "A"

424th INF

Group photos of Company A, 424th Infantry Battalion, 106th Infantry Division taken at Camp Atterbury.

(Courtesy Camp Atterbury album)

Left: Major-General Alan Jones, the commander of the 106th Division. During the Battle of the Bulge, he was relieved of his command and replaced by General Ridgway. *(Courtesy of National Archives)*

Above: Training of 106th Division Infantry at Fort Jackson 1943 under live fire situation. *(Courtesy National Archives)*

Artillerymen of Battery B, 592nd Field Artillery Battalion, double-check brass cases used for practice so that they can be reused again. Fort Jackson, S.C., April 28, 1943. *(Courtesy National Archives)*

A posed photo as "Round 50,000" is loaded in the breech as the crew of a 105mm howitzer looks on. *(Courtesy National Archives)*

Gun crew of Battery B, 592nd Field Artillery Battalion, 106th Infantry Division, stacks 155mm projectiles in preparation for practice firing near the post, Fort Jackson, S.C., April 28, 1943. *(Courtesy National Archives)*

Left: Group photo of Headquarters Battery, 589th Field Artillery Battalion. *(Courtesy of Jim West, Indiana Military)*

Left: Group photo of Headquarters Company, 422nd Infantry Regiment, taken at Camp Atterbury, Indiana. *(Courtesy of Jim West, Indiana Military)*

Above: Second Lieutenants 589th Field Artillery Battalion: Francis O'Toole (killed at Limberg during a bombing while a POW), Graham Cassibry (Air Medal recipient, survived the war), Earl Scott (an L-4 pilot, later Virginia Air National Guardsman), and Willard Crowley (survived the war). *(Courtesy National Archives)*

Below: Group photo of Service Company, 590th Field Artillery Battalion taken at Camp Atterbury, Indiana in May 1944. *(Courtesy of 106th Infantry Division Association)*

Left: A GI stops to rest while digging a foxhole in the Ardennes. Foxholes were a refuge for the 106th Infantry Division soldiers during the first days of the Battle of the Bulge. *(Courtesy of National Archives)*

Below: Lieutenant Ivan H. Long (center) talks to members of his Intelligence and Reconnaissance Platoon of the 423rd Infantry Regiment, 106th Infantry Division. The platoon maneuvered through 18 miles of German concentrations of infantry and armor units without the loss of a single man, December 16, 1944. *(Courtesy National Archives)*

Above: First Lieutenant Krynski, 331st Medical Battalion, 106th Division, asks a British MP for location of medical supply depot in Belgium as his driver waits. The 331st was caught up in the German counteroffensive and had to abandon medical supplies and other equipment. *(Courtesy National Archives)*

Right: High winds whip drifts against hedgerows and buildings in Wanne, Belgium, south of Stavelot, held by the 424th Infantry Regiment, 106th Infantry Division. *(Courtesy National Archives)*

Members of Battery A, 591st Field Artillery Battalion, 106th Infantry Division, unpack 105mm shells and prepare them for firing. Belgium, January 5, 1945. *(Courtesy National Archives)*

Brigadier-General Herbert Perrin, Assistant Division Commander, 106th Infantry Division. *(Courtesy National Archives)*

Major Arthur Parker III, commander of the 589th Field Artillery, led a group of fewer than 300 soldiers in defense of the crossroads at Baraque de Fraiture. *(Courtesy of National Archives)*

Children of Anthisnes, Belgium, flock around Sergeant John J. McCauley, who is attached to an Ordnance Company of the 106th Infantry Division, while Corporal Joseph Legg, Jr. looks on. December 30, 1944. *(Courtesy National Archives)*

American POWs being marched behind the German lines during the Battle of the Bulge. The 106th Infantry Division had over 6,000 soldiers captured and sent to German POW camps where they would remain until the end of the war. *(Courtesy of National Archives)*

Stalag IX–B was a German prisoner-of-war camp in Bad Orb, Germany where many 106th Infantry Division POWs were sent after their capture during the Battle of the Bulge. *(Courtesy National Archives)*

John Gatens was in Battery A, 589th Field Artillery Battalion. He was able to escape the encirclement on the Schnee Eiffel, but was later captured at Parker's Crossroads in Baraque de Fraiture and was freed from Stalag IXB. *(Courtesy of John Gatens)*

John Schaffner, Battery B, 589th Field Artillery Battalion, escaped from the encirclement of the 106th Division and fought at Parker's Crossroads in Baraque de Fraiture as a scout and an artillery observer. *(Courtesy of John Schaffner)*

Combat infantrymen of Company A, 1st Battalion, 424th Infantry, 106th Infantry Division, clean weapons in snow-covered Wanne, Belgium, January 14, 1945. *(Courtesy National Archives)*

The bullet-holed sign for Baraque de Fraiture, Belgium only tells part of the story of where members of the 589th Field Artillery Battalion of the 106th Infantry Division fought alongside other soldiers from several other Army units to try and hold the strategic crossroads. *(Courtesy National Archives)*

An aerial photo of Baraque de Fraiture, Belgium after the battle at Parker's Crossroads on December 20–23, 1944. *(Courtesy National Archives)*

Deep mud in a road near Losheimergraben, Germany, made travel almost impossible for ordinary vehicles. Supplies brought in as far as possible by trucks are transferred to Weasels that can cross mud holes easier. 2nd Battalion, 424th Infantry Regiment, 106th Infantry Division. February 19, 1945. *(Courtesy National Archives)*

Captain H. P. Bailey (left), checks and arranges for their passage into front-line areas. A member of the Military Government unit of the 106th Infantry Division, he also tells them of civilians in the vicinity who need medical treatment, Hunningen, Belgium. *(Courtesy National Archives)*

Soldiers fire smoke shells from 81mm mortars supporting infantry of the 424th Regiment, 106th Infantry Division as they advance on a pillbox, February 28, 1945. *(Courtesy National Archives)*

G.I. ingenuity created this crude but efficient battlefield shower out of discarded pieces of wood and a patched sprinkling can. 591st Field Artillery Battalion, 106th Infantry Division, February 23, 1945. *(Courtesy National Archives)*

Golden Lion Division soldiers, 2nd Battalion, 424th Infantry Regiment, in Belgium find some recreation as they listen to the 106th Infantry Division Band and drink coffee served by Red Cross workers in Losheim, Belgium, March 3, 1945. *(Courtesy National Archives)*

Left: Members of the 106th Signal Corps, 106th Infantry Division, set a booby trap at the head of the stairs at a mine school of the 81st Combat Engineers near Honsfeld, Germany. March 3, 1945. *(Courtesy National Archives)*

Right: Infantrymen of the 106th Infantry Division cross a small foot bridge in snow-covered woods near Berk, Germany. March 5, 1945. *(Courtesy National Archives)*

Left: This photo of the infamous German prisoner of war camp, Slaughterhouse Five, in Dresden, Germany. This was where many 106th Division POWs were sent after being captured, including future author, Kurt Vonnegut, who named his best-selling fiction book after this prison. *(Courtesy National Archives)*

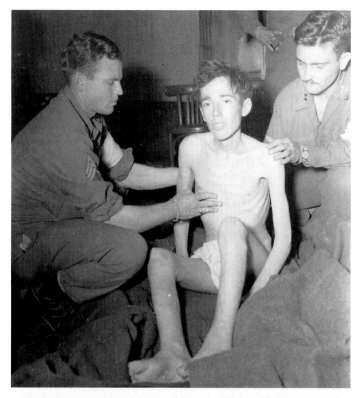

Starving American soldiers released from Nazi prison camps. Part of a group of 350 American soldiers taken prisoner by the Germans during the Battle of the Bulge. These pictures show the result of a 35-mile forced march to Bad Orb, Germany, lack of proper medical attention, forced labor in a rock mine, and a starvation diet. *(Courtesy National Archives)*

Private Samuel P. Archino (left) and Private First Class Arthur B. Jebens examine a war souvenir. The two buddies worked together in the Department of Agriculture, fought together in the 106th Infantry Division, and were prisoners of war in the same German camp. *(Courtesy National Archives)*

Major General Stroh, surrounded by the guidons of the companies of the two regiments is placing the streamers as the men lower the guidons in a salute to the General, August 4, 1945. *(Courtesy National Archives)*

RMS *Queen Elizabeth* arrives in New York Harbor with 14,860 troops, including many with the 106th Division. August 30, 1945. *(Courtesy National Archives)*

draft-age son into hiding to avoid conscription into the German Army. The SS soldiers approached the house, and within minutes the GIs surrendered peacefully. They were led out of the village to a small, muddy field. Over the next several hours, all 11 were inhumanly tortured, beaten and eventually shot or bayonetted to death. Their bodies were discovered by a patrol from the 99th Infantry Division that was directed to the site by villagers. What they discovered there was horrific: legs had been broken, many had bayonet wounds to the head, skulls crushed. Some of the victims' fingers had been cut off. Army investigators were called to the site along with Signal Corps cameramen to record the grisly find.

No one was ever prosecuted for these war crimes and it remained largely undocumented save a couple of grainy photographs taken by Army investigators. The case was officially closed in 1947. Remarkably, at the time, in an act of rare compassion, the SS didn't take any reprisals against the Langer family. Some have speculated that the person who betrayed the Langers might have extracted a promise from the Germans not to take any retribution in exchange for the information. The Langer family claimed that they knew the person who betrayed them but they flatly refused to reveal the name of the alleged traitor. The Germans would have harbored a sort of ethnic kinship with the locals because that area of Belgium had been seized from Germany under the terms of the Treaty of Versailles. (On May 23, 2004, a memorial to the "Wereth 11" was formally dedicated near the location of the massacre. The late Dr. Lichtenfeld, a respected friend of author Martin King and who initially uncovered the story, wrote the first comprehensive account on the subject of African-American GIs in World War II, finishing it just before his death.)

Billy Jackson, Anti-Tank Company, 424th Regiment

I went to Camp Atterbury and joined the 106th Infantry Division. There I was placed in the 424th Regt., Anti-Tank Co. I was issued a carbine to carry … it was a lot easier than carrying the M1 rifle. It was not as good as the M1 for accuracy or distance, etc. I was captured by the Germans for seven hours, but the reserves of I Company, 424th Regt. came to our rescue and freed us and they in turn captured the Germans that held us. During the German attack, one of my buddies pulled out a German bullet that had lodged under his chin and gave it to me. I still have it. Years later, I tried to give it to his wife or ex-wife but she wouldn't take it. I lost a lot of buddies in the snow. I am proud of what I went through but not again.

Major General Middleton had attached the 168th Combat Engineers to the 106th Infantry Division. At 1030 hours that morning, on the orders of General Jones, Lieutenant Colonel Thomas Riggs took over command of the 168th Combat Engineers. Their three companies, together with 40 men from the 81st Combat Engineers Battalion HQ and its A Company plus a platoon of infantry, were ordered to take up defensive positions five miles east of St. Vith at Heuem and to hold at all costs. With reconnaissance reporting Heuem already taken, the unit dug in on the eastern slope of the Prümerberg ridge, roughly a half mile east of St. Vith. By 1300 hours, having persuaded a unit of the 14th Cavalry to stop their retreat and provide support whilst they dug in, the 168th took up positions either side of the Schönburg–St. Vith road and, within a very short time, they faced the first probing attacks of the German advance.

John Schaffner, Scout, Battery B, 589th Field Artillery Battalion
About 0400, on the morning of the 17th, the battalion was ordered to move out for the new position. By now the enemy was astride the only exit from the C Battery position so that it was unable to move. The Battalion C.O., Lt. Col. Kelly, and his Survey Officer, stayed behind and tried to get infantry support to help extricate this battery but they were not successful. The infantry had plenty of their own problems. C Battery never was able to move and was subsequently surrounded and all were taken prisoner, including the Battalion C.O., Col. Kelly, and the Survey O.

While all this was happening, I was given orders by Capt. Brown to take a bazooka and six rounds, and with Corporal Montinari, go to the road and dig in and wait for the enemy to attack from "that" direction. This we did, and were there for some time waiting for a target to appear where the road crested. We could hear the action taking place just out of sight, but the battery was moving out before our services with the bazooka were required. As the trucks came up out of the gun position we were given the sign to come on, so Montinari and I abandoned our hole, and bringing our bazooka and six rounds, climbed on one of the outbound trucks. I did not know it at the time, but my transfer from A Battery to B Battery was a lucky break for me, since Capt. Menke, A Battery C.O., got himself captured right off the bat, and I probably would have been with him.

A and B batteries moved into the new position with four howitzers each, the fourth gun in A Battery not arriving until about 0730 hours. Lt. Wood, with the section, struggled to extricate the howitzer with the enemy practically breathing on them. Battalion HQ commenced to set up its C.P. in a farmhouse almost on the Belgium–Germany border, having arrived just before daylight. At about 0715 a call was received from Service Battery saying that they were under attack from enemy tanks and infantry and were surrounded. Shortly after that, the lines went out. Immediately after that a truck came up the road from the south and the driver reported enemy tanks not far behind. All communications went dead so a messenger was dispatched to tell A and B batteries to displace to St. Vith.

The batteries were notified and A Battery, with considerable difficulty got three sections on the road and started for St. Vith. The fourth piece, however, again was badly stuck and while attempting to free the piece, the men came under enemy fire. The gun was finally gotten onto the road and proceeded toward Schoenberg. Some time had elapsed before this crew was moving.

Battery B then came under enemy fire and its bogged-down howitzers were ordered abandoned and the personnel of the battery left the position in whatever vehicles could be gotten out. I had dived head first out of the ¾-ton that I was in when we were fired on and stuck my carbine in the snow, muzzle first. In training we were told that any obstruction of the barrel would cause the weapon to blow up in your face if you tried to fire it. Well, I can tell you that it ain't necessarily so. At a time like that I figured that I could take the chance. I just held the carbine at arm's length, aimed it toward the enemy, closed my eyes and squeezed. The first round cleaned the barrel and didn't damage anything except whatever it might have hit. As the truck started moving toward the road, I scrambled into the back over the tailgate and we got the hell out of there.

Headquarters loaded into its vehicles and got out, as enemy tanks were detected in the woods about 100 yards from the battalion command post. Enemy infantry were already closing on the area. The column was disorganized. However, the vehicles got through Schoenberg and continued toward St. Vith. The last vehicles in the main column were fired on by small arms and tanks as they withdrew through the town.

As the vehicles were passing through Schoenberg on the west side, the enemy, with a tank force supported by infantry, was entering the town from the northeast. Before all the vehicles could get through they came under direct enemy fire. The A Battery Exec., Lt. Eric Wood, with the last section of the battery, almost made it through, however, his vehicle towing the howitzer was hit by tank fire and he and the gun crew bailed out. Some were hit by small-arms fire. Sgt. Scannapico tried to take on the tank with a bazooka and was killed in the attempt. The driver, Knoll, was also killed there. The rest of the crew was taken prisoner, but Lt. Wood made good his escape (and that's another story). Several other vehicles came down the road, loaded with battalion personnel and were fired on before they entered the town. These people abandoned the vehicles and took to the woods and with few exceptions all were eventually captured.

Major Goldstein's 589th Field Artillery, HQ Battalion had already surveyed the next position south of Schönberg, and everyone was getting ready to withdraw. Things weren't long good for Battery C though. The enemy was astride their only exit. Lieutenant Colonel Kelly had gone down to the infantry positions with the hope of getting help. However, the infantry had their own problems, and weren't going to pull out with the rest of the battalion. Extricating Battery A cannons was not going to be an easy task. They'd gotten them in five days ago using the corduroy road left by the 2d Infantry Division. The heavy trucks and melting snow had churned the road into an icy quagmire that caused the trucks to sink to their hubs. While the men of Battery A pushed, pulled, and dug out the trucks and cannons, artillery and small-arms fire was homing in and hitting the whole area. Snow pounded their sweat-covered faces, brought in on winds that howled through adjacent trees with every possibility that those same trees could be hiding a German patrol. When it was all done they were covered in mud, grime, freezing snow and they were all thoroughly exhausted.

Brigadier General Bruce Clarke met Jones at his HQ in St. Vith at 1030 hours. Jones had been waiting for Clarke and the 7th Armored Division since early that morning. There was some welcome news. At least General Hoge's CCB 9th Armored had arrived and were making their way to Winterspelt in the hope of reaching the 424th Infantry. Jones remained sedate and precise when he informed Clarke of his knowledge of the situation, which didn't allow for much enthusiasm. The 422d and 423d Infantry Regiments on the Eifel were effectively surrounded and the German pincer had closed. With the phone lines out, and the

Germans jamming their radio frequencies, Division had only sporadic radio contact with these men stranded out on the Schnee Eifel.

Colonel Devine's 14th Cavalry Group up north had been severely mauled and its current ability to fight was regarded as doubtful. When Devine had arrived at the St. Vith HQ the previous day his reports were regarded as being garbled and largely incoherent. Jones didn't personally see or talk with Devine and throughout the long night the cavalry commander paced the halls. Devine left the 106th Division command post at about 0800 hours, December 17, without having been given any specific instructions.

In the course of the afternoon Devine ordered the remnants of his two squadrons to fall back in the direction of the village of Recht. Owing to a problem of misconstrued orders, both squadrons ended up on the congested St. Vith–Poteau highway. As soon as night set in Colonel Devine set off toward the 106th Division command post with most of his staff. This small group was ambushed near Recht. Colonel Devine and two of his officers abandoned their vehicles and only narrowly managed to escape. Devine didn't get back to his own HQ in Poteau until five hours later. He had suffered a slight wound from the ambush.

What then transpired has long since been the subject of speculation but for all intents and purposes, he appears to have suffered a mental breakdown caused by extreme nervous exhaustion. Other reports indicate that the symptoms he displayed were more conducive to PTSD or "combat fatigue." At that moment command of Devine's unit was effectively handed over to Colonel Damon of the18th Cavalry Reconnaissance Squadron. As dawn broke on the following morning, Devine was evacuated, ostensibly on the basis of being neither physically nor mentally in a condition to continue his command.

Troop B of the 32d Cavalry Reconnaissance Squadron was engaged in a bitter fight at Andler and had lost contact with the 106th Division on their southern flank. Despite all this, as far as General Jones was concerned, there was still some reason for optimism, particularly now the 7th Armored Division was on the way. He suggested that Clarke's CCB could begin by attacking toward Schönberg to break the ensuing encirclement of the Schnee Eifel. Unfortunately Clarke was compelled to inform Jones that the only elements of the 7th Armored Division anywhere near St.

Vith were him and his three fellow travelers. Regarding the eagerly anticipated arrival of the 7th Armored Division, Clarke told the general of the 106th that he couldn't be specific at the time other than to say they would be there soon, which might not be soon enough for two of the 106th regiments fighting for their lives out on the Schnee Eifel.

Sergeant John P. Kline, M Company, 423d Infantry Regiment

German activity was reported along our front on the 17th (remember the Bulge started on the 16th). The commander called me back to the command post. He informed me that I should be prepared to move my gun to his area to protect the command post. While visiting with him, I noticed that he was very nervous. His .45 Colt pistol was on the table, ready for action. Our Master Sergeant who was also present seemed equally concerned. Later I was to learn the reason for their anxiety. I suspect, in retrospect, that they had been made aware of the German breakthrough yet did not yet know the importance of the news.

While in the vicinity of the command post bunker, I watched a U.S. Army Air Corps P-47 Thunderbolt chase a German Messerschmitt 109 through the sky. They passed directly in front of us. Our area, being one of the highest on the Schnee Eifel, gave us a clear view of the surrounding valleys. The P-47 was about 200 yards behind the Me 109 and was pouring machine-gun fire into the German plane. They left our sight as they passed over the edge of the forest. We were told later that the P-47 downed the Me 109 in the valley.

As it turned out, my machine gun was not moved to the command post. During the night of the 17th we heard gunfire, small arms, mortars and artillery. We also could hear and see German rocket fire to the south. The German rocket launcher was five-barreled and of large caliber. The rocket launcher is called a "Nebelwerfer." Due to their design, the rockets make a screaming sound as they fly through the air. Using high explosives, but not very accurate, they can be demoralizing if you are in their path of flight.

Lieutenant Robert Howell, 424th Infantry Regiment

I was in the 424th Regiment. We were in the front lines for only a few days before the German attack on December 16, 1944 in the Battle of the Bulge. The Battalion Supply Officer was killed in the first day or two and I was asked to serve as the Supply Officer for my battalion by the Battalion Commander. I remember going to St. Vith, our Division Headquarters, for a supply of food for our troops that were fighting in the front lines. At St. Vith people were milling around all over the place. It was a disturbed group of people. It was just learned that out front the 422d and 423d regiments had been surrounded. There were no happy faces to be seen; the German threat to the area was obvious. My jeep was parked in the parking area at Division Headquarters.

Out of the building came General Jones, our Division Commander. He was teary eyed and appeared stunned. He knew that his son, a 1st Lt., was out there with a regiment that was surrounded and that the planned rescue of the two surrounded regiments by the 7th Armored Division would not take place. We could have spoken but there was not anything to say. It had become obvious that it was a major German attack. I picked up boxes of canned food, what I could find, and returned to the front where the cans were passed out to the men of the 424th Regiment in their foxholes. It turned out that all the cans of food contained orange marmalade. The men tore into the cans with their bayonets and that was all they had to eat for two days, orange marmalade. Many of the 424th Regiment men were lost in battle. We were rescued by the 82d Airborne Division which probably kept us from being surrounded and taken prisoner.

By the morning of December 17, the 14th Cavalry Group's new positions extended along a five-mile line from Andler in the south to Hepscheid in the north. The 18th Reconnaissance Squadron, attached to the 14th Cavalry, could only field E Troop and F Company, which were the only units still intact; its reconnaissance troops had been largely obliterated during the previous day. The 32d Squadron appeared to be in a marginally better condition, as they had only lost Troop A at Honsfeld, where they'd fought alongside the 99th Division's 394th Regiment and had come up against a whole column of Kampfgruppe Peiper's 1st SS Panzer Division Leibstandarte SS Adolf Hitler who by dawn were heading down the Krinkelt–Büllingen–St. Vith road.

Sometime during the early afternoon General Jones sent a message to Colonel Reid and Brigadier General William Hoge, commander of the 9th Armored Division giving permission to proceed with their planned attack, but only on the condition that they retreated across the Our River during the night to establish a more defendable position. Hoge saw no reason to retake lost territory and needlessly expend lives so he ordered the 27th Armored Infantry Battalion and the 14th Tank Battalion to prepare to fall back. During the night December 17 both the CCB and the 424th Regiment accomplished successful withdrawals across the river. In the process the 424th were forced to abandon a lot of their equipment but once the withdrawal was complete they soon established a new line running from Maspelt in the north to a location approximately halfway between Burg Reuland and Beiler in the south. CCB held the area from Weppelerand (northeast of Steinebrück) south to Auel.

These U.S. units hadn't been entirely successful in their attempts tackle the 62d VGD but they had effectively disrupted their timetable causing them to fall 24 hours behind schedule. Manteuffel had remarked that timing was an imperative for the German offensive if they were to succeed in their initial objectives.

In 1943, three good friends from Boston joined the U.S. Army together. James Hanney, Frank Galligan and Robert Zimman were still together December 17 as soldiers of the 168th Combat Engineer Battalion on the Prümerberg. They had made foxholes in the frozen earth by first tossing hand grenades to loosen it up and then "digging like hell." Biting Siberian winds swept over that ridge and calf-deep snow only served to make a bad situation worse, and, on top of that, like other U.S. units in the area, they'd been ordered to hold the position at all costs, and hold they would with every ounce of courage and tenacity they could muster.

Meanwhile General Jones was getting to the end of his tether. At 1730 he ordered the 424th to withdraw immediately. The regiment had fought well against superior numbers but the addition of CCB 9th Armored hadn't produced the expected results so it was time to cut their losses and withdraw to the west bank of the Our. During the course of the previous evening Jones had contacted General Middleton to air his concerns for the regiments out on the Schnee Eifel only to be told by Middleton of the importance of retaining these positions. Jones felt that Middleton was evading his responsibilities and decided against ordering a full withdrawal. Nevertheless after the phone call Middleton addressed his subordinates and said, "I just talked to Jones. I told him to pull his regiments off the Schnee Eifel." He could have been more specific and given precise orders during the call, because up until that point he'd done an excellent job of plugging the line. It's possible that he didn't entirely appreciate the gravity of the situation with the 106th. It's also possible that due to a bad connection some of the information exchanged between the generals was unintelligible or misinterpreted. Without an actual transcript of the conversation it's hard to determine. Nevertheless Jones remained calm, composed and apparently confident that the 7th Armored was going to arrive as scheduled. By the evening of December 17 he knew that this wouldn't transpire. Brigadier General Bruce Clarke, commander of CCB, 7th Armored Division, requested command of the defense of St. Vith and Jones acquiesced even though he outranked Clarke and the 7th Armored Division commander, Hasbrouck. Jones allegedly told Clarke, "I've thrown in my last chips. Your combat command is the one that will defend this position. You take over command of St. Vith right now."

The 106th had risen to the challenge and put up a terrific fight so far but even seasoned U.S. veterans along the front line were reeling from the shock of this fresh Nazi onslaught and numerous cases of combat fatigue were being reported at the time. The 106th were indeed well trained and capable but there's a world of difference between an exercise and real "all out" war. Nothing could have prepared them for the psychological consequences of facing a determined enemy that was armed and equipped with a terrifying armory of weapons. One of the great strengths of the U.S. Army in World War II was their capacity to deal with situations as they arose and take the necessary action autonomously on the basis of received and perceived information. They could operate independently down to squad level if required and it was this capacity to engage and improvise that bought valuable time on innumerable occasions during the Battle of the Bulge. Initially the Germans were better prepared, but they couldn't operate with any degree of autonomy below regimental level. Whereas a GI could think on the hop, the German army needed orders, specific orders, regarding strategic disposition, movement and resupply.

December 18 both regiments were still in good fighting condition, and had incurred relatively few casualties. They still had and adequate food, rifle ammunition, and a full basic load for their mortars. The reinforcements and expected supply drops never materialized. Consequently the following morning both regiments were instructed by Division Headquarters to move west to St. Vith but a lot can happen in a battle over 24 hours. The next 24 hours would be even more crucial than the last.

After action report: 81st Engineer Combat Battalion

17 to 21 December. A Co. (less third platoon missing since 0800, 16 Dec 44 and first platoon missing since action near Auw) moved to vicinity Rodt, Belgium, at 0900. At approximately 1100 the first platoon of Co. A reported to the HQ at Rodt having entered St. Vith, and reported to Div HQ during the night. At approximately 1200 H&S Co. and Co. A moved to a defensive position 1,000 yards east of St. Vith. This position held for five days against repeated attacks by the enemy ... Co. B attached to the 423d Inf. Regt. was not heard from after the patrol was reported entering Bleialf. Co. C attached to the 424th Inf. Regt. fell back with the withdrawal of the Regt. after preparing the Bailey Bridge at (870773) for demolition. At the Our River, 23 vehicles of the 424 Service Co. were winched across the river and evacuated to the rear, having been found abandoned. At approximately 2300 on 21 Dec 44 units of Co. A and H&S Co. began arriving at Div. fed echelon at Vielsalm. Belgium.

CHAPTER 6

A LOT OF SHOOTING

Elements of the 7th Armored Division finally arrived in the town of St. Vith at 0100 hours December 18. Meanwhile between Monschau in Germany and Echternach in the south of Luxembourg, the tentacles of over 50 German columns were extending their devastating reach into the Ardennes. Manteuffel's Fifth Panzer Army was homing in on St. Vith from three directions because this was the place where five highways and three rail lines converged. He was complying with an indirect order that had originated with German Sixth Army commander Josef "Sepp" Dietrich and that had been passed on to Generalfeldmarschall Model. Dietrich wanted the road network that emanated from St. Vith to provide support for his troops heading toward the River Meuse in the west. In a vain effort to stem this violent tide, the 7th Armored began taking up positions on what has since become known as the "Goose Egg." It started out as the "Horseshoe" but as the area diminished in the east and west it took on another semblance, hence Goose Egg. During the night, the U.S. Army defenses had been reinforced along a salient around St. Vith that arced roughly 15 miles from point to point.

John Gatens, Battery A 589th Field Artillery Battalion

After this halt, orders were received from the Division Artillery Commander, General McMahon, to proceed to the west and be prepared to take up positions in the vicinity of Recht. The battalion was halted at 0100 and remained on the road until 0700 when it began moving forward again. At about 0800 the column was halted again and word passed down that enemy tanks and infantry had attacked HQ Battery, 106th Div. Arty. on the same road to the west. The column was turned and pulled off the road into a clearing. A perimeter defense was organized and a roadblock set up with two guns covering the approach from the north. A noon meal was served. Orders were next received to withdraw to the vicinity of Bovigny. What was left of the battalion loaded up and proceeded to the designated place in good order.

The preceding night the Germans had dropped parachute troops into the area near St. Vith. They were not in great strength but they did a lot of shooting and spread confusion along the communications routes west of St. Vith.

At Bovigny the C.O. of the 174th Field Artillery Group requested that the three howitzers remaining with the battalion and the personnel be sent to positions near Charan. This was agreed to and the battalion was split into two groups: Group A composed of the three 105 howitzer sections, Fire Direction Center people, most of the officers, and part of our meager ammunition supply. I was with this group. Group B was composed of the remainder of the battalion plus some men from the 590th Service Battery.

Group A departed for Cortil, went into position and laid the guns to fire on Charan. The town was reconnoitered and no enemy was found so the group was withdrawn to Bovigny for the rest of the night. Observers were sent out with the outposts and preparations made to fire on any enemy coming on the scene. Group B left Bovigny and traveled west through Salmchateau and bivouacked for the night on a side road near Joubieval.

Sergeant John P. Kline, M Company, 423d Infantry Regiment

Our column did not come under fire until we were near our destination, a heavily wooded area (Linscheid Hill, Hill 546) southeast of Schoenberg. As we approached the logging trail, near Radscheid, we were shelled by German 88s. My driver drove the jeep into the ditch on the right side of the road. A bazooka-man who had hitched a ride on the jeep flipped over the right rear wheel. As we hit the ditch, his weapon fell apart. The rocket fell out and landed in the mud alongside of me, where I had fallen. Fortunately the bazooka rocket did not arm itself. As I picked myself up, I noticed a pair of German binoculars lying in the ditch. I picked them up and hung them around my neck. They were probably left there by German troops who had been patrolling in this area. I have often thought, "What if they had been booby trapped?"

A point where my memory fails is that I cannot remember what happened during the night of December 18. It would have been logical to set up defensive positions and sleep in shifts, which we probably did. However, my mind is completely blank about the events of that night. M Company men I have met in recent years, 1988 and 1989, tell me that we spent most of the night trying to get our jeeps out of the mud. The number of vehicles on the road and an unusually warm spell caused the fields to be very muddy. The weather turned much colder and stayed that way until after the end of January.

General Jones had ordered an air drop that never transpired and had instructed the two regiments trapped on the Schnee Eifel to fight their way out. Once more the "fog of war" element appears to have played a part because initially Jones had said, "Our mission is to destroy by fire from dug-in positions south of Schoenberg–St.Vith road. Ammo, food and water will be dropped. When mission accomplished move to St. Vith–Wallenrode–Weppler."

The lack of clarity caused some confusion among the regiments who had been instructed to hold and break out from the Schnee Eifel. They were told that once they had extricated themselves from their positions they would be relieved by elements of the 7th Armored Division. When recounting the battle in later years General Jones stated that he issued explicit orders to the 422d and 423d regiments to withdraw from the Schnee Eifel, as he had done with the 424th when he instructed them to retire to the far side of the River Our. Inclement weather conditions had effectively prevented U.S. air support at this time, moreover Jones had encountered some serious administrative obstacles when he had attempted to arrange the air drop.

Richard Sparks, I&R Platoon, 423d Infantry Regiment
We found the end of the column about three quarters of a mile outside Buchet on the road to Halenfeld. We could hear that the fighting had intensified over near Skyline Drive and the column had ground to a halt. We were told to hold our position and be alert for any enemy movements in our rear. And hold we did, for five or six hours. During our wait, Hank Iversen had found an abandoned 2½-ton truck and, taking three of the fellows with him, went back to the schoolhouse and loaded up all our barracks bags, rejoining us a short time later. We had hated to leave all our

possessions and were bound and determined to get them out if we could. Some of the second squad also went back into Buchet to check out the headquarters buildings for any classified material that might have been overlooked when they moved out. They found quite a lot of papers laying around and, to be safe, had quite a bonfire.

Late in the afternoon, the convoy got moving again, the troops having fought their way past Skyline Drive, suffering heavy casualties in the fighting. The 1st Battalion had been nearly wiped out with the exception of A Company that was serving as their rearguard. Lt. Col. Nagle came to Ike [Long, commander I&R Platoon] about this time and told him to have the platoon establish a roadblock at the crossroads south of Radscheid near a corduroy road called "Engineers Cut-off" that had been built by the engineers to serve as a shortcut between the Bleialf–Schönberg road and the Bleialf–Auw road. (Skyline Drive). Half of our little force was to hold the roadblock at all costs and the other half were to occupy a hill overlooking the Ihren valley. The 1st squad, in charge of the roadblock, had a backbreaking job during most of the night. We succeeded in felling one tree across the road using a rusty hatchet we found in an abandoned truck and one or two entrenching tools from our jeeps. We would work two or three at a time while the others kept watch at our rear.

During the night, the fighting continued, more intense than before. Ike, trying to keep in touch with headquarters, found that Col. Cavender had moved the headquarters contingent to 3d Battalion CP on a hill overlooking Schönberg. All the vehicles had become bogged down in the mud of the logging trails leading into the Ihren valley and had to be abandoned. The supporting artillery had been ordered to withdraw to St. Vith, and thus was not of much help to the regiment. The troops spent one of their most miserable nights ever, not being able to see the enemy and being constantly fired upon and shelled in the muddy and mainly exposed positions. Ammunition was extremely scarce, food and medical supplies had run out and the regiment was only at about 50 percent of full strength. The I&R was comparatively lucky. The Germans had not tried to come down our way and had not, obviously, spotted our positions so we received no artillery fire. Toward daybreak, spelling each other, we were able to get a few winks of sleep.

In some of our bull sessions stateside, we had often wondered how we would react under combat conditions. We knew we had been trained well. We had proven ourselves in tactical exercises. We knew we could count on each other. We knew we wouldn't panic. Would we be scared? Could fear be controlled? Or even be made to work for us?

Yes, we found as any combat soldier did, that we were scared at times. If we could see and identify what was happening to us, we could do something about it and fear was minimized. But in the middle of an artillery barrage, we could well experience a terrifying, shaking fear. We couldn't see the shells. We couldn't do much about them. We had to have faith that we could duck down far enough to keep from being hit. We also had to have faith that someone somewhere was looking after us and trust that, unless our name was on that particular round, we would be safe.

During this night, with the noise and fighting just a few hundred yards from us, we began to feel some of this trepidation. Tomorrow we would be in the middle of things we couldn't forecast and this knowledge transformed our feelings into a cocky, fine-edged attitude that said we would make it, God willing.

A little later, aware that the decision had been made to save the 7th Armored for the defense of St. Vith, the 422d and 423d regiments were compelled to make it back to St. Vith as best they could. Both regiments tenuously emerged from the cover of their defensive positions and began to attempt to break out toward Schönberg and St. Vith. After destroying excess equipment, the regiments started out abreast at approximately 1000 hours. The reason why neither regiment could reach its objective was that both regiments discovered how disorganized and isolated from each other they were as they were moving. By the end of the third day of fighting all of these attempts were stopped cold due to additional German reinforcements pouring into the Schnee Eifel also moving toward St. Vith. Slowly, as casualties mounted, and provisions and ammunition began to run low, it began to dawn on both regiments that all hopes of relief by the 7th Armored had evaporated and the chances of making it back to St. Vith were gradually becoming untenable. The 106th Infantry Division had already endured three days of almost constant combat in the most deplorable freezing conditions.

Lieutenant Colonel Joseph F. Puett, 2d Battalion, 423d Infantry Regiment
At about 0600 the battalion received regimental orders to move out as the advance guard of the regiment and move to the southwest and do as much damage as possible to a German armored column which was on the St. Vith–Schönberg road with its head about 5 miles from Schönberg. We moved out at 1000 hours with E Co. leading F, H and G companies in column. The leading elements

were fired on at the crossroads of the cut-off road and the Auw–Bleialf road. E Company deployed to the left of our advance, and attempted to push enemy to south and clear road. It was very open country and E Company encountered very heavy MG, mortar and rocket fire.

F Company (less 1 platoon at St. Vith) was deployed to E Co.'s right. After very heavy fighting E Co. with 1 MG platoon and 81mm mortars of H Company succeeded in taking hill 1,500 yards to south of crossroads. During the engagement E Company had approximately 60 casualties, H Company 37 casualties and F Company 16 casualties. The Hill was taken at 1320. Just before this time the enemy reinforced their troops and we were fighting a reinforced enemy regiment and could gain no more, but inflicted heavy casualties on the enemy. G Company at 1345 with 1 MG platoon of H Company and supported by an 81mm platoon attempted to break through to the Bleialf–Schönberg road. They got to this road after heavy fighting, but were unable to advance farther than this road, which ran west [northwest].

In the meantime the 3d Battalion had been committed to our right [north] but could not advance across the road. We continued to attack till dark with all companies committed. By dark at about 1900 hours the battalion had suffered approximately 300 casualties and had no 81mm ammunition and only 2 rounds per mortar of 60mm ammunition. We had lost 5 heavy MGs and 4 light MGs. We had 375 rounds of ammunition per MG left and 16 officer casualties. At dark we consolidated and dug in for the night.

While moving up to the front Colonel Charles C. Cavender, 423d Regiment, received news from General Jones that he would not be getting any reinforcements in the immediate future and in compliance with the orders for the two regiments he was going to redirect their efforts towards Schönberg. Cavender passed the message on with all haste to Colonel Descheneaux and then ordered his 3d Battalion to advance on Lieutenant Puett's right and provide assistance. Puett had successfully repelled a German attack at Bleialf but now their situation was deteriorating and by noon he was dispatching an urgent plea for assistance. It would fall on deaf ears because the state of flux that was affecting both the 422d and 423d prevented any fulfillment of this request. Consequently Puett's attack began to dissipate and lose all momentum. The 7th Armored Division was supposed to move on Schönberg from

St. Vith and relieve the 422d and 423d regiments but this wasn't happening. The I&R Platoon, was ordered to fall in as rearguard and protect the movement on Schönberg from a German attack in the rear.

Lieutenant Colonel Thomas Kelly, Commander 598th Field Artillery Battalion

The situation was hopeless, but some of us were in favor of holding out until dark and attempting to get out in small parties. I thought that had been decided upon and went to dig a slit trench when Descheneaux sent out the white flag. If his command post hadn't been the regimental aid station he could have stood it a while longer—he had been right up with the leading elements in the attack that morning. It's just as well, I guess, that he surrendered; it was just a question of time and we weren't even a threat.

It was a beautiful afternoon in the late fall of 2012 when I (author Martin King) met Eva Maraite. She invited two friends and me into her home and took out her photo albums. She shared her very precious memories of a polite young American who came to their home in December 1944. It was later claimed that Eric Fisher Wood waged a very personal guerilla war against German forces in the forests that surrounded the small German-speaking village of Meyerode. Eva told me of how she helped make warm food for Eric and even how she provided fresh woolen socks for him. She was very proud indeed of her acquaintance; she was one of the last civilians to see Eric alive. Shortly after our meeting she passed away. I got to know Eric's story. There are a few accounts of what occurred after he ran into the woods, most of them erroneous. One even refers to "mountains of Meyerode." I have lived in relatively close proximity to that village for 35 years and I can confirm without contradiction that there are no mountains near Meyerode or in the Ardennes.

December 17, sometime in the late afternoon, local woodsman Peter Maraite was looking for a suitable Christmas tree. He inadvertently discovered two weary American soldiers. Despite having no English language skills, using facial expressions, hand signals and the odd English word, the German-speaking Maraite attempted to convince the wary Americans he was friendly. After a while and with nightfall rapidly descending on the woods, Maraite persuaded them to follow him to his house in Meyerode. The identity of the second American still remains something of a mystery, though it could possibly have been Pfc Lehman M. Wilson of the 82d Airborne Division.

Upon reaching the village, Maraite welcomed them into his large, stone house and sent for a friend to translate. Maraite later described Eric Fisher Wood as "a big young man with confident, smiling face." Wood apparently stated to the family that if he could not get back to American lines, he was going to fight the Germans behind the lines and conduct a war of his own. That night Wood and his companion enjoyed good company, warm food and a comfortable bed for the night.

Sometime later after the GIs had left the Maraite household news began to filter back about brigands harassing German supply convoys and making the forest unsafe. Consequently civilians were banned from entering. Long after the front line had moved farther west, German wounded were seen being brought out of the woods. According to some German solders these "damned bandits flitted like ghosts through the trees." Was that Eric Fisher Wood conducting his own very personal war? In the absence of firsthand witness accounts it's nigh on impossible to determine if it was indeed the man himself but all available evidence suggests that it probably was.

When his body was found it is claimed that there were seven dead German soldiers in close proximity and the American officer still had his papers along with about 4,000 Belgian francs in his pocket. Beside Wood, the body of Pfc Lehman M. Wilson of the 82d Airborne Division was also recovered from the site. Lieutenant Wood was a dedicated, driven man. Major Elliott Goldstein, the battalion's executive officer, attributed A Battery's low casualty rate specifically to Wood's assiduousness and professionalism. During their first few days on the line, he made the men dig deeper, well-protected shelters near the gun line in case of sustained counter-battery fire. Local Belgians erected a small monument to the lieutenant. It stands on the site where the bodies were discovered. To this day the villagers beautifully maintain the simple plaque. Lieutenant Wood was a undoubtedly a hero even before the events around Meyerode occurred and whatever happened there, it's safe to say that Wood didn't go down without a fight: that wasn't his way of doing things.

Meanwhile up on the Prümerberg ridge the 168th Combat Engineers were performing admirably holding their positions against repeated enemy incursions. They were eventually reinforced with infantry from the 38th Armored Infantry Battalion, which brought much needed mortar support and two Sherman tanks. As German forces continued their onslaught, men from the 168th not only defended their own positions but also provided flexible reinforcements to plug the line when and where necessary. Helped by men of the 275th Field Artillery who had bravely volunteered to stay to provide artillery spotting, the 168th and its reinforcements managed to destroy two further tanks and two assault guns.

James Hanney Jr. was wounded by a piece of shrapnel. He was helped off the ridge by his friend Frank Galligan and taken to a U.S. medical facility some 15 miles west in Vielsalm. James would never see his friend Robert Zimman again and would only discover his fate 65 years after the fact.

The last opportunity to counterattack and break out of the Schnee Eifel had been lost during the previous night before the opposing forces had reinforced. As December 18 ensued, German strength increased, making both regiments vulnerable to further murderous artillery, tank, and machine-gun fire. To exacerbate an already bad situation the 422d and 423d regiments lost all cohesion and any tactical advantage was squandered as battalions and companies found themselves isolated. The courageous stand made by the 422d and 423d regiments out on the Schnee Eifel had severely disrupted the German timetable, compelled von Rundstedt to commit additional reserves and inflicted serious casualties on the whole German Fifth Panzer Army but time was running out. General Jones moved the 106th command post 14 miles west to Vielsalm, in close proximity General Hasbrouck's 7th Armored Division headquarters. Despite all efforts the situation was drawing to an inevitable conclusion.

Albert C. Reed, Construction Platoon, 106th Signal Company
As daylight broke we slowly arrived in Vielsalm, dead tired, but with work to be done, starting immediately. The Construction Platoon found a place to store our stuff in a part of what looked like a Belgian Army installation. Our wire team was immediately pressed in to service laying wires. Two of our three regiments,

the 422d and the 423d, had been captured and killed. The 424th Regiment was the only one left. We were told where to find them. We located the 106th Division HQ where we found Sgt. Hunter.

Sgt. Hunter always controlled the place where all of the wires from our combat and service units came in to the HQ of the division. This was called "the Zero Board." All of the wires started there. Sgt. Hunter knew when a wire was disabled and informed us. As we started trying to find the wire line in trouble, we would tap in to a wire and ring it. Sgt. Hunter would identify the wire, which we would follow and inspect for a break or damage. Periodically we would tap in to the wire. If we got Sgt. Hunter it meant that the break was farther away from him. If we got the unit that we were trying to connect to Zero Board, it meant that the damage was between that spot and the last spot when we had contacted him. To save time we often laid a new piece to wire between those spots rather than look for the damaged place in the wire. We began our work immediately because finding a break in the wire is almost impossible to do after dark. Almost all of our work was laying new lines because the front line of combat was so fluid that they changed completely almost every day. (We ran into Minturn Wright with his Signal Co. radio team while were at the 424th regimental HQ several times. He and I had been good friends when we both went to radio school at Camp Atterbury, Indiana.)

After two or three days I was puzzled because we had put in new lines in four different directions—the west, north, east and south. There is no written record of this but we were apparently surrounded. I told Sgt. Hunter about it and he said, "We are surrounded, but don't tell anybody" So I didn't. I suppose he didn't want anybody to panic. I didn't know it then, but I later figured out that I was, for two days, affected by "combat fatigue." It is now called Post-Traumatic Stress Disorder. It affected me in these ways: I did not speak to anyone, even if they wanted to carry on a conversation. I could not register an opinion to myself about anything or make any decisions. I always stared straight ahead with my eyes, never moving them to the side. To see anything not in my direct line of vision I would turn my head until my eyes lined up with what I wanted to see. I could not willfully stop any of these things that went on. There were others but I cannot remember them. They were too weird. Sometimes one of them pops fleetingly in to my mind but is immediately forgotten.

CHAPTER 7

WE NEVER SURRENDERED!

During the early morning hours of December 19, messages from the 423d Infantry began to filter in at the new 106th HQ in Vielsalm. On the basis of this information General Jones learned that both regiments had started attacking westward and that was all he knew. The next looming concern was the situation around St. Vith. Hasbrouck, responsible for the northern half of the horseshoe and his tightly knit defensive line, was in relatively good shape.

General Bruce Clarke's line in front of St. Vith was also in good shape. All reports appeared to indicate that his men were not going to concede St. Vith. They were confident that as long as they had ammunition they would hold. Lieutenant Colonel Roy Clay and his 275th Field Artillery Battalion was firing in three directions. Major Don Boyer and Lieutenant Colonel Thomas Riggs were piling up dead Germans in front of St. Vith and on the Prümerberg ridge the 168th Combat Engineers continued to mount a historic defense.

There was some consternation regarding the south of the horseshoe. Hoge's CCB 9th Armored tied in well with Clarke's CCB 7th Armored. However, there was still a gap of several miles between Hoge and Colonel Alexander Reid's 424th Infantry; after four days of tough fighting they were nearly out of food and ammunition. Below Reid was a no man's land. All they could ascertain at the time was that there was strong German activity at Gouvy, ten miles south of Vielsalm. Other than that, nobody knew what was going on down there, and that had the potential to jeopardize the entire St. Vith–Vielsalm sector.

The 423d Regiment, now down to around half its strength, had assembled to the east of Schönberg. Their 3d Battalion was positioned to the left while the 1st was on the right. Neither battalion had incurred serious casualties up until that point, but two companies from the 1st Battalion had been misplaced out on the Schnee Eifel during the previous night's march. The numbers in the 2d Battalion had been significantly reduced due to having endured almost three days of constant combat. The grueling march had thoroughly exhausted the 1st and 2d battalions. To make a bad situation worse all three battalions were running dangerously low on mortar and machine-gun ammunition. Directly to the rear of their positions the 590th were down to a meager 300 rounds to check the imminent German attack. Somewhere out on those snowbound hills to the east was the 422d Regiment but at the time nobody knew precisely where they were.

John Schaffner, Scout, Battery B, 589th Field Artillery Battalion

December 19 in the afternoon, what was remaining of the 589th Field Artillery Battalion arrived at the crossroads at Baraque de Fraiture to establish some kind of blocking force against the German advance. Whether or not there was any intelligent planning involved in this move I really don't know. I had the feeling that nobody knew anything, and that we would resist here in this place as long as possible and hope to get help before we were blown away. There were approximately 100 men and three 105mm howitzers to set up the defense at this time.

The weather was cold, wet and foggy with some snow already on the ground. Visibility was variable, clearing from maybe 50 yards to two or three hundred on occasion.

I didn't even know who was in charge of the rag-tag group that I was with until I saw Major Elliot Goldstein out in the open, verbally bombasting the enemy (wherever they were) with all the curse words he could think of, and at the top of his booming voice. I thought at the moment that he wouldn't be around too long if there were any Germans out there to hear him. Apparently there were none, he drew no fire. I was taking cover behind the rear wheel of one of our trucks at the time and felt rather naked.

For almost six hours the 590th Field Artillery Battalion had inched through the snow-covered fields and woods east of Schönberg, and come to rest in the valley behind a location marked on their maps as "Hill 536." As dawn arrived the tired GIs grabbed space in any and every available vehicle in an attempt to procure some rest. As daylight filtered in forward observers scanned the narrow valley in front of their position. They had no idea where the enemy was, but they were sure that they were exposed and completely vulnerable. Steep, densely wooded slopes rose to the right and left. In front, to the right, was a half-frozen swamp. Directly in front was a rapidly flowing stream some six to eight foot wide that was now full of abandoned vehicles left by the infantrymen who had long since forged ahead. Batteries A and C were forward near the stream. Battery B was about 200 yards to the rear near a curve in the forest edge. The aid station was set up in the scrub pine along the lower edge of the far slope across the stream. As early morning wore on the artillerymen got about their business.

Not far from there, at Hill 504, at the same time, the 423d's Colonel Charles C. Cavender conducted a quick reconnaissance of his positions and men before returning to his HQ to plan his breakout attack. By 0830 hours, Cavender's battalion commanders had assembled and the briefing began. The regiment would attack in a column of battalions echeloned to the right rear. 3d Battalion, already near the Bleialf–Schönberg road, would lead the main effort following the road into Schönberg. The line of departure for 1st and 2d battalions would be the wood road running along the crest of Hill 536. The time of attack would be 1000 hours. After issuing his orders Cavender looked at his watch, "It is now exactly 9 o'clock." With that, Cavender's men stiffened to salute, and then suddenly the Germans opened up.

The powerful German artillery battery in Schönberg lobbed a volley on the regimental command post, killing the 1st Battalion's commander Lieutenant Colonel Craig outright, and wounding several officers and men. The others ran for cover as the barrage continued unabated for over half an hour. When it ended German infantry began an attack from the direction of Bleialf and immediately overran the 590th Field Artillery Battalion position. Cavender reacted quickly and while ordering the commencement of the planned counterattack, he instructed the battalion commanders to move covering forces to the rear.

Lieutenant Colonel Thomas Kelly, as did almost everyone else, dove into the first slit trench he saw. When he looked up, he saw the tense white face of a corporal. "Is this your slit trench?" Kelly asked.

The corporal just nodded, while Kelly hopped out, pushed him into the trench, and jumped in on top. It sounded to Kelly as if every tree in the forest was simultaneously blasted from its roots. As an artilleryman Kelly knew the sounds of incoming salvos, and for the next 30 minutes this one had a little bit of everything in it as it swept the area. When it stopped hundreds of guttural shouts and the sounds of intense small-arms fire came from the hollow south of the hill.

John C. Rain, Battery B, 589th Field Artillery Battalion

After about three days of moving around, the remnants of the 589th were divided into two groups, one half going to Baraque de Fraiture to defend the crossroads and the other half going the other way out of danger. Regrouped and moved back—stopped at what we thought to be an important crossroads—deployed with only three howitzers and about 100 men from the 589th. Joined off & on by a few tanks and half-tracks with quad 50 AA guns. The Germans came.

General Alan Jones had a vested interest in keeping tabs on the situation because as far as his son Lieutenant Alan Jones could tell, 1st Battalion was off to a rough start. A Company was lost somewhere near Oberlascheid. D Company had taken a serious pounding in the opening barrage: they lost their CO, two of three platoon leaders, and a host of men. Suddenly, a stream of men from B Company came running up the hill from below and headed back up over the top. Then the shelling started again. This time it resembled a creeping barrage, methodically starting at the bottom and moving yard by yard up the hill.

The 2d Battalion, to the right and rear of 1st Battalion as the assault on Schönberg opened, moved to the right of the Bleialf–Schönberg road and onto the apex of Hill 506 just southeast of Schönberg. When the 1st and 3d battalions came under heavy fire, Lieutenant Colonel Joseph F. Puett slipped 500 yards east and pushed on until his unit was abreast of the 1st. Separated by a deep gulley, Puett was well aware of the rigorous fire and the fighting on his left. While he could see Schönberg and the German 88s and tanks, he couldn't do much about them: they were just too far away.

F Company was on point for the 2d Battalion attack on Schönberg. When the firing started they ran into a German roadblock; the first shot rang out, sending the scouts, flank security, and everyone else to the ground.

The Germans ran for cover while the Americans dispatched the first German truck with a rifle grenade. In the confusion one GI obediently followed the man ahead of him. It didn't occur to the GI at the time that they were both heading in the wrong direction. It wasn't until he gained on him that he realized the helmet was not that of a GI: he'd been following a German.

Despite having his rifle pointed at the German soldier, he didn't have that killer instinct and couldn't envisage the prospect of shooting him in the back. His next surprise was finding that his German lead had walked him right into the sights of a German machine-gun nest. When the Germans saw the GI with his rifle pointing at them they immediately raised their hands. Seeing this, the German lead man turned, dropped his rifle, and raised his hands too. For a few seconds the GI felt like Sergeant York, but dismissed that glorious thought when he saw a bunch of GIs from F Company had also arrived with rifles pointed.

One squad was ordered to charge across a road in the woods. Every time they reached a clearing, they drew fire, hit the dirt, and changed direction. Finally, they made the road. With tracers flying up and down the road, the sound of burp guns on one side and mortar fire on another, they knew that they were caught in a triangle of fire and that they were done for.

At Hill 504 on the Andler–Schönberg road two unknown lieutenants from the 1st Battalion discussed the possibility of surrender even though most of the men remained defiant and vociferously argued against this option. Nevertheless they were overruled, and the officers ordered surrender. When the firing abated the lieutenants gave a medic a white handkerchief and elected him to go out onto the road. A few moments later some other GIs reluctantly ditched their rifles and also headed onto the road.

In the forest just east of Skyline Drive Phil Hannon and the engineers were raiding the kitchen trailers before they dug them out. He and four other engineers had volunteered to fill the crater in the road and come up with a load of gravel to extricate the truck and trailers stuck hub deep in the muck. They grabbed a few D bars and some fruit juice, which was better than nothing. Finishing their snack, they started bailing water from the crater and filling it with gravel when suddenly, men and trucks came bursting out of the woods—it was a total scramble. GIs were hanging on the trucks any place they could.

"We're getting out—pile on," said the GIs.

That sounded like a good idea to Hannon, but he wasn't leaving empty handed, and raided the kitchen trailers again. With a carton of D bars under his arm, he started hailing a truck. He'd been carrying grenades for days, using the buttonholes in his jacket to hold them, and none had fallen off yet. However, this time, of all times, one did with a thud, knocking the pin out. Fortunately, the weight of the grenade stuck in the mud kept the handle from kicking off. It didn't matter. Everyone scattered. All, that is, except the one guy Hannon thought would be the first to crack under the pressure: the kid simply picked it up, walked to the edge of the field by the road, and threw it.

The explosion brought the convoy to a dead stop. GIs dove to the ground, sprawling all over the place. That was Hannon's chance, as he scrambled onto the closest truck. When they began moving again, it was apparent that the 37mm anti-tank gun they were towing kept them from keeping up with the convoy. The driver stopped, and one of the GIs jumped out and unhooked the thing. It usually took two men to do it, but this soldier was motivated, and practically threw it off the hitch. Their truck had now lost its place in the convoy. Unlike maneuvers, where an umpire would have called them on it, they simply crowded their way back in, now moving along at a good pace. That was until they started out of some little village where a Tiger tank was raising hell with the lead vehicles.

"Sure doesn't sound like we're getting out," said one of the GIs.

In the back Hannon and his friends were catering to their stomachs. "Throw me that peanut butter," said another, when the lead jeep hit a landmine.

On the hillside John Kline's M Company machine-gun platoon provided their heavy weapons support to the infantrymen of L Company on the road below. Then the shelling began again. The hills were raked by artillery. The woods were raked by artillery. There was terrible confusion. Kline and his squad were pinned down at the edge of the woods and had no place to go. His gunner, Smitty, was hit in the leg by shrapnel. Forty-three years later Kline would learn that Smitty lost his leg in a German hospital and had in fact taken shrapnel wounds to his stomach that caused him problems for the rest of his life.

Kline found a trench near a tree scooped out by one of the infantrymen the previous night. While it offered some protection, his feet stuck out, and he ended up taking shrapnel in his right Achilles tendon. In the excitement and trauma of the battle he didn't even know it. At one point, Kline felt a piece of metal slam into the ground a foot from his head. The jagged shrapnel, 18 inches long and four inches wide, was smoking hot when he turned to look at it. When it cooled he picked it up: this was no 88 or mortar shell. The Germans were using their anti-aircraft Flak guns, the shells of which exploded on contact with the treetops and showered everything below with a rain of steel.

Sergeant John P. Kline, M Company, 423d Infantry Regiment

12/19/44: Battle positions. In early morning of the 19th I received orders to position my 30-cal water-cooled machine gun in the edge of the woods overlooking Schoenberg. I was high on a hill, overlooking a slope leading into a valley. I could see, about 1,000 yards to the northwest, the rooftops of Schoenberg.

Company M, 423d Regiment, my unit, was assigned to support L Company, a rifle company who were preparing to enter Schoenberg. They were advancing down the slope, attempting to enter Schoenberg along the Bleialf–Schoenberg road, which was several hundred yards in front of my gun position. The town and area around was infested with Germans, but from my position I saw no sign of them. I saw little, except the rooftops of Schoenberg ahead of us, and a few of our troops on the slope below us.

A rifle company, Company I, 423d, was waiting on orders to proceed down the hill in support of L Company. It was about 0900 when we were suddenly hit by very heavy artillery fire. It seemed that all hell had broken loose. The shells were exploding all around us, on the ground and in the trees. Men were screaming for medics. I heard that M Company's Commander, Captain Hardy, had been killed and the Executive Officer, Captain Weigers was blinded by a tree burst. There was a terrible lot of confusion at that time. I thought to myself that the officers could be from one of the rifle companies. That was not so: they were our officers that were hit by tree bursts.

All radio contact between the 422d and the 423d had been lost. While the right-wing battalion of the 423d was attempting to advance northwestward, it was discerned by the left-flank troops of the 422d who, mistaking this movement for a German flanking attack, poured small-arms fire into the draw where the men of the 423d were moving. In the brief exchange of fire which followed both these inner-flank units became considerably disorganized.

Finally it was numerical enemy superiority that checked further movement. Around 1400 hours tanks were heard approaching from the north. In a last desperate flare of optimism the Americans assumed that these were friendly tanks: they weren't. The Führerbegleit Brigade had been ordered forward to support the LXVI Corps attack on St. Vith. En route from Auw to Schönberg, the panzers arrived at the fork where the road split toward Schönberg and Bleialf just in time to give the *coup de grâce*. The tanks rolled through the battalions on the right while the German infantry poured in from the woods. At 1430 hours the regimental commander decided to surrender that part of his regiment that was disorganized and entrapped.

The last message from the 422d arrived at 1600 hours that day and from the 423d at 1800. They were addressed to Lieutenant Colonel Earle B. Williams, the division signals officer, and were signed by sergeants who were in charge of the regimental radio teams. Both messages were in code and contained identical information: "We now are destroying our equipment." That was all. After negotiations to determine that the Germans would feed the Americans and provide care for the wounded, the surrender was completed about 1600 hours.

Sergeant John P. Kline, M Company, 423d Infantry Regiment

We disabled our weapons by breaking them on tree trunks or by taking them apart and throwing the parts in different directions. After that the Germans led us to a clearing in the forest and directed us to throw down our equipment, e.g. ammo belts, packs, hand grenades and trench knives. I quickly disposed of the German binoculars that I had found earlier.

We were led in a small column down to the Schoenberg–Bleialf road in front of the rifle companies. There were Germans on one side of the road and Americans on the other. They had been facing each other in a fierce firefight, from ditch to ditch. There were many dead, both Americans and Germans. The wounded were still crying for help. As we approached the Schoenberg road, it seemed that hundreds of Germans rose up out of the field.

There was a German truck burning in the middle of the road. Behind the truck was an American infantryman lying in the middle of the road. He was dressed like an officer, but with no insignia, as would be normal in combat. His was wearing his winter uniform, a heavy winter coat, ammo belt and canteen. He was lying on his back, as if he were resting. The body had no head or neck. It was as if somebody had sliced it off with a surgical instrument, leaving no sign of blood. All my life I have had flashbacks of that scene and I still find it hard to believe. I always wonder how it happened. He was the only soldier, either American or German that I saw laying on the road. But there were many wounded and dead in the ditches and fields as we were led out of the woods.

The Germans then walked us in columns to Bleialf (recorded in my diary as St. Beliat), where they herded us into a church courtyard. I probably recorded the church name by mistake.

It had turned dark and the temperature was dropping. Most of us were without overcoats. We had only our field jackets and our winter issue of "olive drab" uniforms with long johns. I recall that I wore two pair of pants, my long johns and my field jacket. We had to sleep on the ground. I remember how nervous I was. Every little sound was amplified. I wondered what was going to happen to us when daybreak came. We had had nothing to eat since early morning, December 18th.

Phil Hannon was tired, hungry, and cold, but he was still an American soldier, and expected to be treated as such when the order came down the line to throw up his hands. The men didn't say much when the Germans started rounding them up. Hannon pulled out his wallet and looked at the pictures of his family and home. Their smiles engraved on his mind, he tore them up: he didn't want the Germans leering at them. Pulling out the 1,000 franc note he'd been carrying, he tore it up, and tossed his wallet into the mud. No German was ever going to carry that, he thought grimly. Around him GIs were busy paying respects to home, shaking themselves back to reality, and milling around to find their buddies.

Over the next two hours, Hannon's platoon slowly grew as GIs started showing up. Those with food passed it around. Officers gave orders to get rid of everything from helmets to knives and canteens. Finally, their German guards motioned them down the hill. Men would hit a slippery spot and tumble head over heels, get up cursing, and continue double-time like sheep.

Hannon made the run down to the bottom of the hill. The stream at the bottom stopped him. With a running jump he tried to clear it, and instead fell in waist deep, filling his boots with the ice-cold water. For the next hour, half walking, and half swimming, he passed burnt-out American trucks and weapons. It was a sad sight.

Wondering what was going to happen to them, Hannon and his fellow POWs finally arrived in a small village. They weren't sure which village. When they arrived they saw GIs standing in the square watching the Germans learning to drive their trucks and eat their chow. Hannon and the men had a few laughs watching them puzzle over the gearshift. One managed to get a truck into reverse and couldn't seem to find forward. Another managed to get a truck into second gear, and, seeming to believe that's how it ran, went screaming around the square. Hannon thought that they should have burned all the vehicles. With the coming of darkness, the assembled were herded into a courtyard. Hannon found an apple tree, and managed to pick up a frozen apple from the ground.

"You will spend the night here. This is where your latrine will be," said their guard, motioning to the highest corner of the courtyard.

"If anyone tries to escape, all will be shot," he finished, leaving a handful of German troops behind. Tired men crowded together in the small courtyard, lying on top of each other to keep warm as a drizzle began. The GIs closest to the latrine cursed the law of gravity when it overflowed and ran down hill onto them. For a time they sang Christmas carols, filling Hannon's mind with thoughts of home. At first, the guards didn't seem to mind. However, as the night wore on the guards made it clear that the noise was keeping them awake and threatened to shoot the prisoners.

Richard Sparks, I&R Platoon, 423d Infantry Regiment

As dawn arose, the squad holding the hill overlooking the Ihren valley were relieved by remnants of Fox Company of the 422d, who had somehow wandered out of their assigned area in all the confusion. The squad returned to the roadblock and reinforced our small group that had been there throughout the night. The weather continued snowy and foggy, the fighting continued in the valley to our west and it was evident that the troops were being severely battered. Shortly, we moved our jeeps and the 2 [and-½-ton truck] down the hill a few yards and lined them up on a small dirt road within sight of the fighting, all the while maintaining the roadblock at the crossroads. In an attempt to establish communications with

Division, Ike sent two of the radio jeeps up onto Skyline Drive to try to get a message through to Division.

Skyline Drive was under direct observation by the Germans and was zeroed in by mortar and 88 fire. One at a time the jeeps would go down the road for a few yards and stop to try to key the message on the radios. Usually the message could not be completed before shells started dropping around the jeeps. Then it was down the road for a few more yards and try again. After a couple of passes back and forth, it became impossible to make any more attempts. Both jeeps came back to the platoon position with holes in the back of the radios and one of the drivers had a nice dent in his helmet from shrapnel. We assumed that the message never got through. Meanwhile, Ike had headed out to find regimental headquarters to see what the situation was. From our semi-concealed positions on the road, with the valley on our left and a hill and tree line on our right, we saw, at about 1,000 yards, a group of American soldiers of about company strength under a white flag of surrender. So far the I&R had not been spotted in our position on the hillside and we had not been fired upon. Ike returned about 1200 hours and said Col. Cavender had indicated that he would be surrendering the regiment to the Germans at 1600 and that any troops who wished had permission to take off and try to work their way back to American lines. There was no question of what the I&R would do.

As we started to move the jeeps and the 2 further along the road, a barrage of 88s landed all around us. We had been spotted. We hit the ditches, and, between shell bursts, we'd pop up and grab any ammunition we could, fired rounds into the radios, threw grenades under the hoods of the jeeps and took off over the crest of the hill to our right. The last thing we did was to throw an incendiary grenade into the back of the 2 and, from the top of the hill, looked back and saw the truck and all our personal belongings enveloped in flames and black smoke. After reaching the crest of the hill, we proceeded rapidly eastward across Skyline Drive, skirted Oberlascheid, then across open fields for about a mile, crossing a small stream on the way. We assembled in some heavy woods at the top of a small hill and stopped to rest and get organized. We had escaped the 88s with just the clothes on our backs—field jackets—and no overcoats or overshoes. We were in good shape as far as ammunition was concerned since everyone had grabbed all he could carry from the jeeps. All cartridge belts were full. I was carrying a "grease gun" and had about ten magazines stuck in the pockets of my field jacket. Mowery, who had the other one, had a similar amount. "Irish" Sheehan, in his *inimitable fashion, had removed his gas mask and had stuffed the carrier with a dozen or so K-ration bars, our only source of food. As we rested, Ike and Casey went back to Oberlascheid to reconnoiter and soon called us down to the village.*

Assembled there were about 150–200 American GIs, the remnants of various units, under the command of Major Helms, Regimental G-3. In the bunch, was a Lt. who had his jeep loaded with all his officer's gear and other booty that he was bound and determined to get out. It took a direct order to get him to abandon his precious possessions. Capt. Nauman was there with what was left of the men from A Company, and also Lt. McKinley with men from A&P Platoon plus a few other stragglers. What a motley looking crew we were—dirty, wet, tired—with some that only could be classified as walking wounded. Major Helms insisted that we try and mount an attack on Schönberg. Ike tried his best to convince him that it would be far better to abandon the few vehicles and try to infiltrate through the German lines back to St. Vith. The major would have none of this and ordered the I&R, along with Nauman and McKinley's groups, to fall in as rearguard for the attack. The column had no sooner started out than 88s started to hammer the column.

The I&R and the other two groups in the rear, dropped down into a small ravine and made their way into a patch of woods out of sight of the enemy. Here we reorganized with Capt. Nauman and A Company in a column on the right, and the I&R and McKinley's group on the left. Ike designated Sam Bordelon as lead scout because of his knowledge of French. Ozzie Spier, who spoke fluent German, was to follow Sam. Bill Morris's 1st squad was next in line, with me and my "grease gun" near the head of the column to provide covering fire if necessary. Bob Jones and the 2d squad followed, with Mowery near the end providing covering fire to the rear. Irish took up position as rear scout. Ike and Casey moved along the column to wherever they were needed. Thus, in that single-file fashion, the I&R started their little hike. We moved out in an easterly direction into a patch of woods to get out of sight of the enemy. Directly in front of us we saw a small German village, probably Schlausenbach. For some reason, Capt. Naumann and A Company immediately took off to attack the village that seemed to be swarming with Germans. Knowing that to try and to help A Company would be futile, Long's and McKinley's groups made a hard swing to the northwest away from the village and pulled up to the edge of the patch of woods.

By this time it was probably about 1600 hours and growing dusk, making visibility in the fog even more impossible. We could hear German vehicles in the distance; coming soon to the main highway from Auw, we cautiously crossed it one by one before the Germans came into sight. In the ever-increasing darkness we could see, off to our left, another small village, probably Laudesfeld. We had no intention of blundering into the village in the dark. This territory was too busy for us to hang around in. We were next to a fast-flowing stream and in we went as quietly as we could, wading across it in water up to our waists, ultimately gaining the woods on the other side. The shock of the cold water was almost enough to do us in, but we continued moving in the woods parallel to the stream until we had passed the village on the other side. We could clearly hear German voices. We moved on about a quarter of a mile, to the top of a nearby hill, where Ike called a halt. We were in bad shape. We could go no further without rest.

Looking to our right, we could see the glow of the German fires 800 to 1,000 yards away. Hoping that the Germans would mistake us for some of their troops, Ike gave us the OK to scoop out three or four pits about a foot deep in the frozen ground and start small fires so we could try to dry out. As the fires were lit, we huddled around them trying to hide them from the German view. We melted snow in our canteen cups, shaved some of the K-ration bars into the water with our trench knives and got a little warm liquid in our bellies. The small fires didn't do much to warm us up. We didn't dare build them up too much for fear we would be seen. We huddled together in small groups, hoping the shared body heat would allow us to rest. A couple of the fellows took off their boots to try to rub warmth into their feet but found they could barely get them back on. Their feet were too badly swollen. One of the guys had managed to grab a blanket when we left our jeeps, and we cut it up in strips to wrap around our hands. And so we sat, leaning against the tops of trees knocked off by artillery fire, and tried to rest for a few hours. Our minds were foggy with fatigue. Our only thoughts were of survival.

A day or two before the fighting began A Company's Captain Naumann had given away his officer's liquor ration, a bottle of Johnny Walker Red Label. As the men prepared to leave Oberlascheid the liquor was generously distributed. There wasn't quite enough for everybody to take a sip, but that didn't matter. Nobody had eaten in the past 24 hours and all it took was a sip to boost desperately sagging spirits.

Meanwhile Colonel Descheneaux assembled his staff together at the command post. A GI standing nearby heard the colonel say, "My God, we're being slaughtered!" Descheneaux was a conscientious and erudite man; he had no desire to sacrifice the lives of his men so he asked his commanders to put forward their suggestions and opinions. They were unanimous in their reluctance to surrender but realized that there were not many alternatives available. A few proposed attempting to escape under cover of darkness but Descheneaux rejected this and emphasized to his men that his primary intention was save the lives of as many men as he could even it meant being court-martialed.

Word went out to the ranks to make preparations to surrender along with orders to destroy all weapons. As the sound of rifle butts smashing on the frozen ground reached the colonel's ears he couldn't contain himself anymore and burst into tears. A few young GIs sought to comfort him but now he knew it was all over.

Lieutenant Colonel Joseph F. Puett, 2d Battalion, 423d Infantry Regiment

At 1300, seeing that the other battalions were held up by fire to our left front, I sent message to regiment asking to be allowed to attack these enemy positions. At 1400, not having received any kind of communication, and realizing how difficult communications were due to heavy woods and hilly terrain, I gave orders to attack to relieve pressure on 1st and 3d Bn at 1430. At 1425, the 422d Infantry came up on us from our right rear and mistook us for enemy and disrupted our plans for attack before we could get them to stop firing.

During the reorganization I sent out patrols to our front and right. At 1515 these patrols returned while I was in conference with regiment commander of 422d infantry and informed me that to our right about 1,500 yards were 35 German tanks and several self-propelled artillery pieces. And to our front were strong German armored forces, and that 2,000 yards to our right front German artillery was going into position facing our formations. I immediately went on reconnaissance to check this information and when I returned was informed by the 422d Regt. Commander Colonel George L. Descheneaux, Jr. that he had ordered all arms destroyed and had sent an emissary to the enemy to surrender, in order not to waste lives needlessly. I then asked permission to withdraw my Bn, around the draw to our left and join my Regiment (423d). This was denied as it might cause the 422d to be shot up needlessly. I then gave orders that anyone in my Bn could try to reach American lines in small groups who so desired. About 50 took advantage of this.

At 1700 the Germans came up and took us in custody. At the time of my return from reconnaissance I had only 387 men left in the Bn and 14 officers, 3 heavy MGs 2 light MGs and 2 60mm mortars with 3 rounds each.

The grandson of western legend Buffalo Bill, William Cody Garlow, was also with the 106th Infantry Division out on the Schnee Eifel. He was with his regiment, the 423d, commanded by Colonel Charles Cavender, when they became surrounded by German artillery troops and attempted to fight their way back to the Allied lines in the west. Just before daybreak on December 19, 1944, Cavender gathered his three battalion commanders and staff in a small open field to discuss their next line of action when a German artillery shell fragment killed the officer standing next to Garlow. After the initial volley, American troops assembled to coordinate an attack westward across the hilly Schnee Eifel, but the entire command was caught in the open where artillery fire was inflicting heavy casualties.

Garlow volunteered to negotiate the surrender although he and several other men had planned to escape through the woods, with the colonel's permission. He decided to hand over his gun and borrow white handkerchiefs to wave as he ran an erratic path down the side of the hill into German-held territory. There he was grabbed and stripped of "his most prized possessions." He spoke no German and was unable to communicate his intent to negotiate a surrender until a young German lieutenant, who spoke English, came to his rescue and ordered his men to return Garlow's watch, a pint of bourbon and candy bars. He was then taken to a major who also spoke fluent English.

The major barked some orders in German, which Garlow soon learned were intended for the young lieutenant to conduct a patrol of nine or ten men to accompany Garlow back to the American positions. Faced with a tense situation, the lieutenant's personality instantly changed. He jabbed Garlow in the back with his MP40. Garlow recoiled and winced under the painful blow. He discovered later that the lieutenant had broken two of his ribs. The lieutenant's previously friendly attitude then returned. Keeping Garlow covered, he let the American guide his patrol up the hill to Descheneaux's CP on the Schnee Eiffel, where they discovered found that Descheneaux was prepared for their arrival.

Garlow, therefore, held what he termed "the dubious honor or having negotiated the surrender of the largest number of American soldiers in the European theater, surpassed only by the Bataan surrender in 1942." Members of the 422d and Garlow's 423d regiments spent the rest of the war in captivity in German prison camps and were awarded purple hearts for the frostbite they suffered as a result of their capture. Garlow was also "unofficially shot in the leg."

By December 19, General Hasbrouck and General Jones were becoming increasingly concerned about the new salient that was developing with St. Vith at the easternmost tip. The most pervasive fear was that the attacking Germans would orchestrate a fresh pincer movement and effectively cauterize St. Vith as they had the Schnee Eifel.

Private First Class Leon Goldberg, D Company, 422d Infantry Regiment (President of the 106th Infantry Division Association)

For several nights we heard noises across the ridge that sounded like heavy equipment moving around. Then on the morning of December 16, German infantry attacked us. I manned my 30-caliber, water-cooled machine gun while bullets sped all around us. We killed three or four Germans, including their lieutenant, captured about 20 soldiers, and thought we had won the war.

Later that day, under orders to attack the town of Schoenburg, heavy German armor and tanks repulsed us. Our artillery support was knocked out and we ran out of food and ammunition.

On the morning of the 19th, a German officer approached, waving a white flag. Our lieutenant followed him behind the lines and discovered that we were completely surrounded by heavy forces. We could have been obliterated in 15 minutes. He had no alternative but to surrender us.

The attempt to counterattack and break out of the encirclement had been an audacious and courageous move but ultimately it had failed. That failure was in no part due to the GIs of the 422d and 423d. They had fought under almost constant bombardment for three long days and nights. They had effectively disrupted the German offensive to such an extent that General Manteuffel later remarked that the Battle of the Bulge was lost on December 18, 1944. If it hadn't have been for the

106th the Germans would have easily swept into the Ardennes and reached the River Meuse on schedule. The Golden Lion Division had performed admirably in the direst conditions and they didn't have to make excuses to anyone.

The surrender of the two 106th Infantry Division regiments was the result of poor communications and overwhelming force. The communication problem became overtly apparent once the fighting started and subsequent radio messages were easily disrupted. This resulted in terrible confusion. Consequently all efforts to organize the 422d and 423d were futile in extremis due to these inadequate communications.

It has been estimated that approximately 6,800 GIs were taken prisoner by the Germans but neither side has ever formally verified this number. There's no doubt that the glaring lack of cohesion due to badly organized strategic dispositions also played an integral part in the disintegration and eventual capture of the regiments but there was considerably more to it than that. General Jones had complained vociferously about sending a green division so deep into German territory but all his objections had fallen on deaf ears.

It's an irrefutable fact that those 106th GIs out on the Schnee Eifel during that bitterly cold winter displayed incredible courage and fortitude despite the overwhelming odds. Veterans of the division relate incredible acts of heroism and sacrifice that have often passed unrecognized. Either way those two regiments of the 106th never surrendered; their superiors surrendered them.

CHAPTER 8

TO FIGHT ANOTHER DAY

The story of the 106th could have ended on December 19 and many historians consider that it did, but even though two of the three regiments were captured almost in their entirety, there was still plenty of fight in the 424th and their story was far from over. The same applied to the 589th Field Artillery who headed west and prepared to make a heroic stand in the face of overwhelming opposition. However, the terrible loss to the 106th wasn't the tragedy as so often described in other accounts on the subject. Those two regiments had mounted a staunch and concerted defense and severely disrupted the Nazi timetable. The whole premise of the Battle of the Bulge hinged on buying time and that's precisely what the 106th did. They did their duty to the best of their ability and held back the tide. They were heroes.

It had become increasingly obvious to all but the uninformed that by the night of 20 December all hope for the two regiments stranded out on the Schnee Eifel had been abandoned. Vague reports concerning pockets of GIs attempting to get back to U.S. lines filtered through to the HQ in Vielsalm but these did little to pacify the overall situation. These nomadic units were broadly divided into three groups. Firstly, there were those very small groups that fought and timorously edged their way back to the American lines collectively or individually. Secondly, there were the larger groups who sustained the fight for a further 48 hours before ultimately being forced to surrender. Thirdly, there were the strays such as Eric Fisher Wood and a few others that wandered through woods along the Belgian–German border and, despite being completely isolated, fought on guerrilla style, in some cases for weeks on end. Most would be captured and many of these self-styled renegades were killed but not until they had caused deep consternation and much disruption to the German forces.

Meanwhile German reinforcements began pouring in from the east and massing in front of St. Vith.

John C. Rain, Battery B, 589th Field Artillery Battalion

After about three days of moving around, the remnants of the 589th were divided into two groups, one half going to Baraque de Fraiture to defend the crossroads and the other half going the other way out of danger.

Regrouped and moved back—stopped at what we thought to be an important crossroads—deployed with only three howitzers and about 100 men from the 589th. Joined off & on by a few tanks and half-tracks with quad 50 AA guns. The Germans came. On the night of Dec 20/21 Ken Sewell and John Schaffner were sent to a foxhole down the road to Houffalize as an outpost. About midnight the German patrol attacked toward the crossroads and the outpost brought down fire on them from the M-16 half-track and the 37mm gun on an M-8. This was only the first attack by the German 2d Panzer Division. One night the word came to come out of the foxholes and go into the stone barn for shelter. Apparently Bernard Strohmier never got the word. He was still in his hole the next morning having killed a German soldier who was lying just in front of the foxhole. He told his relief, "I got my German." Bernard had let them know that we were still there. His being there could have saved all of us from an attack.

During the previous day a small artillery column led by Major Arthur C. Parker had managed to extricate themselves from the tumult of the Schnee Eifel. They were ordered to take up position and establish a roadblock at the strategic crossroads of Baraque de Fraiture roughly 25 miles west of St. Vith. As Parker's unit detrucked and prepared, he was reliably informed that reinforcements would be sent to him as soon as they became available. The situation in the center of the German offensive was still very fluid. Sensing that trouble was on the way and using the three remaining 105mm howitzers from the 589th Field Artillery, Parker began to organize a thin defensive perimeter.

It was actually a prime defensive location. Baraque de Fraiture is a small crossroads that back then only had a few inhabited farm buildings nestled at the apex of the Plateau des Tailles, which rises to over 1,800 feet and is one of the highest points in the Ardennes. It is on the watershed of several tributaries that flow respectively into the rivers Ourthe and the Meuse. Holding these vital crossroads was critically important to the Allies because the N15 Liège road running to the west of this position was the boundary between the flank divisions of the 3d Armored Division and the 82d Airborne Division, neither of which was capable of mounting an autonomous defense in strength. Loss of the junction would potentially allow the Germans access to maneuver in three directions and effectively flank or infiltrate the U.S. First Army line.

Parker's howitzers were initially reinforced with four half-tracks mounted with quad .50-caliber machine guns from the 203d Armored Anti-Aircraft Battalion. Parker received specific orders to organize the defense and deny access to approaching enemy forces. He fully understood the significance of retaining this position due to its strategic location. When he arrived there he found a deserted crossroads, almost completely surrounded by pine forests. His initial objective had been to protect the vital supply route back to the St. Vith area, but after studying a map of the area Parker concluded that this road junction was of much greater importance than was previously assumed at HQ. He ignored direct orders to relocate his howitzers at the time.

During the night December 19/20, Major Parker ordered his men to dig in and managed to persuade several other passing units to provide assistance in his task of holding the crossroads. Among them was a reconnaissance company from the 7th Armored Division, and several dozen assorted stragglers who were in the process of falling back from the east. Those quad fours from the 203d were going to come in handy.

Early on December 19 the 112th Infantry and 229th Field Artillery Battalion had displaced unhindered under cover of a heavy fog and assembled a south-facing defensive front around Huldange in Luxembourg astride the Belgian border. It was here that Nelson received a message from the 28th Division, ordering the regiment to hold the line Lausdorn–Weiswampach–Beiler, which the 112th Infantry had just abandoned. At this moment Colonel Nelson had two contradictory orders, both of which posed a significant risk to his regiment.

Through indirect artillery channels he requested permission to join the 106th Infantry Division, only a little distance away to the north. Nelson also reported to General Jones at Vielsalm and informed him of the problem he now faced. Jones wasted no time in attaching the 112th Infantry to his own division, while assuring Nelson that he would assume full responsibility. The VIII Corps commander approved the attachment. On the morning December 20 Jones ordered the regiment to sideslip back to the east, reoccupy Beiler, and dig in along the east–west ridge line, Leithum–Beiler–Malscheid. This would put them in proximity to the right flank of the 424th Regiment, the 112th becoming another piece contributing to the fast developing "horseshoe" defense of St. Vith.

The 424th had at least been fortunate enough to pull back to a more defensible line on the high ground between Bracht and Burg Reuland. From this location, even though they had lost contact with the 9th Armored's CCB to the north and the 28th Infantry Division's 112th Regiment to the south, they were able to hold their position against the whole 62d VGD. Sometime before dawn a combat patrol of the 2d Battalion, 424th reestablished contact with GIs from the 1st Battalion, 112th Regiment near Beiler who were equally compromised and out of touch with the rest of the 28th Infantry Division.

Back in Vielsalm the news filtered back to General Jones. He immediately assumed command of the 112th Infantry Regiment and dispatched Brigadier General Herbert T. Perrin, his assistant divisional commander to organize the southern flank of the "Goose Egg" and establish contact with the 424th Regiment. Meanwhile the 112th's B Company that had stood shoulder to shoulder on the front line with the 424th for three consecutive days was returned to regimental control.

It had become increasingly apparent to the German high command by December 20 that taking St. Vith was now an unavoidable imperative. That salient had to be eliminated to gain control of its vital road network. The failure or success of the Nazi offensive depended on it. Repeated attempts by the 62d VG Division to break through the breach that existed between CCB, 9th Armored Division and the 424th Infantry Regiment were stoically resisted. By the end of the day Hasbrouck's 7th Armored Division on the northern flank, the northern perimeter of the

Goose Egg, had seen little action due to concentrated enemy efforts to penetrate the southern flank, that hadn't achieved the desired results. The 112th Infantry Regiment, 28th Division had succeeded in consolidating the line and linking up with the 424th Regiment.

On the Schönberg road, after five days of incessant German probes, barrages, and attempts to break through, the 81st Engineers had been reduced to company strength. On the Prümerberg the 168th Combat Engineers had held firm but a renewed German assault comprising six Tiger tanks and a battalion of infantry was coming up the road from Schönberg and heading straight for their position. Neither the "daisy chains" of mines nor bazookas were effective against these German behemoths. Even the medium tanks sent up for a direct shoot out couldn't stop them. The German tanks lobbed flares behind the Sherman's, fired directly at them and almost immediately achieved three direct hits. This caused the remaining Shermans to retreat.

Lieutenant Colonel Thomas Riggs considered the situation with the utmost gravity and ordered his staff to fall back to St. Vith. He picked his way up the hill to the front-line positions, only to learn that he had lost contact with the men north and south of his skirmish line. By this time, the German Tigers were so close that Riggs could hear the German tankers talking among themselves. A few hours before midnight time ran out and he got on the radio to inform the 7th Armored Division that his position had been compromised and penetrated. He told the 7th that there were at least eight heavy tanks and infantry nearby and that he was awaiting orders. Forty-five minutes later Riggs received his reply from Clarke: "To Riggs or senior officer present: Re-form; save what vehicles you can; attack to west to St. Vith; we are forming a new line west of town."

The Germans were heading toward St. Vith. Over the next few hours the survivors of Riggs's 81st Engineers, the 38th and 23d Armored Infantry battalions reinforced by Lieutenant McKinley's men from St. Vith, the 87th Reconnaissance Squadron, and the 31st Tank Battalion, pulled back under fire. All over the eastern side of St. Vith men repeated the orders to one another: "Go west! Go west!" The 168th Combat Engineer Battalion was the only unit not to have its lines breached.

Exhausted from six days of continuous fighting, the defenders of the Prümerberg initiated a nerve-wracking game of cat and mouse as they began to pull back south and west in small groups. Even though some were taken POW by the Germans, others managed to escape and rejoin the rest of 7th Armored. The 168th, along with the other defenders of St. Vith, received a Presidential Unit Citation for bravery.

Back at a U.S. aid station in Vielsalm medics carefully removed James Hanney's boots only to discover that frostbite had rendered his feet useless for the duration. James moved from Boston to Florida in 1955 but until the day he died in 2012 he never managed to get his feet warm again.

Howard L. Bryant, F Company, 424th Infantry Regiment

I remember 1944 when we moved up on the line. All nice and quiet with no problems. Then noises in the night like engines roaring, tracks clattering, etc. When reported the word came back, "They play that stuff over loud speakers to keep you guys awake." One evening at dusk a Spitfire screamed across the German lines just above the treetops. Boy did those "loud speakers" ever shoot back! He made it OK, but that was the last plane we saw until Christmas Day. That night Jerry crunched through the snow on patrol. The only flare we had was a dud. Then one morning all hell broke loose. Screaming Meemies and all that. Nothing left above ground, ammo dump blown up, but most of us in good shape. The Platoon Sergeant handed me and Pfc Clifford Freilinger a bazooka and one round of ammo to go down the hill and stop any tank trying to cross the creek. Also, be sure to get the infantry following the tank. "Yes Sir," no doubt even crossed our mind, but no tank came. "Praise the Lord."

We got out by hoofing cross-country. Snow filled canteen cups out of a jeep track. Several days no food. One evening near St. Vith, our company cook had a small pot of hot water with a few potatoes in it. "Fellows, I wish I had more for you." He had tears streaming down his face. I wish I could remember his name. Next day we hitched a ride out of there with some 7th Armored half-tracks. Found food, crab apples buried in horse manure and later a half-eaten can of Spam laying beside the road. Next day clear skies. Lots of bombers going east.

Field Marshal Sir Bernard Law Montgomery's staff car drove with all haste from his 21st Army Group HQ at Zonhoven to Lieutenant General Courtney Hodges' First Army HQ at Chaudfontaine in the Ardennes.

Sometime earlier Eisenhower had called Monty at his HQ regarding the situation. It's been well documented that Eisenhower's contentious decision to put Monty in charge of the northern section of the Bulge was not well received by other U.S. commanders. General Bradley had already briefed Hodges on the coming change for First Army.

When Montgomery rolled into First Army HQ around noon he was well aware that Eisenhower was prepared to sanction his proposal of giving up ground to gain reserves. Monty was known to be a cautious commander who courted publicity, didn't easily make friends and didn't have many among the higher echelons at SHAEF. His supercilious and aloof attitude often alienated him from his subordinates; many didn't regard him as the right man for the job. Eisenhower had endured numerous altercations with Monty over the past few months and in later years referred to him a psychopath, but at the time he had been left with little alternative. There's also the distinct possibility that this was more of a political choice than a strategic one. Monty would do the job, but he would do it his way and only go on the offensive from a position of numerical and tactical strength. This made him popular with the rank and file because his way of fighting was designed to incur the least number of Allied casualties.

The town of St. Vith, a vital road junction, remained the hub of resistance to, both Manteuffel's Fifth Panzer Army and Dietrich's Sixth Army. The defenders, led by the 7th Armored Division, including the remaining regiment of the 106th U.S. Infantry Division, with elements of the 9th Armored Division and 28th U.S. Infantry Division, all under the command of General Bruce C. Clarke, had successfully repelled all German attacks and significantly delayed the German advance.

Monty breezed into Hodges' HQ and haughtily addressed the officers and staff in attendance. "Well, gentlemen," he clasped his hands behind his back and took a deep breath before saying in a somewhat disturbingly jocular tone, "I gather a difficult situation has arisen. Now do tell me the form."

Montgomery then sat quietly and listened to the situation brief before suddenly springing to his feet with, "Gentlemen, will you please excuse me," and promptly leaving the room to have lunch alone. Shortly thereafter he returned and began eyeing the map laid out on the table before the officers and staff. Monty predicted that the Germans, having passed through Stavelot, would wheel north across the Meuse near Liège. "Therefore," he said with furrowed brow, "an immediate counterattack is out of the question," He went on to suggest to Hodges that he should assemble a corps northwest of Marche for a counterattack. Then he returned to the map and drew his finger across it from north to south as he said, "But first we must sort out the battlefield, tidy up the lines." The officers in attendance looked at one another aghast at this suggestion.

The primary job at hand, Montgomery concluded, was to pull everyone out of the St. Vith pocket. Hodges shook his head in disagreement and was visibly exasperated: he couldn't believe his ears. Was the Field Marshal serious? The St. Vith "bulge" was precisely what they needed in preparation for a counterattack. Hodges had already appropriated the bulk of Middleton's VIII Corps for Bradley so they could hold Bastogne. He'd kept control of Hasbrouck's 7th Armored Division, Jones's 106th Infantry Division, and the town of St. Vith. Moreover he had already placed Major General Lawton "Lightning Joe" Collins's VII Corps in reserve behind the River Ourthe between the town of Marche and the River Meuse. To seal the gap behind the Goose Egg and provide additional support to the defenders of St. Vith, he'd attached them to Ridgway's XVIII Airborne Corps and sent Gavin's 82d Airborne in to close the gap between the rear door to the Goose Egg at the Salm and Ourthe rivers. Monty's new plan of action would effectively negate all these arrangements.

Ridgway had displayed exemplary leadership throughout. Despite the increasingly grave situation as the German attacks gained momentum, he remained fearlessly on the move and could frequently be found in the thick of the fighting, organizing defenses and counterattacks and always leading by example. It was not unusual for a GI in a front-line foxhole to suddenly find his corps commander next to him. Ridgway had little regard for officers perceived as weak or indecisive who were usually relieved of command on the spot. He would demonstrate his capacity for instant dismissal more than once during the course of the Battle of the Bulge.

In order to protect the river crossings on the River Meuse at Givet, Dinant and Namur, Monty had taken the precaution of ordering the few available units he had to hold the bridges on December 19. This had led to a hastily assembled force comprised from rear echelon troops, military police and Army Air Forces personnel. The British 29th Armored Brigade, which had turned in its tanks for re-equipping, was told to take back them back with immediate effect and head to the designated area. Consequently XXX Corps who were at that moment in Holland began their move south on December 20.

While Hodges and Montgomery were discussing the situation, Lieutenant Colonel Frederick Schroeder interrupted the proceedings with a letter from Hasbrouck for his old friend, First Army Chief of Staff, Brigadier General William Kean.

Kean, glanced at it, and then made his announcement. "Gentlemen, I think you'll find this news from St. Vith interesting," he said, and then read the letter verbatim to the assembled officers and staff:

Dear Bill
I am out of touch with VIII Corps and understand XVIII Airborne Corps is coming in. My division is defending the line St. Vith–Poteau both inclusive. CCB, 9th AD, the 424th Inf. Regt. of the 106th Div. and the 112th Inf. Regt. of the 28th Div. are on my right and hold from St. Vith to Holdingen. Both infantry regiments are in bad shape. My right flank is wide open except for some reconnaissance elements, TDs and stragglers we have collected and organized into defense teams at road centers back as far as Cheram [Chérain] inclusive. Two German Divisions, 116 Pz and 560 VG, are just starting to attack NW with their right on Gouvy. I can delay them the rest of today maybe but will be cut off by tomorrow.

VIII Corps has ordered me to hold and I will do so but need help. An attack from Bastogne to the NE will relieve the situation and in turn cut the bastards off in rear. I also need plenty of air support. Am out of contact with VIII Corps so am sending this to you. Understand 82d AB is coming up on my north and the north flank is not critical. BOB HASBROUCK

Hodges had what he needed to sway the argument in his favor. "In the light of this new information," stated Hodges, politely but firmly, "Ridgway's XVIII Corps will have to keep driving forward toward St. Vith to Hasbrouck's relief."

Monty was well known for his intransigence but this was one of the rare occasions when he sensed that this wasn't the time to impose his agenda, therefore he allowed Hodges' plan to remain for now. They would hang onto St. Vith and the Goose Egg.

"I agree that the chaps in St. Vith must be helped," said Montgomery. However, if there was to be any compromise it had to be done on his terms. General Ridgway was to proceed east to Vielsalm to open up the escape corridor. Then, as soon as the men inside the Goose Egg were pulled out, the defensive lines were to be shortened.

"After all, gentlemen," he concluded, "you can't win the big victory without a tidy show."

With his new understanding of First Army's situation, and his plan clear to Hodges, Montgomery left. However, he was concerned about Hodges' health. The man looked like a candidate for a heart attack, but it would be another general who suffered that fate.

Over at Baraque de Fraiture Parker's team was still too few in number to offer any serious resistance but they would dig in and hold on for the duration. This was going to be a hard fight.

John Schaffner, Scout, Battery B, 589th Field Artillery Battalion

Most of the night was spent in the foxhole. All was quiet on the front line. When I was relieved during the night to get some rest, I tried to find a dry place in the stone barn to lay down. The floor was deep in muck, but the hayrack on the wall was full of dry hay so I accepted that as a good place to sleep. Pushing the cows aside, I climbed into the hay. I guess that the cows just didn't understand, because they kept pulling the hay out from under me until I became the next course on their menu. Anyway, it wasn't long until I was outside in another hole in the ground.

In the meantime at Vielsalm December 19, the Service Battery returned to the Division. After having been surrounded, they used their bazookas, machine guns and carbines to kill or wound the bulk of the enemy forces opposing them. They succeeded, after a four-hour battle, in clearing the enemy from the road in front of their CP, and driving the few that remained into the hills surrounding their position. Using white phosphorus grenades for a smoke screen they were able to move all of their personnel and equipment from the position with the exception of a few men. Finding the road to Schönberg blocked, they took to the woods where they were joined by personnel from other outfits. By moving at night they passed through the German lines and joined the 9th Armored Division. Then they returned to the division at Vielsalm. They immediately went from there to join the elements of the battalion at Baraque de Fraiture. They provided the kind of support that can only be given by determined men who have proven themselves in battle.

Group B withdrew from Joubieval to the vicinity of Phillipeville via La Roche and Dinant. Camp that night was on a road in front of a French-style chateau owned by a Belgian Count. It was a refuge from the war for about 100 orphaned Belgian children and operated by the Count and his wife with a Belgian Army Chaplain as spiritual adviser. The Count and the Chaplain were very friendly and allowed many of the men to get cleaned up and listen to their radio to get some news. (It was disquieting to hear a report of German paratroopers in the immediate area. The report proved to be false later.) Part of the night was spent in the chateau and part in the vehicles, with a double guard on the column.

1600 hours: Returned to Baraque de Fraiture and went into position to form a roadblock against attack from the south or west. Joined by elements of the 203d AAA and 87th Reconnaissance. 2400 hours: German patrol reported in front of minefield to the south. Fired on [them] with our 50-cal machine gun.

Sergeant John P. Kline, M Company, 423d Infantry Regiment

Left Bleialf 0800, we were on the road until 2300 that night. We had no water or food except for the snow from the ground. During the march, as we were going through a very small village, the Germans stopped us in front of some civilians. They made us take off our overshoes and give them to the civilians. That was when I discovered that my right overshoe had been ripped open by shrapnel. The shrapnel had cut through my rubber overshoe, leather combat boot and heavy sock. It had then cut around, but not through my Achilles tendon. It was a small wound, but had it gone any deeper it would have cut my tendon and I would have been unable to walk.

There was much evidence in the area that a large-scale battle had taken place. I remember as we were leaving Bleialf walking through a small village. It could have been outskirts of Bleialf, or some small village nearby. There were German troops in American jeeps. They were opening ration boxes and meat cans. They were eating our Christmas dinner. My guess is that this had been our battalion supply depot. As we walked through the area, I was surprised to see my jeep with four Germans in it. I was positive it was mine. I had personally painted my son's name "Teddie" on the jeep, and the name was there.

There had been had been a real shoot-out, with hand to hand fighting. There were dead Americans and Germans lying in doors, ditches and hanging out of windows. The in-fighting must have been fierce, for some of the bodies were on top of each other.

As we left the town and just before we made a slight right turn that led us into the country, I saw a two-story stone building. Its upper floor was occupied by several young women, who waved at us through the open windows as we went by. I have often wondered if they were brought along by the Germans.

The road we were on eventually took us through Pruem, Germany, the town that I could see from our positions on the Schnee Eifel. We ended up that evening sleeping in an open field near Gerolstein, Germany.

The southern half of the St. Vith perimeter defenses was still relatively intact. The 424th Regiment was still fighting fit. Task Force (TF) Jones, an outfit compiled from the 7th Armored Division, was defending the extreme right wing near Gouvy and Cherain and holding well. General Hasbrouck knew full well that if this TF caved everyone within the horse-shoe perimeter was in danger of being outflanked and trapped. He ordered the TF to fight a holding action against the enemy and fall back to the small town of Gouvy in the west, adding that keeping that road open was an imperative. So far all troops had held the line but time was running out and decisions had to be made. Maybe it was time to relinquish St. Vith?

During the afternoon December 21, a heavy German assault, led by tanks and accompanied by intense artillery, rocket, and mortar fire, overran the 81st Engineers positions. Colonel Riggs ordered his men to break up into small groups and attempt to escape to the rear. Most of the survivors including Colonel Riggs were captured by the Germans. The 81st Engineer Combat Battalion received the Distinguished Unit Citation, praising its "extraordinary heroism, gallantry, determination, and esprit de corps."

The ensuing story of what happened to Colonel Thomas Riggs turned into a remarkable adventure. Along with other prisoners he was force-marched over 100 miles to a railway marshaling yard in Germany. During that march Colonel Riggs lost 40 pounds in weight. From there he was transported and interned in a prisoner of war camp northwest of Warsaw. He escaped from the camp and surviving on snow and sugar beets, he headed for the Russian lines. Late one night members of the Polish resistance discovered him. Later on he joined a Russian tank unit. After some time with the unit, Colonel Riggs joined a number of former Allied prisoners of war on a train to Odessa. From there, he went by ship to Istanbul and then to Port Said in Egypt. When he arrived there he reported to American authorities.

After his ordeal Riggs was eligible for medical leave in the States, but he politely refused and insisted on rejoining his old unit, who were at that moment in Western France. On his way back to the unit, Riggs stopped in Paris for a debriefing and made his first contact with his unit when he ran into some engineers from the 81st in a bar. It was the first news they'd heard from him since St. Vith. He had quite a story to tell them.

Silver Star
The President of the United States of America, authorized by Act of Congress, July 9, 1918, takes pleasure in presenting the Silver Star to Lieutenant Colonel (Corps of Engineers) Thomas J. Riggs, Jr. (ASN: 0-25356), United States Army, for conspicuous gallantry and intrepidity in action against the enemy while serving with the 81st Engineer Combat Battalion, 7th Armored Division, in action in Belgium, from 17 to 23 December 1944. Lieutenant Colonel Riggs' gallant actions and dedicated devotion to duty, without regard for his own life, were in keeping with the highest traditions of military service and reflect great credit upon himself, his unit, and the United States Army.

General Orders: Headquarters, 7th Armored Division, General Orders No. 23 (January 23, 1945)

Action Date: December 17–23, 1944

CHAPTER 9

PROPERTY OF THE REICH

It would be nigh on impossible to cover all the POW accounts of the 106th Infantry Division—that would take another volume—so the ones selected in this chapter are representative of many of the stories. Around 6,800 106th Infantry Division soldiers were now prisoners of war and considered property of the Reich. Over the past few days they had been rounded up and were now huddled together in groups in various villages and towns astride the Belgian–German border. They were unshaven, weary and thoroughly disheartened at having been forced to surrender by their commanders. A German guard strutted arrogantly up and down in front of one particular column while imparting the latest news from the front in broken English.

"American prisoners, the war goes in Germany's favors! American and British forces are thrown back in a catastrophic defeat until they reach the North Sea! Germany will therefore win the war after all!"

Nobody actually believed the news but true or false it did cause consternation. The POWs faced a very uncertain future when they began their forced marches east with neither food nor water to sustain them.

Phil Hannon marched away with the rest of his platoon. It was a tragic panorama to witness as they began their march in columns of fives. Colonel Cavender and Lieutenant Colonel Puett held their heads high and led the column. After six hours of steady walking they stopped at a village that was occupied by a panzer grenadier unit. Hannon had been looking forward to the stop because of the promise of food and water. Instead, they were stripped of their overshoes and had half a dozen potatoes tossed at them from a window. The ensuing scramble by starving GIs appeared to be a source of amusement for the Germans, who weren't known for their sense of humor.

Hannon gathered a couple of canteens and helmets and motioned to the guards letting them know he wanted *wasser*. He was lucky that he picked a Polish guard who gathered a half-dozen GIs and took them up the street to his billet. Not only did the guard let them fill up all their containers with water, he brought a bucket of boiled spuds, telling them to fill up their pockets for their comrades. Hannon loaded his overcoat pockets to the brim. Back in line he made sure everyone in his platoon got two each. An hour later, they counted off and marched on. Some of the men were suffering from trench foot, hypothermia and frostbite but they had to keep moving. Stopping could mean instant death. Empty stomachs and dry mouths only exacerbated a bad situation. When they occasionally stopped men would check the ditches on the roadside, break the ice on the dirty, half-frozen, puddles and streams, and drink their fill. Eating the ice helped a little too. This is what it meant to be a prisoner of the German Army in 1944.

Most of the 422d Regiment was force-marched 35 miles to Gerolstein and from there was marched or moved by boxcar deeper into Germany. A significant number of the officers and men were transferred to Bad Orb. Others were scattered throughout German POW camps. A number of officers reached Poland, from which they made a winter march of several hundred miles, finally arriving at Hammelburg, where the officers from Bad Orb meanwhile had been relocated. Colonel Descheneaux spent the remainder of the war as a POW in Stalag XII-A and later in Stalag IX-B where he contracted tuberculosis.

Sergeant John P. Kline, M Company, 423d Infantry Regiment

12/21/44: At Gerolstein we were awakened at 0600, and given our first food since breakfast on December 18. They fed us hard crackers and cheese. Seven men to one can of cheese. We left Gerolstein during the evening.

12/21/44: Arrived Dockweiler Dries 2300. Billeted in an old German barracks. During the three and one-half days there, we were fed one ration of very weak potato stew. Received two bread rations of one loaf split between five men, and one ration of cheese, one small can between four men. We were each given two old German Army blankets. They were old and worn, but did give us some warmth. They would prove to be lifesavers as time went on.

12/22/44: During the night the road alongside the barracks was strafed and bombed. We could not see the plane, but in the moonlight we could see that it was a British Spitfire. The English usually flew night missions, the Americans flew during the day. The weather was clearing and cold. There were many planes in the sky, so we will probably be moved during the night, to avoid the possibility of being strafed.

12/23/44: No reason given for our delay. Someone said there had been a lot of prisoners taken. Maybe they were not sure what to do with us because of the large numbers. I am sure, from what I can see, we were clogging their transportation system.

12/25/44: Christmas Day, Dockweiler Dries. On the march by 0630, marched all day and night, no water, or food, except snow.

No Christmas, except in our hearts.

One of the most grueling experiences the 106th GIs had to endure was a 35-mile forced march with hardly any sustenance. The only water available was collected from heaps of snow that lay at the side of the road. When they arrived at German railway stations and marshaling yards, they were packed into boxcars reminiscent of those used to transport Jews to the concentration camps. The packed railway wagons would often be shunted around from one railway siding to another for days on end, and each boxcar presented a claustrophobic hell as between 65 and 90 soldiers were crammed inside with virtually no means of sanitation. The GIs were reduced to relieving themselves in their helmets. The human effluence would then be thrown out of the ventilation hatches located in the upper corner of the car.

Germany was experiencing serious food shortages at the time so little consideration would have been given to the needs of POWs. Initially each soldier was given six slices of *ersatz* bread, which could contain sawdust and potato peelings.

If the situation of the POWs in Limburg, Germany wasn't bad enough less than a week after their capture, collateral damage occurred when a squadron of RAF bombers inadvertently destroyed an officer barracks. Due to excessively high winds, marker flares from the pathfinder plane blew off course, away from the rail yard target to the POW camp. Forty-eight officers were presumed killed with 39 bodies positively identified.

Sol Kravitz, 424th Medical Battalion

During the Battle of the Bulge, I was captured in Belgium while taking care of a wounded soldier. I was taken back toward Germany in the freezing snow and I saw many terrible sights, including soldiers surrendering and some being shot as they surrendered. I saw dead soldiers piled very high on the ground, some without shoes. I even saw dead horses without heads.

We were marched many miles to Limburg Stalag X11-A. There, I was interrogated and given a German dog tag. That night the prison camp was bombed and our officers were killed. The next day my number was called and I was told to stand with three other guys. I soon learned that we were all Jewish. We were given a shovel with which to dig our own graves, but two bombs landed nearby and exploded. As we dug ourselves out of the debris, I realized somehow I was spared. Later I was put into a boxcar with the wounded and for five days we had nothing to eat until we arrived at Luckenwalde III-A. There the wounded were taken away. I was given a bowl and a spoon and a small loaf of bread, which I shared with six men; that was it for the day. Often we would stand out for roll call in the cold for many [hours], it was freezing and we would stand there until the Germans got the count correct. After several months, I was marched many miles to Stalag X1-A, then forced to march another 18 to 20 miles a day; nobody dared fall out or they would be shot. As a column, we were bombed by friendly fire and strafed by our own planes.

During the night of December 23/24, 1944 the RAF and USAAF launched one of their most intense bombing raids on Germany. When the dust had settled at the POW camp in Limburg 68 U.S. Army soldiers had been killed. That very same night a stationary train full of American POWs in a marshaling yard in Koblenz was also bombed. One particular truck suffered a direct hit killing all occupants but the bodies of these unfortunate men weren't removed until two days later.

American 106th POWs at Stalag IX-B in Bad Orb were suffering from lice infestations and the devastating physical effects of inadequate nutrition. One soldier described the ubiquitous lice as being the size of grains of rice. They would collect in the armpits and crotches and left blotchy red bite marks all over the body that caused an extremely disagreeable, stale smell. Various methods were used to remove them. A lighted candle was fairly effective but the skill of burning the lice without burning your clothes was only learnt with practice. As well as causing frenzied scratching, lice also carried a disease known as pyrexia. The initial symptoms were shooting pains in the shins followed by a very high fever. Although the disease wasn't fatal on its own it could effectively disable any soldier for the duration. Compounded with other health problems it could even cause death. The POWs were eventually forced to shower in a foul-smelling delousing agent while their clothes were steamed. None of them cared about the nasty smell.

Gifford B. Doxsee, HQ 3d Battalion, 423d Regiment
I was taken prisoner in the Battle of the Bulge, December 19, 1944 when the Regimental Commander, Colonel Charles Cavender surrendered the remnants of his regiment to the Germans outside Schönberg, Belgium.

The evening our train brought us from Limburg to Muhlberg, our captors first put us all through a "delousing" station. We were forced to remove all our clothes, go into a shower room naked and be thoroughly showered with hot water, which felt wonderful. Our clothes were sent through a chemical delousing treatment room while we were showering, so they came back purified if not washed. But before we could put our clothes back on, we had to endure inoculations, probably a good idea in principle, but one which hurt at the time because the needles were put into our breasts rather than in arms or elsewhere. After receiving the inoculations and then dressing, we were taken to piles of overcoats and each given one. I received the coat originally used by a Belgian soldier, unbeautiful but wearable and much appreciated.

At the Muhlberg camp there were prisoners of many nationalities, including Russians. Each group was housed separately in different compounds within the larger camp. But somehow it was possible for the differing groups to move back and forth during daylight, and we saw Russians come many times into the British noncommissioned officers' compound where we were housed temporarily, seeking food. Russia had never signed the Geneva Convention on treatment of prisoners in wartime, and since the Russian government mistreated Germans held in the USSR, the Germans felt quite able to reciprocate. Hence, these Russians were literally starving, and to fend off death as long as possible they wandered into the compounds of other nationalities to scrounge the garbage and leftovers that Allied prisoners would not eat.

We remained at the large prison camp near Muhlberg, Germany, for about 14 days until sent off to Dresden January 12 as part of an arbeitskommando work group. Only one of the 150 POWs who eventually moved to Dresden was given a blue coat with the letters USSR painted or stenciled on the back in yellow. That coat made him the single most conspicuous member of our arbeitskommando and it was ironic that he should be the individual later caught by the SS carrying off a quart jar of canned string beans from the cellar of a bombed-out Dresden home, an offense for which he was tried, found guilty, and executed.

A hundred and fifty GIs got off the train from Stalag IV-B at Mühlberg, and began their march through Dresden. Among them was another typically unshaven, tired, and hungry GI by the name of Kurt Vonnegut. The welcoming speech, given by a rather short middle-aged man with a Hitler moustache, was long winded. Whatever he was saying it was very loud and emotional. The first thing they were told was they were at Arbeitskommando #557 and their new quarters was known as Schlachthof Fünf—Slaughterhouse Five. The next thing they were told, or more correctly asked, was if any of them wanted to fight the Russians on the Eastern Front. There were no takers. The directions continued. They would be allowed two postcards home every other week. During the intervening week, they could send one letter. They would be up before dawn and work until dusk. Most importantly, if any of them plundered anything while out on their work detail, they would be shot. What wasn't completely clear to the POWs was whether "they" meant the perpetrator, or all of them.

Dresden, long known as Florence on the Elbe, was a beautiful Baroque city full of churches and fine buildings of brick and stone lining the wide and stately streets. The slaughterhouse was a large compound enclosed on three sides by a bend in the River Elbe that ran through the heart of Dresden.

Their new home was a large concrete-block structure, originally built to slaughter livestock, divided into three sections. The western and central part of the building had been converted into sleeping quarters lined with double-decked bunks. Along the walls, piping and faucets ran atop shelving where meat had been prepped and butchered. The eastern third was the kitchen. In the back, of course, was the latrine.

In another stalag, in direct breach of the Geneva Convention, German officers and guards began singling out Jewish or Jewish-looking POWs from the ranks of American POWs. In some cases a GI could find himself sent to Berga, a satellite camp of the infamous Buchenwald concentration camp, purely for misbehaving.

A group of about 350 men was selected from among the more than 2,000 American prisoners initially taken to the Stalag IX-B prisoner of war camp at Bad Orb, 50 miles north of Frankfurt. It was here that the prisoners were gathered on the parade ground. The commandant then gave the order for all Jews to step forward. One of the survivors, Joseph Littell, recalled how nobody moved. The commandant repeated the order but was again met with a deafening silence. Unable to contain his frustration the commandant took a rifle and struck Hans Kasten, the leader of the group of American POWs with a powerful, withering blow that knocked the man clean off his feet. When Hans shakily stood upright he was felled once again. The commandant stated in no uncertain terms that he would kill ten men every hour until all the Jews were positively identified.

A group numbering 350 was eventually assembled under great duress. Only 80 of them were actually Jewish; others such as 106th GI Hans Kasten selflessly volunteered. Then there were those who were handpicked by German guards purely on the basis that they were regarded as "looking Jewish." Kasten was in a particularly volatile situation because he was an American of German parentage. He was told repeatedly the only thing worse than a Jew was a German who had turned against his own country. After several weeks the group was loaded into boxcars without food or water, arriving at Berga on February 13, 1945. Although labeled by the Germans as part of Stalag IX-C, in reality it was in fact a slave labor camp. Its inhabitants, made up of many nationalities, were subjected to a harsh regime of forced labor excavating a large underground slate mine intended as the location for a future factory.

The Nazis policy of "extermination through work" became overtly apparent to these unfortunate Americans. They were accommodated in barracks adjacent to the camp and treated exactly the same as other forced laborers in the German Reich. They slept in three-level bunks, and had to survive the consequences of 12 hours a day hard labor in dangerous, dusty tunnels on *ersatz* bread and thin soup. There were no washing facilities and prisoners had to relieve themselves in a hole in the floor. They were beaten with alarming frequency and as a result many succumbed to this inhumane treatment.

"The purpose was to kill you but to get as much of you before they killed you," said former 106th Division POW Milton Stolon. Gangrene, dysentery, pneumonia, and diphtheria were some of the diseases that made life even more intolerable for these POWs. In the space of just two months 70 POWs died. Berga had the highest death rate among all the POW camps.

John W. Reinfenrath, B Company, 423d Regiment

I was sent as part of the 350 to Berga. Upon arrival at Berga we were marched to newly constructed barracks on a hill about a mile from the town. There were four barracks. The barracks were surrounded by barbed wire fences and guard towers. The barracks were one-story wooden buildings with two large rooms and a common entryway. Most of each room was taken up by wooden bunks. They were double bunks with corn shuck mattresses and stacked three high.

At night we were locked in and had to use the wooden boxes provided for latrines, which leaked some or overflowed. They had to be emptied each morning into the outdoor slit trench latrine. Those who got this job were ones who tried to escape, were caught stealing or were unlucky enough to be picked by the guards.

I was taken into the compound where the prisoners from Buchenwald were. I thought that this was the end and almost didn't care, I was in so much pain. There were other GIs there. We all had to take off all our clothes, which at that point didn't make me feel any better. However, our clothes were put into a large box-like room within the big room we were in. The clothes were being heated to kill the body lice. I don't think it did much good because nothing was done to get the lice that were on our body. The prisoners in the compound did all of the work with our clothes, putting them in the "box" and then dumping them out in one big hot pile where we had to sort through to find our own. There was a prisoner there who was a doctor. He saw that I was in pain and sent one of the other prisoners to get something for me. He brought back a small bottle with and eyedropper cap. The doctor had him squirt a few drops into my mouth. Within a minute the cramps were gone.

While we waited for our clothes, we talked to the doctor who spoke very good English. He said that the best thing to do was to eat only dry toast and stay in bed for a couple of days. I thought the chances of that were dim to nothing. He also said the Americans were getting close and that we were going to be moved. I asked him what was to happen to prisoners in the compound. He replied in a matter of fact voice as though he was talking about the weather, "Oh, they will probably shoot us."

The inhumane treatment of these American POWs, many of whom hailed from the 106th Infantry Division, was correspondent to that endured by civilian concentration camp inmates. Moreover these GIs had no recourse to the rights afforded other POWs under the Geneva Convention. At the mercy of their German captors, they were brutalized, terrorized and often starved to death. Most of the Berga American soldiers' Red Cross aid packages were withheld. When one medic suggested that certain soldiers needed to be hospitalized he was sent to work in the mines. Almost all of the GIs suffered from a plethora of critical illnesses such as diarrhea or dysentery. According to two Nazi supervisors two Berga POWs were shot dead while trying to escape.

While only a handful of GIs were forced to work at night—the civilian workers usually worked the night shift—on the rare occasions that they did temperatures at times fell as low as 20°F to 30°F below zero. One American POW later attested that whenever a civilian laborer collapsed he was immediately shot.

The majority of 106th POWs were dispatched to Stalag IX-B and IX-A, while others ended up in other camps around Germany, including Stalag XII-A in Limberg, Stalag IV-B in Mühlberg and Stalag VIII-A in Görlitz.

Sergeant John P. Kline, M Company, 423d Infantry Regiment

The Stalag at Görlitz was in a desolate, wind-swept area. There were the usual two fences of barbed wire around the perimeter, with guard towers. There was a wire, about knee high about 50 feet from the inside fence. If they caught you there you could be shot, and probably would have been. I have not heard of any attempts to escape—where would you go and where would you get the strength to try? There was a large barren area back of the barracks, used for recreation and exercise. It being mid-winter, I only ventured into that area a couple of times, to see what it was all about.

The buildings were single-story wood frame and would accommodate, normally, about 500 men. (I have no idea of the number in each building at the time I was there. They were extremely over-crowded.) They were quite large and separated into two sections. There were no regular beds. They had wooden platforms, about four high, that we slept on. Very much like in a chicken coop. All we had to spread on the slats were our two thin blankets. I carried bruises on my hips and upper legs for months after I was liberated. They were caused by the hard boards I slept on in camp, as well as from the floors in the many buildings we slept in during the evacuation march.

I don't remember the barracks as being too cold. There was some sort of small stove, but not much fuel. We were out of the wind, and the many bodies huddled close together probably accounted for the warmth. I did not catch a cold during my captivity. I did come down with a very severe cold during my first sick leave at home.

The toilet (latrine) was outside and it could not be used after lights out. There was a small open pit toilet in the corner of the barracks, for emergencies during the night. Heaven forbid if you had to use it, for it was usually occupied. The small convenience of toilet paper was non-existent. There was a washroom with an industrial-type wash basin, with spray nozzles for washing your hands. Unfortunately the nozzles did not work. Fortunately there was another ordinary faucet on the wall that did work, so we used it. The washroom was always ice cold. There were no "Hilton Hotel" towels nor toilet paper for our use.

Before being liberated, over the course of two months John Kline would have to suffer a 415-mile march from Stalag VIII-A to Helmstedt. When he was liberated at 1000 hours, April 13 he wrote in his diary: "An American artillery captain just walked into the infirmary with a large box of cigarettes, chocolate and K-rations. He says he is happy to see us. If he only knew how happy we are to see him. I couldn't help it, I had to cry."

Private First Class Leon Goldberg, D Company, 422d Infantry Regiment (President of the 106th Infantry Division Association)
My dog tags put me in a potentially dangerous situation. On them was the letter H for Hebrew. There I was, a Jew, about to be taken prisoner by

Adolf Hitler's army. We knew the Nazis had passed laws against Jews and that the Gestapo rounded up Jews, but we didn't know what was done with them. We hadn't heard anything about concentration camps or gas chambers.

We were herded into a group and ordered to march. We marched for eight days, from sun-up to sundown, and slept in the snow or in a clearing if one was near. We were given a piece of bread once a day and, on occasion, a tablespoon of molasses.

The second phase of the journey was the most wretched. At a train depot, we were loaded onto windowless boxcars and made to stand shoulder to shoulder in rows. It was so tight that if you picked your feet up from the ground, the pressure from the other guys' bodies would hold you up. The worst was that Allied planes overhead shot at our train, believing the boxcars were transporting goods for the Germans. It was our own guys shooting at us! The bullets ripped right through the boxcars and made this whizzing, zipping sound. Guys in my boxcar got hit: one was standing right next to me. There was nothing we could do for them. All those who were hit were left by the side of the tracks when the train stopped. This part of the journey went on for five days.

On December 31 we arrived at Stalag IV-B, a British non-commissioned officers' prisoner of war camp near the middle of Germany. This was the first time we had to show our dog tags. British soldiers registered us and none of them commented on the H on my tags. I was merely assigned to one of the barracks. The bunks inside were set edge to edge and piled three high to the ceiling.

There was no heat, no blankets, and no change of clothes. We wore the clothes we had and were allowed to rinse them just once a week. A meal was bread, watery soup and sometimes a small potato. POWs were allowed to shower once a week, with 30 seconds of hot water and 30 seconds of cold, in concrete rooms with spigots in the ceiling. British soldiers who had been in the POW camp the longest imparted this and other vital information to the newly arrived Americans. The most important thing they told me was to keep moving. We were given time to exercise outdoors, and the British said, "Keep your body moving or you'll die."

We had a secret radio. It was kept in pieces in different barracks so the Germans wouldn't find it during inspections. But it worked very well, and we could get the BBC on it, so we knew what was going on with the war.

The POWs already knew about the battle in the Ardennes when we arrived at Stalag IV-B. They also knew that the Russians were closing in from the northeast while the Americans made progress from the southwest. The best news of all: there were other Jews in the camp.

As I got to know the other prisoners, I told them I was Jewish and asked if they thought I'd be mistreated. They said I wouldn't and that there were other Jews in the camp. I sought them out. I found Jewish soldiers from England, Australia, and the Middle East who'd been captured in various campaigns. They had been at Stalag IV-B for a long time—years in most cases—and had not been tortured.

I couldn't understand why. Jews who fought in the German army during World War I were sent to concentration camps, as were Jews from the Soviet army held in POW camps. Stalag IV-B's Jewish POWs could've been loaded into boxcars and shipped to nearby Buchenwald, which wasn't liberated until April 1945.

I believe that the officers in charge of Stalag IV-B were different from those elsewhere in the German military. They saw us as soldiers first and as Jews second, if at all. I believe this to be true.

In mid-May 1945, five months after arriving, we awoke to find the Germans had abandoned our camp. Soon Russians arrived and eventually they escorted us through the German countryside. With a group of seven other Americans I headed out to find the American lines. We were on our own.

We walked three days before we met an American armored unit, cleaning their equipment. They put us on a plane to Paris, where we were hospitalized. I remained at an Army hospital for over five months, suffering from hepatitis and severe hypothermia on my feet. The hypothermia caused nerve damage that still brings me pain.

I was cleared to leave Europe on July 4, 1945. After arriving at La Guardia Airport in New York, I was bussed to an army base nearby for overnight. The next morning I was flown to an Army hospital in Atlantic City where I remained until December 1945, when I was discharged.

The price paid by those who were taken prisoner was a high one indeed but they did their duty. They had displayed extreme resilience and fortitude, which sapped all the courage they could muster. All were emaciated and many were gravely ill, having survived incarceration by a cruel and soulless enemy, and many were so physically and mentally traumatized that they would never speak of their experiences again.

CHAPTER 10

HOLDING THE CROSSROADS

When he ordered his men to take up position at the crossroads Major Arthur C. Parker had allegedly said something to the effect of "We will run no more. Here we will stand and fight and here we will make a difference." It sounds defiant and courageous now but one can only assume that after days of enduring sustained combat, the statement didn't go down all too well with some of his men but they accepted their fate and got to work. Parker was a man they could follow anywhere. He had the guts, the determination and the insight to see it through.

For the survivors of the 589th Field Artillery Battalion there could have been no more terrifying prospect than the one facing them when they dug in at Baraque de Fraiture. Dense mist obscured depth of vision and every noise would have resonated through the all-encapsulating gloom as they waited and waited. Freezing weather conditions caused temperatures to dip to well below zero as the men did everything they could to stave off the numbing cold. They knew that the Germans were heading their way and there had already been a few exchanges, but that's about all they knew. GIs huddled in foxholes, checked their rifles and machine guns and kept their heads well down. The nights had been long and bitter on that exposed plateau in the Ardennes in the winter of 1944. Teeth chattered and fingers froze on the triggers as tense moments passed in anticipation of the approaching storm. The cold subdued the fear and the longing for warmth eradicated almost all other considerations.

They knew that the Germans could strike at any minute and they knew that they could be blown to pieces or maimed beyond recognition but they had a job to do. Thousands of miles from home and about to face a desperate enemy, some of these young GIs talked in hushed tones while others attempted to get an hour or two of troubled sleep. The first couple of days had been deceptively quiet but it was becoming apparent that something big was going to go down. Around midnight December 20, a group of German bicycle scouts arrived on the road. This forward German patrol allegedly numbering around 80 men approached the crossroads from the direction of the town of Houffalize roughly 12 miles south of Baraque de Fraiture. The actual number of Germans has never been precisely determined but it's entirely possible that they numbered less than half of what is stated in other accounts. As soon as their wheels and boots were heard crunching the snow, the U.S. half-tracks opened up with their quad-four machine guns. Bullets and tracers pierced the early morning gloom and within seconds fountains of blood were sprayed onto the virgin snow as fragments of German bodies began flying in all directions. The dead and wounded were grenadiers of the 560th VGD. They'd inadvertently stumbled across a daisy chain of mines in close proximity to the crossroads OP, which alerted the defenders. A further concern was that a German prisoner they captured said that he was a member of the 2d SS Panzer Division who had been given the job of scouting out the route of advance of the German assault.

Unbeknown to the young GIs at Baraque de Fraiture, the location was going to be the prime objective allocated to the infamous 2d SS Panzer Division Das Reich ("The Empire"), who intended to use this vital crossroads to break through to the Ourthe valley and progress from there to the River Meuse. The task of crushing American resistance at Baraque de Fraiture was given to SS-Obersturmbannführer Otto Weidinger and his SS Panzergrenadier Regiment 4 (Der Führer). When the Germans began probing, sporadic attacks at this crossroads they had scant idea of the numbers they were up against. The usually good German intelligence and reconnaissance had failed to estimate the strength or the number of units dug in there. John Schaffner had other considerations.

John Schaffner, Scout, Battery B, 589th Field Artillery Battalion

Next morning at the crossroads the weather remained miserable, cold, wet and foggy with a little more snow for good measure. If the enemy was around, he was keeping it a secret. The day went very slowly. (This kind of time is usually spent getting your hole just a bit deeper, you never know how deep is going to be deep enough.) Now and then one of our guys would pop off a few rounds at something, real or imagined.

The Battalion, on order from the CG, Div. Arty. was to prepare to move closer to Vielsalm to draw equipment and supplies but that never happened. Some men and supplies were sent to us from Vielsalm. The enemy was reported in Samree by an observer and firing data was computed using a 1:50,000-scale map and a safety pin for measuring a firing plot. Two rounds were fired for adjustment and then two volleys fired for effect. The observer reported, "Mission accomplished."

We were joined by some people of the 203d AAA, 7th Armored Division equipped with three M-16 half-tracks mounted with a brace of four .50-caliber machine guns and an M8 Scout Car with a 37mm cannon. I thought at the time, I'd hate to be in front of that quad-50 when it went off. Little did I know at the time that I would be. This weapon was positioned to fire directly down the road to Houffalize. We were also joined by a platoon of the 87th Recon Squadron. Plans were made for coordination of fire from all weapons, outposts were manned and telephone communications installed.

Group B: Established contact with Division CP at Vielsalm and was ordered to return there which was done via Dinant and Marche. They arrived at Vielsalm in a complete blackout. This group spent the night in a very warm shower room in one of the Belgian Army barracks.

Group A; Later in the evening, Captain Brown sent me, with another B Battery GI, Ken Sewell, to a foxhole in the ditch at the side of the road to Houffalize, about a couple hundred yards out from the crossroads (hard to remember the distance exactly). We were the outpost and had a field telephone hookup to Captain A.C. Brown's CP. Captain Brown told us to just sit tight and report any movement we observed. There was a "daisy chain" of mines strung across the road a few yards ahead of our position to stop any vehicles. The darkness was made even deeper by the thick fog that night, with a silence to match. Now and then a pine tree would drop some snow or make a noise. I think my eyelids and ears were set on "Full Open."

So, here we sat in this hole in the ground, just waiting and watching, until about midnight, when we could hear strange noises in the fog. It was very dark and our visibility was extremely limited, but, we were able to discern what was making the strange noise as about a dozen Germans soldiers riding on bicycles came into view. They stopped in the road when they came on the mines. Being unaware of our presence, not ten yards away, they stood there in front of us, in the middle of the road, probably talking over what to do next. We could hear the language was not English and they were wearing "square" helmets. Sewell and I were in big trouble. This was a first for us, to be this close to the enemy. Thinking that there were too many for us to take on with a carbine, I took the telephone and whispered our situation to Captain Brown. His orders were to, "Keep your head down and when you hear me fire my .45 the first time we will sweep the road with the AAA quad 50s. When that stops, I'll fire my .45 again and then we will hold fire while you two come out of your hole and return to the CP. Make it quick!" And that's the way it happened. That German patrol never knew what hit them. On hearing the .45 the second time, Ken and I left our hole, and keeping low, ran back toward our perimeter. I was running so hard that my helmet bounced off my head and went rolling out into the darkness. I thought, "To hell with it" and never slowed down to retrieve it. I lost sight of Ken and honestly don't remember ever seeing him again. (I heard many years later that he was captured along with Bernard Strohmier, John Gatens and others after the Germans took the crossroads.)

By calling out the password "Coleman," I got safely past our perimeter defense and was then shot at (and missed) by somebody at the howitzer position as I approached it. After a blast of good old American obscenities they allowed me through and I reported to Captain Brown. (The official book says that there was an eighty-man patrol from the 560th Volksgrenadier Division and the 2d SS Panzer Division out there that night. Maybe the rest of them were back in the fog somewhere.)

Meanwhile back at the respective 106th Infantry and 7th Armored Division HQ at Vielsalm, General Ridgway felt compelled to add some clarity and cohesion to the proceedings. He summoned Jones to Hasbrouck's office. Something didn't seem quite right with Jones. He'd seemed listless and distracted and hadn't exhibited any interest in the coming day's operation. Ridgway wasn't impressed with the command structure of the Goose Egg, regarding it as being overly complex. With his deputy chief of staff taking down the order, Ridgway dictated his changes. He appointed Jones deputy commander of XVIII Corps and put the entire operation under the command of Hasbrouck and 7th Armored Division. He made Hoge Hasbrouck's deputy, and appointed

Brigadier General Perrin, then deputy commander of the 106th Infantry Division, its temporary commander. Once all the command changes had been allocated, Ridgway turned to Hasbrouck and said, "Bob, start pulling your people back as soon as possible".

Ridgway had noticed that Jones was indeed a bit listless. The man was gravely ill and there's every indication that he'd had to contend with some serious health problems during the previous days. The accumulated stress of having two regiments captured and not knowing the whereabouts of his own son, Lieutenant Alan Jones serving with the 423d, was weighing heavily on the general. At that time Lieutenant Jones was listed as missing in action, and it would be some time before news arrived that he was a POW. Just after midnight, Jones succumbed to the accumulated stress and collapsed unconscious onto the HQ floor. He had suffered a serious heart attack, and was immediately sent to an evacuation hospital in Liège.

On the night of the 22d two M7 Priests from the 5th Armored Division arrived. Combined, the initial U.S. forces at Baraque de Fraiture increased from 110 to around 300 soldiers. The timely arrival of reinforcements at the crossroads coincided with probing attacks by the 560th Volksgrenadier Division who were in the process of feeling out the American positions. During one of these attacks mortar shell fragments wounded Major Parker, and despite his protestations he lost consciousness and had to be evacuated. Major Elliot Goldstein, the original battalion executive officer but actually junior to Parker, took command. On the morning of December 22 Goldstein tasted the crisp pre-dawn air when he heard vehicles moving and the sound of approaching infantry. He immediately ordered his men to open up with everything they had. The cacophony that ensued sounded like a full-scale battle. The previous night temperatures had plummeted and a heavy snowfall had descended on the plateau obscuring many features of the landscape.

A few miles away the 82d Airborne's General James Gavin was examining a detailed map of the area. He noticed that the N15 road from Bastogne to Liège was precariously exposed. He recognized that if the Germans reached this road they would have the means and the possibility of flanking the position of his men further north. Gavin, the youngest general in the U.S. Army decided to take action. He released his

2d Battalion, 325th Glider Infantry Regiment, the regimental reserve, with orders to go to the crossroads immediately.

John Gatens, Battery A, 589th Field Artillery Battalion

Although historians have disagreed as to where the No. 1 howitzer was located, I can place it without question. My 105 howitzer was at the intersection of the Samree–Manhay road, pointing at Regne. Exact opposite corner and across the street from the farmhouse and barn. On December 20, a tank from the 3d Armored Division showed up. He parked in the road near the farmhouse, with his gun pointing down the road towards Manhay. Of course, we were very happy to see the tankers. One of the men jumped out and walked up to the corner. He was looking in the direction of Regne. He wasn't there too long when he fell to the ground. A few of us went over to see what had happened to him. He had a bullet hole in his forehead. Unfortunately, he didn't have his helmet on, only the soft tanker's hat that they wear. Needless to say, no one went wandering around after that. That's why I can't say where the other two howitzers were. I never did visit with them, and I didn't see them from my position. Immediately after the tanker fell, it was determined that he was hit by a sniper in the woods down the Regne Road. I was given an order (I can't remember by whom) to fire a few rounds into the trees. We never heard from anyone down there after that.

At the 7th Armored Division HQ in Vielsalm, General Hasbrouck waited for word that his two harassed combat commands on the front line of the Goose Egg were ready to disengage. His G-2 told him that the 2d SS Panzer Division was heading for Baraque de Fraiture and Salmchâteau. If they beat back the 82d Airborne, they would close off the two-mile-wide exit route and he'd lose nearly two entire divisions in the Goose Egg.

Meanwhile the 3d Armored Division's Task Force Kane dispatched a detachment from Manhay south to Baraque de Fraiture, to reinforce the mixed collection of GIs already there.

During the night of December 22/23 the 2d SS Panzer was waiting in the final assembly area in preparation for the impending attack. They had experienced some fuel supply problems that prevented their immediate advance towards the crossroads. In the course of the evening sufficient fuel arrived to allow the 4th Panzergrenadier-Regiment, some tanks, and an artillery battalion to advance. The grenadiers relieved the small reconnaissance detachments of the 560th VGD that had had been keeping a close eye on the crossroads. When they arrived they filed through the woods to set up a cordon west and north of the crossroads. The commander of the 4th Panzergenadier-Regiment consigned his 2d Battalion to the right of the main north–south highway, while his 3d Battalion deployed around and to the rear of the crossroads.

The first wave of attacks against Baraque de Fraiture went in just before dawn December 23, when the German 2d Battalion orchestrated a surprise attack. At around 0430 hours a combined assault was made by SS patrols on the crossroads area. A bitter fight ensued before they were eventually driven back by the men from the 325th Glider Regiment. The initial attacks were successfully repulsed, and an SS officer and NCO were taken prisoner by the U.S. defenders but it was far from over. It was in fact the start of what was going to be a long and bloody day.

A complication arose for the defenders when the Germans intercepted communications from their forward observers using captured American radios. Later that morning Lieutenant Colonel Walter B. Richardson of Task Force Y, 3d Armored Division sent additional infantry and a platoon of tanks to the crossroads. Throughout the morning heavy German mortar and artillery fire rained down on the heads of the defenders and as noon approached the barrage increased in momentum.

John Schaffner, Scout, Battery B, 589th Field Artillery Battalion

It seems that the Germans had come closer each time our perimeter got smaller, and were ready to end it. The sequence of events on this day I cannot accurately recall but I was in and out of foxholes and, on occasion, running into the shelter of the stone building for a warm-up (or thaw-out). The fog would roll in and out, giving us limited visibility. I would fire at anything I saw moving around in range of my hole. This weather was tough on us, but I think it was to our advantage from a defensive point of view. I'm sure our enemy was not able to determine exactly what he had to overcome to take the crossroads. Whenever he came into view we would drive him back into the fog. Our ammunition was running out. I had one clip of carbine rounds and could find no more. Word had come around that when the ammo ran out and the Germans came it would be every man for himself, escape if you could, otherwise a surrender was prudent.

I never heard this as an order directly from an officer but it did not take a genius to assess our situation. We were apparently surrounded, but the Germans were taking the easiest route, the hard surface roads. That left the fields open.

Late afternoon, probably after 1600, the final assault came. Mortars, small arms and fire from tanks. I was in the stone building, sitting on the floor with my back to the wall. Harold Kuizema was with me. This room must have been a kitchen at one time because I recall a wood-burning cook stove and a GI who I didn't know trying to heat something at it. Something big hit that wall and exploded right over our heads into the room. It must have hit high or it would have gotten the both of us. As it was, it filled the room with debris and dust. That was all the motivation we needed to leave there. To wait for another one never crossed my mind. We (Harold and I) went to the front door. They were coming and we were going. It was that simple. Some of our people were going to the cellar. I didn't like that idea. So once outside I crawled to the road and the ditch. There were some cattle milling about on the road and much smoke so I got up and ran through the cattle to the ditch on the far side and once again dropped down to avoid the German fire. On this side of the road was a snow-covered field very open, but it was "away" from the attack so that's the direction I took. Not far into the field Harold went down. As I got to him I saw two GIs approaching from the other direction. It was apparent that Harold was not going any farther on his own so between the three of us we moved him the remaining distance to the shelter of the woods and into the company of a patrol of infantrymen from the 82d Airborne Division. When we reached the shelter of the woods and I looked back at the crossroads, the whole sky seemed to be lit up by the flames from the burning building and vehicles. Our wounded man was evacuated, and I received permission to tag along with these 82d Airborne Division GIs, which I did until late sometime the next day (December 24) when I was able to locate some 106th Division people. There were some vehicles from the 589th with this group that were not with us at Parker's Crossroads, and one was loaded with duffel bags—mine was with them. Another miracle, clean underwear and socks.

Major Elliot Goldstein had driven over to Manhay to beg Lieutenant Colonel Walter Richardson of the 3d Armored Division to urgently give him some reinforcements to assist in holding the crossroads. Richardson wasted no time in complying with the request and ordered a platoon of tanks to head down there at once.

Major Elliot Goldstein, 589th Field Artillery
Colonel Richardson knew we needed help when he saw the two SS prisoners. While we had not had access to any intelligence, he had access to his Division's intelligence and knew what we didn't know—that there was a major attack coming our way and that it was important to hold the crossroads. He ordered Lieutenant Colonel (then Major) Olin F. Brewster to accompany me back to the crossroads so that he could take command of the defense. He ordered a platoon each of armored infantry and of medium tanks and a company of paratroopers from the 509th Parachute Infantry Battalion to go to the crossroads immediately. The 509th was able to get into the crossroads prior to the German attack. The other units were held up by a German roadblock. (I was so shocked by the events which followed that my memory of the sequence of events is cloudy, but Major Brewster's recollections set out below aided my memory.) We drove towards the crossroads from Manhay. We were stopped before we got to the crossroads by troops who said we couldn't proceed down the road. Major Brewster and I parked the jeeps and walked towards the crossroads, keeping well off the road. My memory is very vivid, however, of a round, fired by a tank, going by us in the center of the road. It looked as though it was only six feet off the ground, and flying in a flat trajectory. It was close, so we took to the woods and tried to reach the crossroads through them. We were never able to get close, and meanwhile, artillery shells were bursting in the treetops and showering shell fragments in the area. We finally concluded that we couldn't go farther and retreated. It was the saddest day of my life. I had accomplished my mission, but too late, and I felt that I had let down the brave men who had fought so valiantly, and whom I'd left behind.

The principal emotion I felt was anger, anger at myself for not succeeding in extricating my command from the trap; anger at the Germans; anger at the commander, whoever he might be, for not having sooner sent aid to us. Although I had escaped almost certain capture or death, I felt neither happy nor relieved since the men I commanded were being overrun. I thought all our efforts had come to naught.

The ground was prepared for the final attack as sometime around 1600 hours German artillery hammered the U.S. positions for 20 minutes. As the shelling abated two panzer companies moved ominously towards the crossroads. Silhouetted by crepuscular light and with freshly turned snow, the foxholes and gun positions were easily discernable to the approaching Germans.

Shortly after, the GI defenders' blood ran cold as they saw eight German Mark IV tanks escorted by a horde of highly motivated SS Panzergrenadiers coming right at them. The initial wave approached from the south as the subsequent wave approached from the west accompanied by half-tracks. The 589th's howitzers began blazing away and within moments they'd taken out two Mark IVs. Suddenly another wave of SS Panzergrenadiers and two Panther tanks emerged along the road from the direction of Salmchâteau in the east. Two Sherman tanks had already been destroyed and the Panthers quickly notched up two more.

As twilight turned to darkness and nightfall descended on the crossroads it appeared as if the very gates of hell had been blown wide open. Dense Ardennes mist descended on the position as SS troops were swarming in and returning fire from all directions. The GIs fought with every ounce of strength they could muster to stave off wave after incessant wave of determined SS. The Sherman's frequently scored close-range direct hits on the Panthers just to see their shells impotently bounce off the thick armor plate of these almost indomitable German tanks.

John Gatens, Battery A, 589th Field Artillery Battalion

Major Goldstein, knowing that the situation was now hopeless, that we were out of ammunition and medical supplies, took off [to get reinforcements]. If he had stayed, he would have realized that the order to withdraw was still in effect. We possibly might have been around to fight another day.

At about 1530 in the afternoon all hell broke loose. Captain Brown came around and told us to be ready—when the artillery attack stopped the infantry and tanks would be coming in. Half of my crew were in the house getting warm. I made a run for it to get my men back to the gun to be ready for the assault.

Once inside, I got my men together, but we never did make it back to the gun. I was standing in the doorway ready to go when a shell hit. The concussion picked me up and sent me flying against the back wall. I sat there a few minutes in a daze. I had to feel for my legs and arms to make sure they were still there.

At about this same time the farmhouse itself was now being hit with incoming shells. The roof was on fire and some of the fellows were trying to put the fire out. In this building there were also some wounded men. Our main concern at this point was how we were going to help them. Our concern was soon ended. The shelling stopped and at the same time there was a German tank outside the door. His gun was pointing in the door. A German officer shouted out, "Are you coming out or do I tell this guy to fire?" No one can be a hero when a tank is staring down your throat.

Some of the surrounding area men had already been rounded up and were standing in rows on the road. We filed out of the building and joined the rows of men. They made us remove our overcoats so they could search us. They took anything of value. I was wearing my wife's (although not at that time) high school ring. That was gone. The other items were money, cigarettes and chocolate (every GI had a few concentrated chocolate bars called D bars that didn't melt. They were hard and you had to scrape off shreds, or if you had good teeth you could break off a chunk), my gloves, my wool knit cap and my fountain pen. For some reason they would not take wedding rings. Either they were superstitious or they had some respectability. It was now approximately 1750 hours. The weather was bitter cold, but now I had no overcoat, gloves or wool knit cap. It was a cold helmet and field jacket from here on. How I made that winter with just those clothes I'll never know.

Gradually the defenders began to succumb to the ferocity of the German onslaught as their casualties mounted. Captain Junior R. Woodruff, F Company, 325th Glider Infantry frantically radioed his battalion commander to inform him that holding the crossroads was becoming untenable. The perimeter defenses were gradually disintegrating. The captain's request to vacate the position was initially denied in the hope that further reinforcements would arrive to save the situation. When this didn't transpire Colonel Charles W. Billingslea, 325th Glider Regiment reluctantly gave his permission to his men to move back and set up on the highest ground north of Baraque de Fraiture.

German tanks were now in dangerously close proximity to the perimeter and to all but the dead or fatally wounded it was becoming glaringly obvious that the crossroads would soon be irrevocably lost. All three of the 589th Field Artillery Battalion's howitzers had been abandoned along with two assault guns of Task Force Kane, the quad-four half-tracks and every vehicle belonging to the troop of 87th Armored Cavalry.

There could have no more terrifying prospect for a young GI waiting in a foxhole than to see the vague silhouettes of well-armed SS troops looming menacingly out of the fog in their direction. In some cases vicious hand-to-hand fights ensued as the Germans lunged at the GIs in the foxholes filling the tainted night air with agonized screams. Some managed to hole up for a while in a farmhouse but after it was repeatedly attacked they were compelled to abandon the position and struggle back to their own lines. Some made it, some didn't.

Superior weight of arms and material finally began to subdue the defenders. But that ad hoc combination of U.S. troops had bought valuable time again. The 106th Infantry Division artillery unit, the 589th, had been virtually annihilated and had ceased to exist as a fighting outfit but they had done more than their fair share of the fighting and inflicted terrible damage on the 2d SS Panzer Division. That damage would inevitably lead to their demise. Gradually while the more fortunate wounded survivors were extricated back to the safety of their own lines, other U.S. soldiers that had remained to the last were taken POW. These latter faced a particularly daunting prospect as rumors abounded concerning a group of POWs who had been savagely murdered by another SS unit at another crossroads farther north, not far from Malmédy. A few officers and men fought or slipped through to friendly lines, but from the 116-man Glider Rifle Company, only 44 survived to rejoin their unit.

The scant remnants of the 589th Field Artillery Battalion were assembled in the vicinity of Eronheid, then moved to Hoyment December 25, and told they would be reorganized. After drawing equipment, in preparation for the reorganization, the battalion was moved to Xhos December 27 and was notified that it would be officially disbanded. On January 1, 1945 the majority of the personnel remaining were transferred to the 591st Field Artillery Battalion and the 592d Field Artillery Battalion.

SS-Obersturmführer Horst Gresiak commander of the 2d Battalion, 2d SS Panzer Regiment, described the action at the crossroads as the most violent and the toughest battle that he experienced during the entire war.

General Gavin later wrote a letter to Major Parker about his heroic stand at what became known as and would forever be referred to as "Parker's Crossroads":

Dear Major Parker

Through correspondence with Henry D. Heaian, who was with the 106th Infantry Division in the Battle of the Bulge, I have learned of your whereabouts. 1t is a little late for to be writing you about the Battle of the Bulge, but I have been totally unaware of your whereabouts through the years.

*In the Battle of the Bulge, I was commanding the 82nd Airborne Division and we were originally given the front from Trois-Ponts to Vielsalm, including Thier Dumont. We got into very heavy fighting when the 1st Regiment of the 1st SS Panzer Division broke through the Engineers' front and occupied Stoumont. We then had the remainder of the Division at Trois-Ponts. At the same time, in twenty-four hours it came clear that the Germans were bypassing us, moving to the west [and] turning north when the opportunity presented itself. The 7th Armored and part of the 28th Infantry Division and a few of the 106th came through our lines. I was in the town of Fraiture the afternoon when you made your great stand at the crossroads. I had sent a Company from the 325th under Capt. Woodruff, to the crossroads to help hold it, so I started over in that direction myself. The fire was so intense, however, that there was no way of getting there without crawling through the woods, and it was a distance away. I decided that I had better get some more help, so I sent to the extreme left flank of the division for the 2nd Battalion of the 504th, where it had the 1st SS Regiment of the 1st Panzer Division bottled. In doing so, we uncovered the Germans and during the night of Christmas Eve they slipped through the 505th Parachute Infantry. Nevertheless I got the 2d Battalion of the 504th to back up the crossroads come what may. **The stand that your defenders made at the crossroads was one of the great actions of the war** [authors' emphasis]. It gave us at least twenty-four hours' respite so I thank you for that, and all the brave soldiers who were under your command.*

With best regards
James A. Gavin
Lieutenant General (retired)

CHAPTER II

THE GOOSE EGG AND BEYOND

As dusk descended on his HQ in Vielsalm, General Robert Hasbrouck hurriedly packed his papers. In the distance he could hear the ominous growl of German tanks pummeling centuries-old cobblestone roads as they headed for Vielsalm. Shells rained down on the place that had served as his HQ for the past five days but now it was time to get out and get out fast. The enemy had already zeroed the village of Salmchâteau. During the night 22 December 1944, vehicles of the 7th Armored Division and its attached units disengaged from their positions and prepared to begin an orderly withdrawal from St. Vith, and surrounding areas. That same night Hasbrouck and Colonel Ryan methodically worked out the plan for withdrawal. It would begin with a systematic extraction of the units on the most easterly perimeter that would syphon gradually into the main routes leading to the bridges. Their withdrawal would be covered by rearguard holding actions along the roads and trails. General Ridgway of the 82d Airborne Division estimated that it would be possible to complete the withdrawal under cover of darkness within 14 hours.

The 7th Armored's CCB, under the command of Brigadier General Bruce Clarke, had held their ground and defended well for seven days against the perpetual attacks of Manteuffel's Fifth Panzer Army. Now, at 0600 hours, December 23, on the orders of Field Marshal Montgomery they planned a daylight withdrawal from the "Fortified Goose Egg." Artillery, tank and engineering units were earmarked to move first, followed by the infantry units making their preparations to withdraw at 1600.

Hasbrouck had sent the message to the 112th Infantry Regiment's Colonel Nelson to withdraw a few hours previous. The 7th Armored Division's CCA held the northern flank against increasing German pressure while the CCB began its withdrawal to the Salm River. The only forces still on east of the Salm at Vielsalm were the machine-gun squads and rearguard of Lieutenant Colonel Moe Boylan's 87th Reconnaissance Battalion, 7th Armored Division. The rear door to the Goose Egg was rapidly closing. It was time to cauterize it and fall back to safer ground. At the very moment that Hasbrouck stepped out his HQ a German tank came around the corner and fired at his lead half-track, setting it ablaze. He and his staff dashed into a waiting jeep, and raced hell for leather toward the last bridge over the Salm River. Seconds before they crossed the bridge the tank released another round that impacted just in front of them, taking out a dispatch rider on his motorcycle. Since December 20, the defenders of St. Vith had been almost completely surrounded inside the Goose Egg, which was essentially a salient within a salient. Opposing the American defenders of the Goose Egg was a German force of approximately 54,000 from two armored divisions and one and a half infantry divisions. In addition to these, the Germans could call on another two panzer divisions and almost two infantry divisions within striking distance, if required. The withdrawal was made easier thanks to a heavy freeze during the night that allowed the use of normally impassable forest tracks.

The 424th Infantry Regiment, 106th Infantry Division and 591st Field Artillery Battalion, were down to 50 percent effectiveness. They'd been fighting non-stop for six days. They were short on sleep, food, ammunition, equipment, and had incurred hundreds of casualties. Holding the line farther west and south of the 424th was Colonel Nelson's 112th Infantry. Like the 424th they had endured had six continuous days of sustained combat. Heavily engaged with enemy units of the 62d VGD, the 112th fought fiercely while attempting to withdraw. The 112th had emphatic orders: to hold the last battalion in position as a covering force until Colonel Nelson received radio orders from General Hasbrouck personally to withdraw. At 1530 hours, Colonel Nelson reported that all units had cleared out behind his covering force and that enemy tanks were closing in. He requested permission to withdraw his 2d Battalion but there was a problem with communications so at 1630, with no word from General Hasbrouck and German tanks within 200 yards of his CP, Colonel Nelson took charge of the situation and ordered the 2d Battalion to withdraw immediately.

Once the 424th Infantry received their orders to displace they managed to head west relatively unopposed, and many of the GIs were able to ride with the 9th Armored's tanks. There were only two railroad bridges and one wooden road bridge to handle the 10,000 GIs and their vehicles leaving the Goose Egg, which was anchored by a two-mile-wide "back door" on the Salm River between Vielsalm and Salmchâteau. This was the narrow corridor connecting the fortified Goose Egg to the rest of the American lines. The 82d Airborne Division was dispatched to secure the eastern part of this corridor, from Salmchâteau–Vielsalm to Trois-Ponts, which they managed to do successfully. By daylight German assault groups had progressed west in the sectors manned by the two 7th Armored combat commands. A battalion of the 424th Infantry being held in reserve at Maldingen was briefly engaged but the general opinion at the Vielsalm HQ was that the German attacks appeared to be dissipating. St. Vith was lost but it wouldn't be in German hands for long.

Edward Prewett, 424th Regiment

We went under cover of darkness and arrived the next morning at Ferrières. There we were allowed to crawl into a hay mound and pass out. We rested all day. The old Johnny on the spot Red Cross was on the ball again. They issued a few razors and blades, a little candy, gum, etc. They couldn't have been nicer. The people of the town were swell. The little kids gave us apples, etc. It seemed the Germans committed some of their atrocities against them there.

We got a little cleaned up and they held a sick call. There wasn't anything that they could do. We all had rheumatism and trench feet. I'd gotten a pair of Arctics at Lommersweiler, but even they couldn't protect us. After the first night our feet were soaked and never given the chance to dry out. I fared better than most because of my few days with the 9th Armored. When night came we moved out of the town and the woods once again was our home for the next couple days.

We didn't have anything but that was nothing new for us by now. Three of us shared one blanket and one overcoat between us. The overcoat, I stole from the 9th Armored and the other guy stole the blanket at Ferrières. We weren't far behind the lines, because we had to keep fires down to the minimum.

The problem was the southwestern section of the corridor where Baraque de Fraiture was located. There were no available reinforcements for this section. The U.S. defenders of this position had held it as long as was humanly possible under the circumstances but now it had fallen and there were other matters in need of critical attention.

South of the crossroads, the Germans had pushed west, while to the east the only crossing point (also serving nearby Salmchâteau) on the Amblève River was the road that ran to Vielsalm. To the north, the road from Baraque de Fraiture (Parker's Crossroads) ran through Manhay to the strategically important city of Liège.

December 23, as darkness approached, F Company, 424th Regiment reached a position in a wooded area north of the Werbomont crossroads and roughly eight miles north of Manhay. This put them in relatively close proximity to General Gavin's 82d Airborne HQ and the 30th Infantry Division. The area is forested and very hilly with deep ravines that are collectively known as the Amblève valley after the river that courses along the base of the valley to the River Meuse in the west.

Irwin Smoler, B Company, 424th Regiment

We, along with the 112th Inf., formed the southern end of the Goose Egg. To get to this point I remember wading the Our River at least twice in freezing waist-high water, holding our rifles over our heads. As part of the "Fortified Goose-Egg," we had helped hold up the Germans long enough for reserves to be brought into place as well as to disrupt their timetable to get to the Meuse River. For this and some subsequent actions, the regiment, along with the other units involved, and all of its officers and men, later received the Belgian Fourragère, a unit citation.

When the order came from General Ridgway on December 23d we began a long daylight withdrawal from the Goose Egg into and through the lines of the 82d Airborne Division, which had come in from theater reserve. We dug in with them, and, as I recall, they didn't look any better than we did, and frankly, I didn't think they were any better soldiers than we were, especially after our recent experiences.

The 424th Infantry were battle-weary and completely exhausted but with the exception of a few damaged or abandoned vehicles, there was little to no evidence that 20,000 soldiers of the 7th, 9th, and 106th divisions had passed through Major General Gavin's 82d Airborne Division area behind the Fortified Goose Egg. With the approval of their commander Colonel Alexander D. Reid, and while a bitterly cold Siberian wind swept over their position, even though there were still Germans in the vicinity, the 424th felled trees and lit fires in an attempt to bring some warmth to their frozen, tired bodies.

Meanwhile, December 24, Christmas Eve, found F Company of the 424th Regiment in the village of Manhay. They were greeted with clear azure-blue skies and temperatures that dipped well below freezing. Visibility was good, and unencumbered by the notorious Ardennes mist, the dawn sun rose above the pines and bathed the countryside in stark bright light. The clear weather would provide Allied planes with an opportunity to sow destruction on the advancing German forces. Throughout the first five or six days of the German offensive the panzer columns had been able to take advantage of the inclement weather and make significant penetrations into the Allied lines. Now with clear skies these same columns were vulnerable to Allied strafing and bombing. F Company was loaded into trucks of the 7th Armored Division and sent south in the direction of the important Manhay road junction.

At Ferrières, not far from Werbomont, another 106th unit, the 423d I&R Platoon, slept soundly that night. As the sun rose in the east they realized that it was the first time they'd actually seen sunshine in over a week. There was no snow and no fog. Soon the sky was filled to the horizon with planes of every description, B-17s, B-24s, and P-38s. They could hear bombs dropping on the German positions in the distance and the clatter of machine guns as the fighters strafed the German columns. There were a few Luftwaffe planes in the sky which led to numerous dogfights as the American planes took them on.

The 2d SS Panzer Division began attacking in the direction of Manhay at 2100 hours on Christmas Eve. The German tank column had a captured American Sherman tank in the lead. Seeing the Sherman, the 7th Armored Division defenders assumed the column was the American 3d Armored Division, which was known to be changing its position. When the Germans suddenly began firing the surprise was absolute and the 7th Armored fell back in chaos. One particular German panzer inadvertently managed to reach as far west as the N15 Bastogne–Liège road and in the process had more than one close encounter with Sherman tanks.

On Christmas Eve 1944 SS-Oberscharführer Ernst Barkmann was part of the lead group attacking the villages of Manhay and Grandmenil. The company moved out at 2200 hours. SS-Hauptscharführer Franz Frauscher, a platoon leader and friend of Barkmann, was in the lead tank. Barkmann moved behind the company commander. Frauscher's platoon began taking hits and one German tank burst into flames. Barkmann was ordered forward to do some reconnaissance. It was a crystal-clear night that allowed good visibility.

Suddenly, Barkmann saw a silhouette off to the right. The tank commander had his upper torso out of the hatch. In the darkness, Barkmann thought it must be Frauscher. He ordered his driver to approach the vehicle. When they were side by side, Barkmann told his driver to cut the engine before he cupped his hands and shouted "What's going on, Franz?" The man in the other turret disappeared in a flash into his tank and slammed his hatch shut. Barkmann suddenly realized the situation he was in. He yelled over the intercom, "Gunner, the tank next to us is enemy. Knock it out!" The Panther's turret started to turn, but the cannon banged against the other tank's turret.

Barkmann immediately ordered his drive to reverse ten feet before giving the fire order. Within moments flames were leaping from the opposing tank. Then two American tanks started rolling out of the woods towards Barkmann's Panther, which fired and hit one of them, causing the other to retreat back into the cover of the woods.

As Barkmann's tank moved forward it arrived at a sizeable open area flanked by woods. It was then that he saw nine American tanks with their guns pointing to the road. Barkmann ordered his driver to continue moving forward regardless and the Americans must have assumed that the tank was one of their own because the Panther passed through the U.S. position without being engaged. Suddenly, there were houses on both sides of the road. Barkmann's Panther had reached what was at that time American-occupied village of Manhay.

Barkmann's tank drove straight past a U.S. HQ before reaching a crossroads. The road to the left led to the village of Erezée. In his haste to get away from Manhay he continued straight ahead in the direction of Liège. But in doing so, Barkmann inadvertently went from the frying pan and into the fire. He ran into the lead elements of a Sherman tank column that were assembled in groups of nine. Parked in between were staff cars with officers in them. The tank crews stood around their vehicles, chattering and smoking. It was a surreal situation and Barkmann estimated that he moved past at least ten companies before getting to the N15 road. Somehow he managed to get back to his own lines and lived to tell the tale of his excursion.

During the early hours of Christmas Eve the surviving units of the 106th Infantry Division's final disposition went into action. The 592d Field Artillery Battalion was attached to VIII Corps. The 591st Field Artillery Battalion was attached to 7th Armored Division. The 112th Infantry attached to CCB 9th Armored were both attached to Ridgway's XVIII Airborne Corps, and then to Gavin's 82d Airborne Division. Major General Hasbrouck appealed for more infantry to support his 7th Armored Division, and with the recommendation of Brigadier General Herbert Perrin, Acting Commander, 106th Infantry Division, was granted the attachment of the 424th Infantry. Perrin was consequently assigned as Assistant Division Commander, 7th Armored Division by Hasbrouck, and the original 106th Infantry Division effectively ceased to exist as a division, but would still be some months before the division was officially deactivated as there was still a war to fight. The 591st, 592d, and 424th still had plenty of fight, and would be tested in the battle for Manhay.

The Germans duly captured Manhay. Allied commanders were concerned that they would head north toward Liège and, in the process, outflank American positions. So early on the morning of Christmas Day, 1944, the 424th were digging foxholes in preparation of a potential German onslaught. As they dug they anxiously watched the nearby hills for signs of the enemy.

Norris E. Van Cleave, K Company, 424th Regiment

Occasional contacts with enemy forces further endangered the withdrawing troops. Soon, only one out of every four men who had gone into battle with the company remained with it. At last we arrived at a place where a Christmas dinner type of meal was being served to American troops. I began to eat ravenously as a respite from the K and C rations. But nearly as quickly as I began I was full, because the sustained diet of concentrated foods had shrunk my stomach.

Now the American armored forces had turned the German offense around, and we were moving up to rejoin the fight. Although I was cheered by the news of victory, I remained disappointed in Christmas. There had been no recent mail from home. I suppose that the breakthrough had separated me from correspondence as well as from most of the GIs I had known best. Overall, it had been a rotten Christmas, like no Christmas at all.

In early evening, near sundown on a cold winter day, we reached the edge of a Belgian village and began to assemble shelter halves to make tents. I shivered at the thought of another cold night without the warmth of fuel. Suddenly, a company runner came by our tent site and told us to remake our packs and assemble with the company. So now we are going to hike some more, I thought. But we didn't.

Instead, we were going to spend a night indoors! The people of that Belgian village had invited all of us into their homes! My tent buddy and I were ushered into a modest frame home by a middle-aged couple and a little preschool girl. We were offered access to a bathtub and beds, but we declined. We explained that we must keep ourselves ready to go at a moment's notice. Really, it had been so long since I had had a bath and a change of clothing that I wouldn't have felt it proper to mar their living conditions.

We spread our sleeping bags on a thick living-room carpet and soon fell asleep. When we awakened, a pleasant smell was emitting from the kitchen. We learned it was waffles, a special Belgian treat they usually reserved for Fridays. I never knew whether that was Friday or not, but the waffles were great. As we bade goodbye to rejoin our company, our host and hostess stood at the door. As we shook hands the eyes of our hostess brimmed with tears. I often have regretted that I didn't get the name of these friends and their village for later contact. I suppose the language barrier kept me from trying to get better acquainted. But I have since accepted that night in their home as the fulfillment of my Christmas season in 1944.

The 424th was ordered to move closer to Manhay. They could have seen American P-38 fighter planes, those with the distinctive twin fuselages, dropping bombs in the hazy outline of the village of Manhay, zeroing in on of the 2d SS Panzer Division tanks and vehicles.

Major General Ridgway ordered Brigadier General Hasbrouck of the 7th Armored Division to retake Manhay by nightfall on Christmas Day. On the afternoon of Christmas Day the 2d Battalion, 424th Regiment and units of the 7th Armored Division were selected for the task. The troops were told to leave sleeping bags and blanket rolls behind to improve their mobility. The fight was on.

CHAPTER 12

TAKING THE FIGHT TO THE GERMANS

It was Christmas Eve 1944, early in the afternoon when Field Marshal Montgomery pulled up to Ridgway's HQ in an open car. He stepped out in his usual officious manner, saluted the guards, and went inside. He immediately told Ridgway that it was essential for the First Army to build a solid northern flank to prepare for a coming counterattack against the Germans that would be conducted by General "Lightning" Joe Collins's VII Corps. Ridgway reserved his opinions for the moment and respectfully listened to what Monty had to say.

The two shook hands and Montgomery was off to Hodges' First Army HQ at Tongeren in the Dutch-speaking part of Belgium. Half an hour later Ridgway's commanders, Hoge, Hasbrouck, Gavin, and others gathered at his HQ. They stood around a map of the Ardennes as Ridgway began explaining his plan to them.

"Starting after darkness, CCA, 7th Armored will withdraw to Manhay and the 82d Airborne to Trois-Ponts," said Ridgway as he indicated the locations on the map. Then Ridgway sat down with pen in hand and wrote his proclamation:

In my opinion, this is the last dying gasp of the German Army. He is putting everything he has into this fight. We are going to smash that final drive here today in this Corps zone. This command is the command that will smash the German offensive spirit for this war. Impress every man in your division with that spirit. We are going to lick the Germans here today.

The U.S. generals would withdraw their units to the line Montgomery had ordered, and not another step. They were going to stand, fight, and defeat the Germans. December 25, the 591st Field Artillery Battalion and some of the service elements of the division were attached to the 7th Armored Division. The 592d Field Artillery Battalion became attached to the XVIII Airborne Corps Artillery.

T/5 Milton J. Schober, F Company, 2d Battalion, 424th Regiment

So here we were in the early morn of Christmas Day, 1944, digging foxholes as protection against the German onslaught which never came. We dug and anxiously watched the nearby hills for signs of the enemy. Hours passed, nothing happened and we began to wonder if our leadership knew what was going on.

We didn't know it then, but Major General Ridgway, our corps commander, had ordered Brigadier General Hasbrouck, of the 7th Armored Division, to retake Manhay by darkness on Christmas Day! In the mid-afternoon we learned that our 2d Battalion of the 424th Regiment and units of the 7th Armored Division were selected for this task. We were given no briefing as to objectives or anything else, but merely told to lighten up for the attack, that is, to leave such things as sleeping bags behind to improve our mobility.

We moved out along the edge of the tree line in a single file on the high ground. In the process of this movement, the activity was noticed by the Germans who started some machine-gun firing, not too intense, but enough for a couple of men to receive leg wounds.

It was late afternoon, in twilight, when we reached the positions from which we were to begin our attack. Word was given for us to emerge from the woods and begin our race downhill across open farmland toward houses along the main highway. As we began our attack and picked up running speed, not a shot was fired by the Germans. Our confidence increased as momentum picked up, and whooping and hollering started, with the troops firing wildly to the front. It was as if we were playing a game of "cowboys and Indians." The open area that we were traversing was 300–500 yards in my recollection, and the only cover provided along that route in our area was a sunken farm road cutting across the fields. I remember running down on to the road and up the mound on the other side with barely a pause. Still no fire from the enemy. But then, about 30 yards behind, it started. Rapid fire machine guns began their stutter and traversed the field from my right across my front. It wasn't difficult to spot their source because of their use of tracer bullets whose entire trajectory could be followed.

Forward movement stopped as if by command, and we hit the ground. Thirty or 40 feet ahead my squad leader, Mike Jerosky, was hit as he reached a wire fence 100–150 feet behind the house toward which I was moving. George Evansco, close to Jerosky, also was hit but much more seriously. I'll never forget his screams for a medic followed by the words, "I'm dying!"

Now the weather had changed, the moon shone bright as patrols of Brigadeführer Heinz Lammerding's 2d SS Panzer Division left the cover of the woods and made their way across the undulating fields and meadows for Manhay. Moving across open fields without their white camouflage wasn't the ideal way to spend Christmas Eve: they were dangerously exposed and simply dark targets for the Allied artillery.

German Fifth Panzer Army commander von Manteuffel was eating his Christmas dinner of American K-rations while reviewing his army's situation with Hitler's adjutant, Major Johann mayer. General Jodl had rushed Mayer to Manteuffel that morning after a call from Manteuffel the previous night in which the general had called for the drive to Antwerp to be immediately abandoned. The 2d Panzer SS Division had been isolated by the Americans, and even though Manteuffel was rushing the 9th SS Panzer from the west and the Panzer Lehr from the southwest to remedy the situation, he wasn't feeling optimistic at the prospects. Manteuffel informed Mayer that if Hitler gave his immediate permission, the Fifth Panzer Army could wheel north, trap the Americans east of the Meuse and achieve a great victory.

The Führer abstained from making an immediate decision despite Manteuffel's insistence that that an immediate decision was what he needed before it was too late. He also begged for reinforcements to no avail. Nevertheless Jodl reminded him of the Führer's express orders that there would be no retreat under any circumstance. After the phone call with Jodl, Manteuffel slammed down the receiver. Now they had taken Manhay the road west was open but they weren't going to go to Liège. Instead they would employ a kind of limited objective strategy and turn directly west towards the hamlet of Grandmènil.

Pfc Donald Beseler, A Company, 424th Regiment looked up at the sky. It was Christmas morning. Beseler didn't know it, but he was lucky he was with 1st Battalion. After a week of terrible weather, it was actually clear, but there were so many accumulated vapor trails from the hundreds and hundreds of Allied bombers and escort fighters overhead it almost looked cloudy. Finally, he thought, the relentless German advance would be slowed, maybe even pushed back. Beseler's happiness was tempered by the news he and the men had heard that morning. According to the rumors a German colonel by the name of Joachim Peiper and his SS troops had summarily executed over 80 GI POWs in an open field somewhere near the town of Malmédy. The news incurred the rage of all U.S. troops who heard it. It would definitely harden their attitudes when it came to dealing with German prisoners. Of course, there were no orders for them to kill German prisoners, but the troops did a lot of talking. It was generally accepted that captured SS troopers wouldn't be spared. The magnitude of the news, however bad it was, still wasn't enough to quench the elation Beseler and the men felt. Allied planes were bombing the living daylights out of the Germans. Maybe the tide was turning. Maybe the German's had reached their high watermark. Only time would tell.

General Hodges had dispatched repeated messages to Ridgway at XVIII Airborne Corps insisting that Manhay must be retaken. He was rightfully concerned that as long as the village remained in German hands there was every possibility that the Sixth Panzer Army would reinforce the salient, putting the Meuse bridgehead and Liège in grave danger. Hodges simultaneously requested Field Marshal Montgomery to send more divisions to reinforce this vital sector between the Salm and the Ourthe rivers.

Major General Mathew Ridgway was furious when he heard about the withdrawal from Manhay and immediately ordered an investigation. Furthermore, he insisted that the gap in the lines be closed regardless of the condition of the 7th Armored Division. As mentioned, he demanded that Hasbrouck retake Manhay by nightfall on Christmas Day. This was going to prove a problematic request for Hasbrouck. His tankers had felled trees across the highways during their withdrawal that would obstruct his tanks and men as effectively as they blocked the German advance.

Hasbrouck wasted no time in ordering his CCA, CCB, and 2d Battalion, 424th Infantry to retake the Manhay–Grandménil sector.

It was early morning Christmas Day when Colonel Alexander Reid, Commander 424th received a call from Hasbrouck instructing him to provide a battalion of infantry to support Colonel Rosebaum's CCA, 3d Armored Division in the retaking of Manhay and Grandménil. Reid was well aware that his 1st Battalion had sustained serious losses at Winterspelt and subsequently outside St. Vith and the Goose Egg. His 3d Battalion wasn't faring much better. The only battalion still fighting fit and capable was the 2d. The men of 2d Battalion hastily boarded the 7th Armored trucks and moved to Harre from where they would drive down the right side of the Harre–Manhay road while the 48th Armored Infantry Battalion drove down the left.

Meanwhile, in preparation for the impending assault by U.S. troops, the Germans had retired to the basements of homes along the approach roads, turning them into ad hoc pillboxes for the duration. After a preparatory shelling the attack went in over fairly open ground, exposing the troops to murderous crossfire from German MGs firing from basements in the two villages. The attack succeeded in getting to within 50 yards of Manhay before it began to recoil under the weight of German firepower. Supporting tanks were held at bay by several 88mm anti-tank guns, subsequently U.S. armor didn't contribute a great deal to the assault.

When E Company's mortar section zeroed one of the German machine-gun positions, the Germans retaliated with heavy mortar and artillery barrages. Consequently every man in E Company was wounded. Their sergeant bravely picked up a 60mm mortar and a few rounds, staggered 70 yards out front, set it up, and took out the troublesome machine gun with three accurately aimed mortar shells.

That wasn't the only feat of heroism that day; there were many more. Sergeant Richard J. Maslonkowski, Chicago, grabbed a .30-caliber light machine gun in his arms and advanced to wipe out an enemy machine-gun nest single-handedly. During the process the machine gun jammed but he repaired it under fire, and pressed on to eliminate the enemy gunners with his last burst of ammunition. Maslonkowski's Silver Star citation is dated March 29, 1945 and signed by Captain Crank,

422d Adjutant to Major General Stroth, who took command of the 106th Division on February 28, 1945:

Staff Sergeant Richard J. Maslonkoski, 36 648 895, 424th Infantry, United States Army, for gallantry in action on December 25, 1945, in Belgium. *When the attack of a rifle platoon, supported by his heavy weapons section, was halted by withering small arms and automatic fire from a nearby woods, Staff Sergeant Maslonkowski, cradling a light machine gun in his arms, arose, firing his weapon. Delivering a devastating hail of bullets at a camouflaged machine gun nest he detected, Staff Sergeant Maslonkowski valiantly moved forward until his gun jammed. Despite incessant hostile fire, Staff Sergeant Maslonkowki cleared the weapon, resumed his advance, killed the two-man crew and destroyed the enemy position. Entered military service from Illinois.*

While E Company were heavily engaged, Lieutenant Thomas Lawrence and his F Company platoon flanked to the left and ran into both machine-gun and tank fire. Lawrence grabbed a grenade launcher, put one onto the tank, and sent it veering off. By dusk, the men of 2d Battalion had gotten to within 50 yards of Manhay before being ordered to pull back to position known as "Hill 522," a few thousand yards north of Grandménil. At this juncture German 88s began taking their toll, resulting in 35 percent casualties for the 2d Battalion. The last remaining, functional regiment in the 106th Infantry Division was ripped to shreds. When they requested assistance in evacuating the wounded, SS snipers systematically picked off the aide men. The 2d SS Panzer Division Das Reich didn't have a reputation for displaying compassion. It had been a section of this division that was responsible for the atrocities at Oradour-sur-Glane in France where they had massacred 642 people, almost the entire population of the village, which was then reduced to rubble.

Howard L. Bryant recalled: "Late Christmas Day we made an assault on a small village. Somebody said 'Manhay' or something like that. My buddy Freilinger took a machine-gun bullet that broke his hip. I got some shrapnel in the thigh. Heard the next day that we lost 130 men in F Company on Christmas evening."

The rest of Christmas night was spent dragging back the wounded and dead through the deep snow on improvised sleds. With Colonel Alexander

Reid's 2d Battalion licking their wounds after their assault on Manhay, the battalions of the 424th Infantry, the last remnants of the 106th Infantry Division, were disbanded and divided among other units. CCA, 7th Armored Division would continue attacking Manhay with the survivors of 424th Regiment's 3d Battalion, while the assault on the adjacent hamlet of Grandménil would fall to 1st Battalion, now attached to CCB 7th Armored Division. It would effectively be the swansong for the 424th and December 26 would be the final day that the original units of the 106th Infantry Division that had entered France three weeks earlier would fight together. They had courageously endured sustained combat since December 16 and had done everything possible to thwart the German advance west. In doing so the 106th had paid a heavy price for their labors.

On the morning of December 26 the 2d SS Panzer Division still held Grandménil and Manhay. General Hasbrouck had no further plans to retake the villages but his troops would be committed in a drive to see the action to its conclusion. The 7th Armored would support the 3d Armored Division's assault on the German positions. A U.S. artillery barrage that lasted over an hour preceded the attack. When the attack went in Allied air superiority tipped the balance in favor of the U.S. troops.

2d Battalion's E Company attacked astride a highway towards Manhay but were eventually forced to take cover in the roadside ditches from punishing enemy mortar, artillery and MG fire sweeping the road. This stopped their advance in its tracks. It was then that something inexplicable occurred. The battalion chaplain Captain Edward T. O'Neill drove down the road while bullets and bombs flew in all directions. The chaplain appeared unperturbed as he calmly administered first aid to some of the wounded in the ditch. Then still under fire he carried a seriously wounded GI to his jeep and drove back up the road to the first aid station. Inspired by the chaplain's action, E Company rose up from the ditches and charged into the outskirts of Manhay, closely followed by the rest of the battalion. At roughly the same time a battalion from 82d Airborne entered the eastern end of the village. General Ridgway had decided to commit the 517th Parachute Infantry's fresh 3d Battalion to provide assistance. After several hours of house-to-house fighting and some mopping-up of stragglers, Manhay was again in Allied hands.

By 0400 December 27, the village had been completely cleared and by dawn airborne engineers had succeeded in clearing away the felled trees that blocked some of the approach roads to Manhay.

Meanwhile, the 1st Battalion attacked and entered Grandménil and fought house to house until they linked up with a battalion from the 75th Division that was moving in from the northeast. Both objectives had been taken.

The towns had changed hands several times during the bitter fighting between Christmas Eve and December 27 but now they appeared to be firmly in Allied control. When the battles for Manhay and Grandmènil were finally over it was the last few men of the 424th Infantry who got to watch the Germans leaving under a continuous hail of Allied fire.

The battle was a seminal event during the Battle of the Bulge as a whole and a turning point for those in the northern central sector. After weeks of withdrawing, regrouping and holding the line, the balance finally appeared to be favoring the Allies. This wouldn't have been the case if the 106th regiments hadn't delayed the initial German advance out on the bitterly cold Schnee Eifel or at the crossroads of Baraque de Fraiture. It was these holding actions and tactical withdrawals that bought valuable time for other Allied units to appear on the scene, but for the 106th a terrible price in casualties had been paid. However, the war wasn't over yet. Ralph Mullendore Garrett, Headquarters Company, 424th Regiment, sums it up:

The physical hardships endured, the constant exposure to rain, sleet and snow in freezing temperatures and on terrain over which it was considered impossible to wage effective warfare, have, so far as I know, rarely if ever been demanded of soldiers of any nations.

CHAPTER 13

DRESDEN: SLAUGHTERHOUSE-FIVE

The plan put forth by Allied military leaders to sequentially bomb one large German city after another was code-named "Thunderclap" and it would directly affect some 106th Infantry Division GIs who were being kept prisoner at a location known as Schlachthof Fünf—Slaughterhouse Five—in the centuries-old Baroque town of Dresden on the River Elbe. The annihilation of this city began during the night of February 13, 1945, when Britain's Royal Air Force sent 800 aircraft to bomb the city. The fires caused by the incendiary bombing resulted in massive devastation. The following afternoon, the U.S. 8th Air Force assaulted Dresden with 400 bombers, then continued with 200 more planes on February 15. A brief respite ensued after these February bombings, but, on March 2, the U.S. 8th Air Force bombed the city again with a further 400 aircraft. Finally, the destruction of Dresden concluded with the 8th Air Force sending 572 bombers over the city on April 17, 1945.

Gerald "Jerry" Lamb, I Company, 423d Infantry Regiment
When they started marching us that's when you started seeing the real horrors of what was going on. They marched us down a ravine. The ditch was running with blood. After being put in boxcars, we were shipped without food or water for a week by train to a German POW camp. There, a British soldier suggested I volunteer to go with a group of 150 soldiers on a work detail. I was then herded onto another boxcar destined for Dresden.

"Dresden is beautiful," he said. "It has parks and statues and hospitals." German troops marched us into a building that was called Slaughterhouse-Five.

In the back were two buildings they had prepared for us as barracks. Before long, he said, leaflets dropped by American planes began falling from the sky. They were written in German. The leaflets read, "We know you are using Dresden which we have not bombed because it is a hospital area for the wounded but you are storing vital parts for airplanes and tanks and if you don't cease and desist, we will bomb you."

We were in our barracks later when air raid sirens went off. Soon you could hear bombs going off. Buildings were on fire and were caving in … and everything was collapsing. When the bombing stopped we were sent out into the city to remove the dead. I went out on numerous work details in the burning city to remove dead bodies. It was like War of the Worlds. Where a person might have been, there was nothing but a black spot on the ground. Inside a train station that had burned and caved in there was a Red Cross room where the children went. We went to that room. Kids and nurses were dead. We had to carry all those kids and throw them onto trucks.

In early April, I and two others escaped and for ten days we were on the run across the German countryside. We ran into Russian troops who directed us to the American troops. The war ended shortly after that and I was sent home.

It seems in the twilight, between wake and being asleep, things sort of come back to you. You don't plan on it or think about it, but suddenly you are back in a different time or space. In war, you are always living on the edge between life and death. You didn't know between this hour and the next if you were going to make it.

American writer Kurt Vonnegut was also private with the 423d Regiment when they were in the process of returning to American lines. Exhausted, hungry, in serious danger of hypothermia and down to a few rounds of ammunition, he and a few other soldiers huddled in a ditch by the roadside. They all fixed bayonets because they had hardly anything else left to fight with. German voices resonated over loudspeakers, calling for the Americans to surrender. When no one got up, the Germans bombarded them with artillery and machine-gun fire. The order to destroy weapons and surrender was duly received and obeyed. Vonnegut watched as his rifle bolt, trigger and piston fell into the snow. He threw the rest of the rifle as far as he could and it landed in a creek. The Germans came in white uniforms and Vonnegut laughed to himself at how stupid it was that the Americans had on green uniforms, as if wars were never fought in winter.

He watched the Germans approach as he put his hands on his helmet and waited. He tried out some of his German, which his parents spoke fluently. The German soldiers asked him if he was of German descent and asked for his last name. They then asked him, "Why are you making war on your brothers?" and told him in time-honored style that the war was over for him. Vonnegut and other American prisoners were shipped in boxcars to Dresden. He described it as the prettiest city he had ever seen. As a POW, he found himself quartered in a slaughterhouse and working in a malt syrup factory. Each day he listened to bombers drone overhead on their way to drop their loads on other German cities. On February 13, 1945, the air raid siren went off in Dresden. Vonnegut, along with other POWs and their German guards, found refuge in a meat locker located three stories under the slaughterhouse. When they emerged the city was gone.

In recalling for the *Paris Review* the aftermath of the bombing, which created a firestorm that killed approximately 135,000 people, Vonnegut described walking into the city each day to dig into basements to remove the corpses as a sanitary measure:

When we went into them, a typical shelter ... looked like a streetcar full of people who'd simultaneously had heart failure. Just people sitting in chairs, all dead. They were loaded on wagons and taken to parks, large open areas in the city, which weren't filled with rubble. The Germans got funeral pyres going, burning the bodies to keep them from stinking and from spreading disease. It was a terribly elaborate Easter egg hunt.

The Allies claimed that Dresden was the location of a major German Army transit area that needed to be destroyed in order to assist the Soviets approaching from the east, but there have been many claims to the contrary. Some say that it had no military value whatsoever. When knowledge of the bombing reached the British public they remained largely oblivious to the damage inflicted on this city and regarded it as retribution for the Luftwaffe's bombing of London and Coventry. In the U.S. details of this aerial bombardment remained classified until 1978 and it has since been estimated that civilian casualties exceeded those incurred by the atomic bomb dropped on Hiroshima although this has never been effectively substantiated. The bombing of Dresden was, is and will always be a contentious subject for historians to debate.

For the 106th Infantry Division POWs located there it was a place where they were forced to endure two frightful months of slave labor, clearing the city of debris and charred bodies, while frequently being spat at, lambasted and assaulted by German survivors. It was horrific work exacerbated by the lack of food. Often POWs scavenged for food in basements where dead bodies were then discovered.

Kurt Vonnegut would later recount his experiences in the legendary book *Slaughterhouse-Five* but he was obviously deeply traumatized by his experiences because he rarely if ever actually talked about them and never attended reunions.

CHAPTER 14

SEEING IT THROUGH

As dawn hailed a new day, the devastation of the homes and roads around Manhay and Grandménil were accentuated by the stark, crystal clear morning light. A once picturesque little farming community in the Ardennes had been almost obliterated and reduced to a fractured, devastated shell of its former self. It seemed like every road and path was littered with the smoldering, burned-out hulks of all types of military vehicles. This was the scene that greeted the weary eyes of the survivors of that key battle. German and American tanks stood immobile and abandoned, some with their turrets completely blown off, testaments to a violent and bloody clash.

Not long after retaking of the two villages of Manhay and Grandménil, they were abandoned as the last remaining 424th men assumed defensive positions on the northern slope of the valley. Behind them was an impressive arsenal of Allied artillery concentrated along a three-mile front, which spanned the highway. Repeated attempts by the Germans to continue their offensive failed miserably as they succumbed to the massed fire of 300 artillery pieces. Some of the artillery pieces were using newly introduced proximity fuses that detonated in the air, and showered the German infantry formations below with lethal pieces shrapnel.

Finally, on the night of December 30, the 75th Infantry Division relieved the 424th. It was a bitterly cold winter's night, a thick layer of snow lay heavy on the ground as the battle-weary men moved toward the rear, their conversations and exchanges drowned by the thunderous Allied artillery barrage.

A mere two weeks had passed since that first terrible barrage hit the 106th Infantry Division positions out on the Schnee Eifel and during that time the division had been almost annihilated. What remained was to withdraw from the fight to a rear area, where the men could finally enjoy hot baths, clean clothes, hot meals, maybe some entertainment and vital replacements to get them back up to combat strength. These 106th men were officially seasoned combat veterans who had endured and survived everything the Germans had thrown at them. Now it was time to kick back … unless you'd been taken prisoner.

Brigadier General Herbert T. Perrin, 106th Infantry Division
January 22, 1945: With the withdrawal of the 424th Infantry from the line on Jan. 18, the major portion of the elements of this division completed a period of 34 days of practically continuous close combat with the enemy. Our Artillery is still engaged. The events of that period are still fresh in our minds and in those of your men. The physical hardships endured, the constant exposure to rain, sleet, and snow in freezing temperatures, and on terrain over which it was considered impossible to wage effective warfare, have, so far as I know, rarely if ever been demanded of soldiers of any nation. Those twin enemies—weather and terrain—have been our greatest problems, for certainly, wherever we have met the German, we have found that he is in no sense our equal. You and your men have met those demands and overcome them by a stubbornness of will, a fixed tenacity of purpose, and a grim and determined aggressiveness of body and spirit. You have accomplished you missions, and no higher praise can ever be spoken of any military organization.

The 424th Regiment was back in action again January 25 when they attacked north of St. Vith in the German-speaking region of Belgium with the objective of securing the main highway running through Amel–Amblève to the northeast. A coordinated infantry-tank attack removed a German outpost at a road junction and by late afternoon they had achieved their objectives. The following morning the village of Meyerode fell, allowing the 7th Armored to retake St. Vith while the 106th took Deidenberg and Born. At this point the understrength 106th had returned more or less to the area where they initially encountered the Germans in mid-December 1944.

From February 28, 1945 onwards, Major General Donald Stroh commanded the division. After a short respite they were attached to the First Army and back in the line on their southern flank near the Belgian town of Hünningen. The 106th Division was given the task of patrolling and probing the thickly sown minefields as they attempted to find a weak spot along a place that they were already well familiar with—the pillboxes, concrete gun emplacements, dragon's teeth and anti-tank obstacles of the Siegfried Line.

In a typical example, accompanied by 81st Combat Engineers, 424th's C Company destroyed a Nazi pillbox. They edged forward while Germans in foxholes outside the pillbox subjected them to a hail of machine-gun and rifle fire. The GIs also had to contend with four rows of anti-personnel mines before they could train their flamethrowers, rifle grenades and bazookas on their target and effectively destroy all opposition. Less than a week later the 106th had passed through the Siegfried Line and was heading towards the River Rhine. Led by the 3d Battalion, 424th Regiment, they pried Frauenkron from the enemy before seizing the towns of Berk, Kronenburg, and Baasem, as it advanced farther east.

General Stroh informed the division that the Reconnaissance Troop along with the 422d and 423d combat teams was to be reconstituted and the 106th would again take its place as a fully organized combat division. March 15, 1945 the division was assigned the Fifteenth Army and briefly moved to St. Quentin, France. From there they went to Rennes, France, where reinforcements were brought in and the 422d and 423d regiments along with the 589th and 590th Field Artillery battalions were reconstituted. For the first time since the division had gone into the line, it was back up to full strength. A strenuous training program was started for the reconstituted units at Rennes and later resumed at Coetiquidan, France.

An impressive ceremony was held April 14 at the St. Jacques Airfield near Rennes. Survivors of the original 106th regiments presented their colors to the new members of the 422d and 423d regiments. While the division stood at present arms on the parade ground, commanders, with the old and new color guards armed with German rifles captured in the Battle of the Bulge, advanced to the center of the field where they exchanged salutes. Colors and guidons were then presented to the new color guard.

A similar ceremony on a smaller scale was held later in Germany by the 424th. The final task allocated to the 106th was to assist in the rounding up of literally thousands of German POWs that had been taken during the last months of the war. Approximately 1.1 million POWs passed through the 106th cages. It was a gargantuan undertaking: receiving, screening, processing, and discharging the hordes of former German soldiers.

Meanwhile the reconstituted units of the division moved to a training area near Mayen, Germany, named Camp Alan W. Jones after the former commanding general. Germany surrendered on May 8, 1945 but the 106th was destined to remain in Europe for another few months.

The men of the 106th had done their job well and could wear their Golden Lion insignia with pride. They had lost more men than any other division and had endured 63 consecutive days of front-line combat. Many had survived and some had died while prisoners of war in the brutal German stalags. They had collectively earned the respect of other Allied divisions. September 1, 1945 they received the news that they were all waiting for: they were going home and they could return to the United States with their heads held high. October 2, 1945 the 106th Infantry Division was officially inactivated at Camp Shanks, New York. The Golden Lion lives on in the hearts and minds of those who were there.

THE AGONY GRAPEVINE

It's fair to state that relatives of the 106th Infantry Division began experimenting with a kind of "social networking" long before home computers arrived. There was no more heartrending prospect in World War II than receiving a visit from an Army officer or chaplain or even a simple Western Union telegram informing relatives that their loved one had been killed or maimed. But what about those who had been taken prisoner or were listed as missing? A few days after the Germans had made their initial breakthrough in the Ardennes in December 1944, some American newspapers had printed a German DNB (Deutsches Nachrichtenbüro) news release, alleging, among other things, that the 106th Infantry Division had been completely annihilated. They added that around 400 survivors were wandering around loose, and would be shortly taken care of. For security reasons, the War Department maintained strict silence on almost every aspect of the Ardennes Offensive, which did little to abate the withering fears and consternation of the families back home.

In early January Secretary of War Henry Lewis Stimson made a brief announcement to the effect that the Division had suffered 416 dead, 1,246 wounded and 7,001 missing in action. He did say that most of the 7,001 missing were presumed to be prisoners. A few days later notification telegrams began arriving at homes across America (mostly between January 10 and 12, 1945). Families of 106th Infantry Division soldiers back in the U.S. could confirm the rumors as fact and that the Division had indeed suffered heavily.

Eventually the truth was revealed and telephones began ringing from coast to coast across America. Photographs were brought to light in an attempt to identify some son's or husband's buddy, and locate his wife, or family. To maintain hope families visited each other and within a short time some order emerged from the initial confusion that had been perpetuated by rumors and misinformation. When Duward Frampton and his wife Annette received the telegram telling them that their son Duward Jr., a soldier with the 422d Infantry, was missing in action they, like every other family receiving one of those terribly curt and matter-of-fact pink messages, had the same question: What did "missing" mean?

They needed to find out precisely what this term implied so they bought a copy of the *Pittsburgh Sun-Telegraph*, and called the parents and wives of every man from the 106th listed as missing in action. In a matter of days, they'd assembled a list that would become known as "The Agony Grapevine." A letter reached New York from California, reporting that this family in Pittsburgh was turning over the names of missing GIs on short wave listening posts. This family turned out to be Mr. and Mrs. D. B. Frampton. When news of their activities got around and the publicity spread they were promptly deluged with a sizeable volume of mail. It wasn't long before the Framptons became the focal point for information about the 106th. Their efforts to disseminate and share information were rewarded when German propaganda radio announced information regarding 106th prisoners of war. The Framptons promptly notified other concerned families. As time progressed the Framptons began to issue a regular circular letter, counseling families as to proper procedure, and publishing tidbits of cheerful information that was heartening to all. By the time they had finished they had amassed a mailing list of over 600 names.

Out in Cleveland, Ohio, a somewhat similar situation developed in the home of Dr. and Mrs. C. R. Woods. Through a mutual friend, they learned that some officer's wife in Chicago had received a letter from her husband stating he was pretty sure most of the boys were prisoners. That started the grapevine in Cleveland and Mrs. Woods was soon receiving telephone calls and letters from a group of around 50 people. Families that had been total strangers became firm friends, and information was interchanged. In New York and other cities and towns, wherever 106th men hailed from, similar groups organized and exchanged information in a similar manner. The faith and courage exhibited by relatives of 106th Infantry Division men inspired many to keep their hopes alive despite the initially depressing news. Eventually word came directly from the 106th POWs who were liberated from the Nazi prison camps, and then they came home.

Many of the friendships that originated through the Agony Grapevine continued for decades after World War II and the spirit that unites veterans and relatives of veterans of this illustrious division lives on.

Private First Class Kenneth R. Johnson, 12,226,733, Infantry, has been reported missing in action in Germany since 17 December 1944.

WASHINGTON 25, D.C.
AG 201 Johnson, Kenneth, R.
PO-CO 014044
20 January 1947

Mr. and Mrs. Raymond C. Johnson
Box 447, Washington Street
Tappan, New York

Dear Mr. and Mrs. Johnson:
I am writing you relative to the previous letter from this office in which you were regretfully informed that a Finding of Death had been made in the case of your son, Private First Class Kenneth R. Johnson, 12,226,733, Infantry, and that the presumptive date of his death had been established as 18 December 1945.

My continued sympathy is with you in the great loss you have sustained.

Sincerely yours,

EDWARD F. WITSELL
Major General
The Adjutant General of the Army

106TH INFANTRY DIVISION: RECORDS & STATISTICS

GOLDEN LION DIVISION

The division insignia is a golden lion's face on a blue background encircled by white and then red borders respectively. The blue represents the Infantry and the red, the supporting Artillery. The lion's face is indicative of strength and power.

COMMAND AND STAFF

Commanding General

1 Nov 44	Maj. Gen. Alan W. Jones
22 Dec 44	Brig. Gen. Herbert T. Perrin
7 Feb 45	Maj. Gen. Donald A. Stroh

Assistant Division Commander

1 Nov 44	Brig. Gen. Herbert T. Perrin (A/Comd. Gen. 22 Dec 44–6 Feb 45)

Artillery Commander

1 Nov 44	Brig. Gen. L. T. McMahon

Chief of Staff

1 Nov 44	Col. William C. Baker

Assistant Chief of Staff G-1
1 Nov 44   Lt. Col. Max Roadruck

Assistant Chief of Staff G-2
1 Nov 44   Lt. Col. Robert P. Stout

Assistant Chief of Staff G-3
1 Nov 44   Maj. Charlie A. Brock
16 Dec 44   Lt. Col. Charlie A. Brock
18 Feb 45   Lt. Col. John R. Kimmell, Jr.

Assistant Chief of Staff G-4
1 Nov 44   Lt. Col. M. S. Glatterer

Assistant Chief of Staff G-5
12 Dec 44   Maj. J. John Miller
1 May 45   Lt. Col. J. John Miller

Adjutant General
1 Nov 44   Lt. Col. F. I. Agule

Commanding Officer, 422d Infantry★
1 Nov 44   Col. George L. Descheneux
5 Apr 45   Col. William B. Tuttle

Commanding Officer, 423d Infantry★
1 Nov 44   Lt. Col. William E. Long

Commanding Officer, 424th Infantry
1 Nov 44   Col. Alexander D. Reid
15 Jan 45   Lt. Col. Orville M. Hewitt
19 Jan 45   Col. John R. Jeter
14 Feb 45   Lt. Col. Robert H. Stumpf

★ Forced to surrender during fighting in the Bulge 18–20 Dec 1944.

STATISTICS

Chronology

Activated	15 March 1943
Arrived ETO	1 November 1944
Arrived Continent (D+173)	26 November 1944
Entered Combat	10 December 1944
Days in Combat	63

Casualties (Tentative)

Killed	462
Wounded	1,573
Missing	6,113
Captured	15
Battle Casualties	8,163
Non-Battle Casualties	2,508
Total Casualties	10,671
Percent of T/O Strength	75.7

Campaigns

Northern France
Rhineland
Ardennes

Individual Awards

Distinguished Service Cross	1
Legion of Merit	6
Silver Star	64
Soldier's Medal	20
Bronze Star	325
Air Medal	10

COMPOSITION
422d Infantry
423d Infantry
424th Infantry
106th Reconnaissance Troop (Mechanized)
81st Engineer Combat Battalion
331st Medical Battalion

106th Division Artillery
589th Field Artillery Battalion (105mm Howitzer)
590th Field Artillery Battalion (105mm Howitzer)
591st Field Artillery Battalion (105mm Howitzer)
592d Field Artillery Battalion (155mm Howitzer)

Special Troops
806th Ordnance Light Maintenance Company
106th Quartermaster Company
106th Signal Company
Military Police Platoon
Headquarters Company
Band

ATTACHMENTS
Antiaircraft Artillery

634th AAA AW Bn (Mbl)	8 Dec 44–18 Dec 44
563d AAA AW Bn (Mbl)	9 Dec 44–18 Dec 44
440th AAA AW Bn (Mbl)	17 Dec 44–25 Dec 44
Btry A (-1 plat), 634th AAA AW Bn (Mbl)	25 Dec 44–19 Jan 45
1 btry, 634th AAA AW Bn (Mbl)	11 Jan 45–19 Jan 45

Armored

CC B (9th Armd Div)	16 Dec 44–21 Dec 44
Co C (-1 plat), 740th Tk Bn	11 Jan 45–19 Jan 45

Cavalry

14th Cav Gp	7 Dec 44–18 Dec 44
18th Cav Rcn Sq (Atchd 14th Cav Gp)	11 Dec 44–18 Dec 44
32d Cav Rcn Sq	16 Dec 44–18 Dec 44

Engineer

168th Engr C Bn	16 Dec 44–18 Dec 44

Field Artillery

275th Armd FA Bn	11 Dec 44–18 Dec 44
401st FA Bn (105mm How)	16 Mar 45–23 Jun 45
627th FA Bn (105mm How)	16 Mar 45–23 Jun 45

Infantry

112th CT (28th Div)	19 Dec 44–23 Dec 44
1st & 3d Bns, 517th Prcht Inf (Non-Div)	11 Jan 45–17 Jan 45
3d Inf (Non-Div)	16 Mar 45–23 Jun 45
159th Inf (Non-Div)	16 Mar 45–6 Jul 45 (still attached)

Tank Destroyer

802d TD Bn (T)	8 Dec 44–4 Jan 45
Co A (-1 plat), 814th TD Bn (SP)	9 Feb 45–16 Feb 45
Co A (-1 plat), 661st TD Bn (SP)	1 Mar 45–3 Mar 45

DETACHMENTS
(Attached to)

Cavalry

106th Rcn Tr	66th Div	15 Apr 45–15 May 45

Field Artillery

591st FA Bn	7th Armd Div	25 Dec 44–30 Dec 44
592d FA Bn	XVIII Abn Corps	25 Dec 44–30 Dec 44
591st FA Bn	82d Abn Div	30 Dec 44–9 Jan 45
591st FA Bn	99th Div	5 Feb 45–13 Feb 45
592d FA Bn	99th Div	5 Feb 45–13 Feb 45
589th FA Bn	66th Div	15 Apr 45–15 May 45
590th FA Bn	66th Div	15 Apr 45–15 May 45

Infantry

424th CT	7th Armd Div	24 Dec 44–30 Dec 44
424th CT	7th Armd Div	23 Jan 45–28 Jan 45
424th CT	99th Div	5 Feb 45–9 Feb 45
422d Inf	66th Div	15 Apr 45–15 May 45
423d Inf	66th Div	15 Apr 45–15 May 45

ASSIGNMENT AND ATTACHMENT TO HIGHER UNITS

DATE	CORPS	ARMY		ARMY GROUP	
		Assigned	Attached	Assigned	Attached
14 Oct 44			UK Base	ETOUSA	
29 Nov 44	VIII	First	(–)	12th	
20 Dec 44	XVIII Abn	First		12th	Br 21st
18 Jan 45	XVIII Abn	First		12th	(–)
6 Feb 45	V	First		12th	
10 Mar 45	(–)	Fifteenth		12th	
15 Apr 45		Fifteenth	Adv Sect, Com Z (Opn & Sup)	12th	

COMMAND POSTS

DATE	TOWN	REGION	COUNTRY
1 Nov 44	Batsford Park	Oxford	England
26 Nov 44	Limesy	Seine-Inférieure	France
11 Dec 44	St. Vith	Liège	Belgium
18 Dec 44	Vielsalm	Liège	Belgium
23 Dec 44	Ernonheid	Liège	Belgium
25 Dec 44	Sprimont	Liège	Belgium
29 Dec 44	Anthisnes	Liège	Belgium
10 Jan 45	Spa	Liège	Belgium
11 Jan 45	Moulin du Ruy (Adv)	Liège	Belgium
15 Jan 45	Stavelot	Liège	Belgium
24 Feb 45	Houchenée	Liège	Belgium
7 Mar 45	Hünningen	Liège	Belgium
15 Mar 45	St-Quentin	Aisne	France
6 Apr 45	Rennes	Ille-et-Vilaine	France
26 Apr 45	Stromberg	Rhineland	Germany
4 May 45	Bad Ems	Nassau	Germany

BIBLIOGRAPHY

106th AAR. (1945). 106th Infantry Division After Action Report. Retrieved from Indiana Military: www.indianamilitary.org/106ID/Reports/53-106th106thAAR-12-1944/106th106thAAR-12-1944.htm

424th AAR. (1944). The 424th Inf. Regt. faced during the Bulge the 62d Volksgrenadier Division. Retrieved from Die Geschichte der 62 ID und Volksgrenadierdivision von 1939 bis 1945: www.62vgd.de

517th PIR. (1944). Benedict James Barrett. Retrieved from 517th Parachute Regimental Combat Team: www.517prct.org/bios/ben_barrett/barrett_b.htm

591st AAR. (1944). 591st1st FAB After Action Report, 31 Dec 1944. UnitHistory.htm

820th AAR. (1945). 820th Tank Destroyer Battalion After Action Report, Dec 1945. Retrieved from *Forte et Fideli*: www.820tdbn.org/Bn_A_A_rpt_Dec.html

Addison, P., & Crang, J. A. (2006). *The Bombing of Dresden, 1945 Firestorm*. Chicago: Ivan R. Dee.

Ahrens, R. (2007). Personal Story. Retrieved from Indiana Military: www.indianamilitary.org/German%20PW%20Camps/Prisoner%20of%20War/PW%20Camps/Stalag%20XI-B/RaymondAhrens/RaymondAhresn.htm

American Red Cross. (1944). World War II POW Camp Map. Retrieved from: www.redcross.org/museum/history/ww2a.asp

Army, U.S. (2011). Service Personnel Not Recovered Following World War II. Retrieved from Defense Prisoner of War Missing Persons Office: www.dtic.mil/dpmo/wwii/reports/arm_m_j.htm

Aspinwall, F. (1953). 589th Field Artillery Battalion History. Retrieved from Indiana Military: www.indianamilitary.org/106ID/Publications/CubInReview/04-UnitHistory.htm

Barnett, C. (1989). *Hitler's Generals*. New York: Quill/William Morrow.

Baron, R., Baum, A., & Goldhurst, R. (1981). *Raid! The untold story of Patton's secret mission*. New York: Dell.

Beseler, D. W. (2002). The War through my Eyes, One Veteran's Recollection of World War II. (T. Van Straten, Interviewer) Unpublished.

Bishop, J. (1974). *FDR's Last Year*. New York: William Morrow & Co.

Blumenson, M. (1974). *The Patton Papers (Vol. 1)*. Boston: Houghton Mifflin Co.

Bradley, O. N. (1951). *A Soldier's Story*. New York: The Modern Library.

Brown, A. C. (Unknown). My Longest Week. Retrieved from Indiana Military: www.indianamilitary.org/German%20PW%20Camps/Prisoner%20of%20War/PW%20Camps/Stalag%20XII-A%20Limburg/Arthur%20Brown/Brown-Arthur.pdf

Brown, C. M. (1981). The History of Camp Atterbury. Retrieved from Indiana Military: www.indianamilitary.org/Camp%20Atterbury/History/history_of_camp_atterbury.htm

Brumfield, V. E. (2006). Personal Story. Retrieved from Indiana Military: www.indianamilitary.org/German%20PW%20Camps/Prisoner%20of%20War/PW%20Camps/Stalag%20IV-B%20Mulberg/Vernon%20Brumfield/Vernon%20Brumfield.htm

C%20Hammelburg/WilliamDevine/WilliamDevine.htm

Castelli, J. (1946). 820th History. Retrieved from *Forte et Fideli*: www.820tdbn.org/Castelli_820th0th_History.html

Cavender, C. C. (1946, November). The 423d in the Bulge. Retrieved from Indiana Military: www.indianamilitary.org/106ID/Publications/CubInReview/04-UnitHistory.htm

Center of Military History, U.S. Army. (1994). *The War Against Germany, Europe and Adjacent Areas*. Washington: Brassey's.

Chatfield, A. I. (2006). Recollections of: Sergeant Arthur I. Chatfield. Retrieved from Indiana Military: www.indianamilitary.org/106ID/Diaries/None-POW/Art%20Chatfield/Art%20Chatfield.htm

Cohen, R. (2005). *Soldiers and Slaves*. New York: Alfred A. Knopf.

Cole, H. M. (1965). *The Ardennes: Battle of the Bulge*. Washington, D.C.: Office of the Chief of Military History, Department of the Army.

Covington, L. (1944). Rhineland. Retrieved from In Memory of Arley Ray Bishop, Second Infantry (Indianhead) Division: http://webpages. charter.net/lindacovington/rhineland.htm

Crandall, R. (1945). What They Did: Other Engineer Tasks in Combat. Retrieved from The World War II 300th Combat Engineers: www.300thcombatengineersinwwii.com/other.html

Crank, H. D. (1953). The History of the 591st Field Artillery Battalion. Retrieved from Indiana Military: www.indianamilitary.org/106ID/Publications/CubInReview/04-UnitHistory.htm

Cub in Review. (1947). The First Annual 106th Infantry Division Association Reunion. Retrieved from Indiana Military: www.indianamilitary.org/106ID/Publications/CubInReview/16-Reunions.htm

Cub in Review. (1949). The Limburg Bombing, Dec 23, 1944. Retrieved from Indiana Military: www.indianamilitary.org/106ID/Publications/CubInReview/06-PrisonerOfWar.htm

Davis, C. (n.d.). History of the Antitank Companies of the 87th Division in Europe. Retrieved from 87th Infantry Division Legacy Association: www.87thinfantrydivision.com/History/347th7th/Personal/000011.html

Deane, J. R. (1947). *The Strange Alliance*. New York: The Viking Press.

Devine, W. (Unknown). Rise and Shine. Retrieved from Indiana Military: www.indianamilitary.org/German%20PW%20Camps/Prisoner%20of%20War/PW%20Camps/Stalag%20XIII-

Disney, W. (Director). (1943). *Der Fuehrer's Face* (Motion Picture).

Doxsee, G. B. (2005). Personal Story. Retrieved from Indiana Military: www.indianamilitary.org/German%20PW%20Camps/Prisoner%20of%20War/PW%20Camps/Slaughterhouse%205%20Dresden/Gifford%20Doxsee/Gifford%20Doxsee.htm

Drash, W. (2008, November 20). After 63 years, vet learns of brother's death in Nazi slave camp. Retrieved from CNN: http://edition.cnn.com/2008/LIVING/11/20/worldwar.two.folo/index.html#cnnSTCOther2

Dupuy, E. R. (1947). *St. Vith: Lion in the Way.* Nashville: The Battery Press.

Eisenhower, J. S. (1969). *The Bitter Woods: The Battle of the Bulge.* New York: G. P. Putnam's Sons.

Elbflorenz (Unknown). Dresden before its destruction. Retrieved from Axis History Forum: http://forum.axishistory.com/viewtopic.php?t=1000

Eve, P. (2000). Personal Story. Retrieved from Indiana Military: www.indianamilitary.org/German%20PW%20Camps/Prisoner%20of%20War/PW%20Camps/Stalag%20IV-B%20Mulberg/PhilipEve/PhilipEve.htm

First Army G-2 Periodic Report. (1944). Enemy Operations and Units in Contact. Retrieved from Die Geschichte der 62 ID und Volksgrenadierdivision von 1939 bis 1945: www.62vgd.de/first_us_army_report.htm

Frank, Stanley. (November 9, 1946) The Glorious Collapse of the 106th. *The Saturday Evening Post.*

Frye, N. A. (Unknown). Personal Story. Retrieved from Indiana Military: www.indianamilitary.org/German%20PW%20Camps/Prisoner%20of%20War/PW%20Camps/Slaughterhouse%205%20Dresden/Norwood%20Frye/Frye-Norwood.pdf

Fuller, W. (2004). Read Axis Sally. Retrieved from Axis Sally, The lights of Broadway shined bright for Mildred Gillars: www.axissally.net/Axis%20Sally%20Encyclopedia%20_2.htm

Gardner, K. (2000). Minnesotan in Dresden. Retrieved from Blogspot: http://minnesotanindresden.blogspot.com/2010/05/slaughter-house-five-schlachthof-funf.html

Gavin, J. M. (1978). *On to Berlin, Battles of an Airborne Commander, 1943–1946.* New York: The Viking Press.

Giarrusso, J. M. (1998). *Against all Oodds: The Story of the 106th Infantry Division in the Battle of the Bulge.* UMI Number: 1392808.

Gilbert, M. (1995). *The Day the War Ended.* New York: Henry Holt & Co.

Guinn, B. (2003). Aquitania "The Ship Beautiful". Retrieved from Royal Regals: Featured Liners: www.bryking.com/aquitania/career.html

Hannon, P. A. (1984). One Man's Story. Retrieved from Indiana Military: www.indianamilitary.org/German%20PW%20Camps/Prisoner%20of%20War/PW%20Camps/Stalag%20IX-B%20Bad%20Orb/Philip%20Hannon/Hannon-Philip.pdf

Harper, D. P. (2004). World War II Propaganda Broadcasts. Retrieved from FReeper Foxhole: www.freerepublic.com/focus/f-vetscor/1196108/posts

Haug, C. (1949). Personal Story. Retrieved from Indiana Military: www.indianamilitary.org/28TH/Diaries/Haug/Haug.htm

Heinzel, M. (2010). Zur Eisenbahnstrecke von St. Vith über Lommersweiler und Bleialf nach Pronsfeld. Retrieved from ZVS – Der Zug-kommt: www.zvs.be/der-zugkommt/?Wissenswertes:Streckenabschnitte:Zur_Eisenbahnstrecke_von_St._Vith_%FCber_Lommersweiler_und_Bleialf_nach_Pronsfeld&print

Hilbers, J. (2000). Battle of the Bulge: One Private's Story. Retrieved from Vittles, Vintages & Voyages: http://vittlesvoyages.com/army-weba.html

Hitler, A. (1926). *Mein Kampf (Vol. 2)*. Boring, Oregon: CPA Book Publishers.

Hoge, W. M. (1993). *Engineer Memoirs: General William M. Hoge, U.S. Army*. Washington D.C.: Department of the Army, U.S. Army Corps of Engineers.

Irving, D. (1977). *Hitler's War*. New York: The Viking Press.

Jackson. (2003, November). Newsletter of The Jackson County Historical Society. Retrieved from Jackson County Historical Society: www.ajlambert.com/denny/stryww2m.pdf

Jeters, R. (1989). Personal Story. Retrieved from Indiana Military: www.indianamilitary.org/German%20PW%20Camps/Prisoner%20of%20War/PW%20Camps/Stalag%20XI-B/RobertJeters/RobertJeters.htm

Jones Jr., A. W. (1949). Operations of the 423d Infantry Regiment 106th Infantry Division in the vicinity of Schönberg, Germany during the Battle of the Ardennes (The Battle of the Bulge). The Infantry School, Staff Department, Fort Benning, Georgia.

Jones Jr., A. W. (2009–2011). Personal Conversations. (K. B. Johnson, Interviewer)

Jones, A. W. (February 3, 1948). A History of the 106th under General Jones' Command. Retrieved from Indiana Military: www.indianamilitary.org/106ID/Publications/CubInReview/03-DivisionHistory.htm

Jones, M. L. (2003). Infantry Platoon Leader, My Experiences in World War II. Retrieved from Indiana Military: www.indianamilitary.org/German%20PW%20Camps/Prisoner%20of%20War/PW%20Camps/Stalag%20IX-B%20Bad%20Orb/LMartinJones/LMartinJones.htm

Judge, D. J. (Unknown). Cavalry in the Gap, The 14th Cavalry Group (Mechanized) and The Battle of the Bulge. Retrieved from 14th Cavalry Association: www.14cav.org/g1-bulge.html

Kelly, T. P. (2001). *The Fightin' 589th*. 1st Books Library

Kline, J. P. (2005). The Service Diary of German War Prisoner #315136. Retrieved from Indiana Military: www.indianamilitary.org/German%20PW%20Camps/Prisoner%20of%20War/PW%20Camps/Stalag%20VIII-A%20Gorlitz/John%20Kline/John%20Kline.htm

Kuespert, A. (October 1948). Secret Weapon of the 106th. Retrieved from Indiana Military: www.indianamilitary.org/106ID/Publications/CubInReview/17-GeneralInterest.htm

Lapp, R. E. (2010). Personal Story. Retrieved from Indiana Military: www.indianamilitary.org/106ID/Diaries/None-POW/Lapp-RoyceE/Lapp-RoyceE.htm

Lichtenfeld, S. (1989). Kriegie 312330. Retrieved from Indiana Military: www.indianamilitary.org/German%20PW%20Camps/Prisoner%20of%20War/PW%20Camps/Stalag%20III-B%20Furstenberg/Seymour%20Lichtenfeld/Lichtenfeld-Seymour.pdf

Littell, J. (1995). *A Lifetime in Every Moment, a Memoir*. Boston: Houghton Mifflin Co.

Liverpool Ships. (1940). The Cunard Liner *Aquitania*. Retrieved from Liverpool Ships: www.liverpoolships.org/aquitania_cunard_line.html

MacDonald, C. B. (1963). *The Siegfried Line Campaign*. Washington, D.C.: Center for Military History, United States Army.

MacDonald, C. B. (1973). *The Last Offensive*. Washington, D.C.: Center of Military History United States Army.

MacDonald, C. B. (1985). *A Time for Trumpets, The Untold Story of the Battle of the Bulge*. New York: Harper Collins.

Manteuffel, H. (1970, January). German General Speaks to 106th. The Cub, pp. 3–4.

Miller, B. (Unknown). Going thru the attic. Retrieved from blogspot. com: http://goingthroughtheattic.blogspot.com/2009_11_01_archive. html

Moon, W. P. (1949). Operations of the 1st Battalion, 422/D (106th Infantry Division) in the Battle of the Bulge, in the Vicinity of Schlausenbach, Germany, 10–19 December 1944 (Ardennes–Alsace Campaign). The Infantry School, Staff Department, Fort Benning, Georgia.

Mosley, R. A. (1961). A New Perspective. Retrieved from Indiana Military: www.indianamilitary.org/106ID/Publications/CubInReview/15-Tours.htm

Nobecourt, J. (1967). Hitler's Last Gamble: The Battle of the Bulge. New York: Schocken Books.

Nordyke, P. (2005). All American, All the Way. Minneapolis: Zenith.

Official Declaration. (1945). Unit Citation: 81st Engineer Combat Battalion (106th Infantry Division) Unites States Army for Conduct in German Counter-

Offensive 16 to 25 December, 1944 with Supporting Narrative. Retrieved from Indiana Military: www.indianamilitary.org/106ID/Awards/81stEngrCitation/81st1stEngrCitation.htm

Palmer, R. R., Wiley, B. I., & Keast, W. R. (2003). The Army Ground Forces, The Procurement and Training for Ground Combat Troops. Washington, D.C.: Center for Military History, United States Army.

Pictures of World War II. Retrieved from National Archives: www. archives.gov/research/military/ww2/photos/images/ww2-112.jpg

Plokhy, S. M. (2010). Yalta, The Price of Peace. London: Penguin Books.

Puett, J. F. (1945). First Report by Lieutenant Colonel Joseph Puett, Movement and Actions of 2d Battalion, 423d Infantry from December 16th to 19th, 1944. Retrieved from Indiana Military: www.indiana-military.org/106ID/Reports/AAR-1.htm

Purple Hearts. (Unknown). Col. George L. Descheneaux. Retrieved from: www.indianamilitary.org/German%20PW%20Camps/Prisoner%20of%20War/PW%20Camps/Stalag%20XII-A%20Limburg/George%20Descheneaux/Descheneau-George.pdf

Quartermaster Review (May/June 1946). Graves Registration. Retrieved from U.S. Army Quartermaster Foundation, Fort Lee, Virginia: www.qmfound.com/graves_registration.htm

Red Cross. (1940). World War II Accomplishments of the American Red Cross. Retrieved from: www.redcross.org/museum/history/ww2a.asp

Reed, A. C. (2005). My Adventures in Europe 1944/1945. Retrieved from Indiana Military: www.indianamilitary.org/106ID/Diaries/None-POW/Albert%20Reed/Albert%20Reed.htm

Reid, A. D. (1947). Colonel Reid 424th Regiment. Retrieved from Indiana Military: www.indianamilitary.org/106ID/Publications/CubInReview/04-UnitHistory.htm

Reinfenrath, J. W. (1997). An American Slave in Nazi Germany. Retrieved from Indiana Military: www.indianamilitary.org/German%20PW%20Camps/Prisoner%20of%20War/PW%20Camps/Berga/JohnReinfenrath/JohnReinfenrath.htm

Riggs, T. J. (1975). An Engineer's Seven Day War. Retrieved from Indiana Military: www.indianamilitary.org/German%20PW%20Camps/Prisoner%20of%20War/PW%20Camps/Unknown%20Camp/Thomas%20Riggs/RiggsThomas_81Eng.html

Roberts, J. M. (2003). *Escape!!! The True Story of a World War II P.O.W. the Germans Couldn't Hold*. Binghampton: Brundage Publishing.

Rodenbough, T. F., & Haskin, W. (1896). The Corps of Engineers. In H. L. Abbot, *The Army of the United States, Historical Sketched of Staff and Line with Portraits of Generals-In- Chief* (pp. 112–125). New York: Maynard, Merril & Co.

Roosevelt, F. (1945). State of the Union Address, January 6, 1945. Retrieved from The American Presidency Project: www.presidency.ucsb.edu/ws/index.php?pid=16595#ixzz1htIAJ2rI

Schaffner, J. R. (Unknown). Army Daze, A few Memories of the Big One. Retrieved from Indiana Military: www.indianamilitary.org/106ID/Diaries/None-POW/Schaffner/Schaffner.htm

Scott, E. (Unknown). Personal Story. Retrieved from Indiana Military: www.indianamilitary.org/106ID/Diaries/None-POW/Earl%20Scott/Scott-Earl.pdf

SHAEF. (1944). Eisenhower Communiqués. Retrieved from BYU, Digital Collections, Harold B. Lee Library: http://contentdm.lib.byu.edu/cdm4/doc_viewer.php?CISOROOT=/EisenhowerCommuniques&CISOPTR=321&CISOBOX=1

Smith, K. (Unknown). Personal Story. Retrieved from Indiana Military: www.indianamilitary.org/German%20PW%20Camps/Prisoner%20of%20War/PW%20Camps/Stalag%20IX-B%20Bad%20Orb/Ken%20Smith/Smith-Ken.pdf

Sparks, R. D. (2003). A Walk Through the Woods. Retrieved from Indiana Military: www.indianamilitary.org/106ID/Diaries/None-POW/Richard%20D%20Sparks/Richard%20Sparks.htm

Speer, S. (2011). Tennessee Maneuvers. Retrieved from Camp Forrest, Tullahoma, Tennessee: www.campforrest.com/tennessee_maneuvers.htm

Starett, G. F. (1946). The Agony Grapevine. Retrieved from Indiana Military: www.indianamilitary.org/106ID/Publications/CubInReview/17-GeneralInterest.htm

Stars and Stripes. (1945). The 106th: The Story of the 106th Infantry Division. Retrieved from Lone Sentry: www.lonesentry.com/gi_stories_booklets/106thinfantry/index.html

Stars and Stripes. (1945). The 9th: The Story of the 9th Armored Division. Retrieved from Lone Sentry: http://search.yahoo.com/r/_ylt=A0oG-dWYGSJtOqncAGIdXNyoA;_ylu=X3oDMTE1a3Y0bzNkBHN-lYwNzcgRwb3MDMQRjb2xvA3NrMQR2dGlkA0FDQlkwM-l8xNDE-/SIG=12ncq5rsg/EXP=1318828166/**http%3a//www.lonesentry.com/gi_stories_booklets/9tharmored/index.html

Stars and Stripes. (January 13, 1945). 424/A. Retrieved from Indiana Military: www.indianamilitary.org/106ID/Publications/CubInReview/04-UnitHistory.htm

Stein, S. (n.d.). Personal Story. Retrieved from Indiana Military: www.indianamilitary.org/German%20PW%20Camps/Prisoner%20of%20War/PW%20Camps/Stalag%20XII-A%20Limburg/MurraySchwartz/MurraySchwartz.htm

Stevenson, R. L. (2000). Personal Story. Retrieved from Indiana Military: www.indianamilitary.org/106ID/Diaries/None-POW/Robert%20Stevenson/Robert%20Stevenson.htm

Taylor, R. R. (1974). Medical Training on World War II. Washington, D.C.: Office of the Surgeon General, Department of the Army.

Tennery, J. H. (2006). Little Soldiers, Big Battles. Retrieved from Indiana Military: www.indianamilitary.org/German%20PW%20Camps/Prisoner%20of%20War/PW%20Camps/Dulag%20VI%20B/Tenery/TeneryDiary.htm

The Cub in Review. (1947). Order of the Golden Lion. Retrieved from Indiana Military: www.indianamilitary.org/106ID/Publications/CubInReview/12-OrderGoldenLion.htm

The Cub. (1958). Birth of the Golden Lions. Retrieved from Indiana Military: www.indianamilitary.org/106ID/Publications/CubInReview/03-DivisionHistory

Time Magazine. (1941). Army Yoo-Hoo! in *Time* Magazine, July 21, 1941.

Toland, J. (1959). *Battle: The Story of the Bulge*. Lincoln, Nebraska: University of Nebraska Press.

Troop Trains. (2006). The New Haven and the Military. Retrieved from: www.kinglyheirs.com/NewYorkStateRailroads/TroopTrain1.html#TroopTrainSlideShow

U.S. Army. (1944). POW Recalls Battle of the Bulge. Retrieved from On Patrol: http://usoonpatrol.org/archives/2011/01/07/knight-recalls-belgium-battle

U.S. Army. (1945). The Ardennes Offensive: Dec. 16, 1944– Jan. 25, 1945. Retrieved from Battle of the Bulge: http://funnytogo.com/stories/battle%20of%20th0the%20bulge/map1.jpg

U.S. Medical Research Centre. (1944). 324th Medical Battalion, Unit History. Retrieved from World War II U.S. Medical Research Centre: http://med-dept.com/unit_histories/324_med_bn.php

U.S. Senate Committee on Foreign Relations. (May 23, 1991). An Examination of U.S. Policy toward POW/MIAs by the U.S. Senate Committee on Foreign Relations Republican Staff. Retrieved from National Alliance of Families: www.nationalalliance.org/vietnam/overview.htm

Unknown. (1941/1943). Jakov Djugashvili Stalin. Retrieved from Histomil: www.histomil.com/viewtopic.php?f=95&t=3991

Unknown. (1944). 7th Armored Division in St, Vith (Belgium) December 21–31, 1944. Retrieved from European Center of Military History (EUCMH): www.eucmh.com/tag/106th106th-infantry-division/

Unknown. (1945). Dresden, 1945. Retrieved from Axis History Forum: http://forum.axishistory.com/viewtopic.php?t=1000

Unknown. (1945). February 13th, 1945: The Firebombing of Dresden. Retrieved from This isn't happiness: http://thisisnthappiness.com/post/387971584/february-13th3th-1945-the-firebombing-of-dresden.

War Department. (1947). Letter Regarding Death of Kenneth R. Johnson, 12226733, January 20, 1947.

Watry, W. J. (2009). Personal Story. Retrieved from Indiana Military: www.indianamilitary.org/106ID/Diaries/None-POW/Watry-WilliamJ/Watry-WilliamJ.htm

Weiner, M. (1987). Personal Story. Retrieved from Indiana Military: www.indianamilitary.org/106ID/Diaries/None-POW/Milton%20Weiner/Milton%20Weiner.htm

Whiting, C. (1970). *48 Hours to Hammelberg*. New York: iBooks.

Yamazaki, J. N. (1995). *Children of the Atomic Bomb*. Durham & London: Duke University Press.

Ziemke, E. F. (1975). The U.S. Army in the Occupation of Germany 1944–1946. Washington D.C.: Center of Military History, United States Army.

INDEX